MW00977268

magic lantern empire

Magic Lantern Empire

Colonialism and Society in Germany

JOHN PHILLIP SHORT

CORNELL UNIVERSITY PRESS
Ithaca & London

First published 2012 by Cornell University Press
Printed in the United States of America

Library of Congress Cataloging-in-Publication Data

Short, John Phillip, 1967–
   Magic lantern empire : colonialism and society in Germany / John Phillip Short.
       p. cm.
   Includes bibliographical references and index.
   ISBN 978-0-8014-5094-5 (cloth : alk. paper)
   1. Germany—Colonies—Public opinion—History.   2. Imperialism—Germany—
Public opinion—History.   3. Imperialism—Social aspects—Germany—History.
4. Popular culture—Germany—History.   5. Public opinion—Germany—History.
I. Title.
   JV2011.S56   2012
   325'.343—dc23   2012021098

Cloth printing   10 9 8 7 6 5 4 3 2 1

For Ruth Binnicker Eckerd
In memoriam

Contents

Color plates follow page 84

Acknowledgments

I have incurred many debts in the time it has taken to complete this work, many more than I can adequately acknowledge here, in far-flung places from Namibia to New York and across Germany. I am grateful for their patience and knowledge to the staffs of so many institutions: chief among them the New York Public Library, Butler Library of Columbia University, the Library of Congress, the Staatsbibliothek Berlin, the Deutsche Bücherei, the Bayrische Staatsbibliothek, the Stadt- und Staatsbibliothek Augsburg, the Ruhrland Museum, the Markt- und Schaustellermuseum Essen, the Museum für Völkerkunde, Hamburg, the Swakopmund Museum, Swakopmund, Namibia, and federal, state, and municipal archives in Berlin, Leipzig, Munich, Bamberg, Nuremberg, and Augsburg. Lengthy and painstaking research in so many places would not have been possible without the financial support of the German Academic Exchange Service.

Volker Berghahn, Atina Grossmann, and Marcia Wright helped me to elaborate and focus this project from its very beginnings. Since then, parts of the manuscript have profited from a diverse range of sensibility and insight, both within my narrow field and beyond it. Thanks to Ritu Birla, Andreas Eckl, David Kurnick, Sara Pugach, Joe Rezek, and to my colleagues in the Department of History. Particular thanks to Molly O'Donnell for her extraordinary generosity in sharing her transcriptions of women's letters from the federal archive in Berlin, as for our many conversations. Friends in Berlin—Christina Gehlsen, Peter König, Niko Härting—and fellow sojourners there—Mark Landsman and Jenny Weisberg—transformed my experience of that city. Mark Ferketish I can hardly thank enough for his invaluable technical assistance, steadiness, and good nature in putting the manuscript together. I owe profound thanks to the staff at Cornell, especially Susan Specter, Gavin Lewis, and Lou Robinson for the many transformations they have wrought. I am grateful to my editor at Cornell, John Ackerman, for the extraordinary care and interest he has shown, and to the reviewers for their encouragement, deep expertise, and incisive comments.

And, finally, to Chad Kia, always there, fierce and laughing by turns.

magic lantern empire

Empire as World and Idea

Colonialism and Society in Germany

> Moreover, from the social point of view the hierarchical value of an
> idea, its intrinsic worth, is without importance. The necessary point to
> consider is the effects it produces.
>
> —Gustave Le Bon, *Psychologie des foules*, 1895

> *Würzburg, 30 January. A* CAMEROON ENTHUSIAST. *A colossally drunken
> man made a terrific racket last night on Domstraße. Too weak to
> stay on his feet, he lay in the street, wallowing with great stamina in
> the dirt, all the while screaming that he wanted to go to Cameroon,
> until finally the police had mercy on him and paraded him in a
> wagon—maybe not to Cameroon, but at least into his cage. From his
> appearance, by the way, one could quite easily have taken him for a
> Cameroon Negro—regarding the dirt, that is.*
>
> —*Münchner Neueste Nachrichten*, 2 February 1886

In December 1885 the new German protectorate of Cameroon material-
izes in the imperial capital Berlin; it attains, in the Colonial Panorama, a
novel reality that is plastic, atmospheric, seamless. Berliners drawn by the
promise of bold advertising and ersatz palms descend into a dim passageway
at the base of the great circular building and reemerge on a platform at its
dark center, now sensitized to the illumination animating the vast scene that
surrounds them. As a local journalist describes it, one suddenly sees, in the
very center of Berlin, "flooded in a whitish shimmering light, a sultry tropical December day; and spreading out all around . . . in seemingly tangible
reality a broad stretch of a foreign world. We are on the hill . . . where Bell
Town once stood. . . . On both sides one looks out across a canopy of palm
and banana trees, beneath which spreads a thickly grown tangle of reeds,
palms, and mangroves. . . . There, to the right, over the treetops . . . rise the
columns of smoke and flames of Hickory Town, burned by our men."[1] How
vivid the tumult of battle as German soldiers fight their way inland, bullets
whistling between the palms, smoke filling the dense jungle, the savage cries
of the enemy breaking into retreat.[2]

The new panorama, offering "one of the 'most current' events as a
subject," is, according to a preview in the papers, expected to "excite a

particularly lively interest."[3] And so colonial Cameroon becomes a subject of representation, of news—of metropolitan knowledge. The panorama is a popular way to bring knowledge of Cameroon to Germany, but it is just one of many. The rise of travel by railroad and steamship will soon begin to make panoramas obsolete, but in the 1880s the new and distant colonial empire commands all available technologies of representation and information to become intelligible to the metropolitan public. Alongside such techniques of verisimilitude, new forms of colonial expertise and authority will arise, and colonial discourses of political economy, anthropology, and geography will develop, which will license individuals and institutions to report on the empire, to describe it and make judgments about it. The growing mass media of panoramas, illustrated newspapers, and the daily press becomes essential to the dissemination, indeed the production, of colonial knowledge in the widest sense, reaching across lines of class and region marking a fractious, divided society. Media constructions of overseas empire, and indeed fabrications of colonial "experience" at such sites as the panorama, become, like actual colonization, agents of the formation of knowledge—of, indeed, a new representation of the global—as of empire itself.

Stories on Cameroon appear throughout the mid-1880s in books, in the daily and illustrated press, and in magazines including *Globus, Über Land und Meer, Westermanns Monatshefte,* and *Die Gartenlaube.* The "news" from Cameroon, expanding with the rush of excitement that attended the founding of the overseas empire in 1884, and with the new mass culture then taking shape, serves here to suggest the formation and dissemination of colonial discourse across a broad German public. The Cameroon story is a vivid instance of the fusion of colonial ideology, mass media representation, and a vestigial bourgeois public sphere into the powerful metropolitan phenomenon of colonialism. This process developed fitfully and then disintegrated over the course of a century, from the barren colonial hopes of the 1840s to the destruction of Germany in the 1940s. But it was in the last quarter of the nineteenth century, as Germans moved to acquire colonies and realize *Weltpolitik,* that colonialism gradually evolved into the formation examined here: the broad, shifting field of refraction, mediation, and dissemination of both discursive and visual representations of the overseas empire, a complex field that traced the contours and convulsions of German society in the period of its most intensified industrialization.

Crucially, colonial discourse originated in the public sphere of bourgeois associational and institutional life—in an organized colonial movement—and it always bore the strong inflection of class difference, the stamp of its social origins. But it was at the same time interstitial, marginal, finding resonance and distortion across the novel terrains of mass society and mass culture. Colonialism encompassed the "official mind" of empire, and its materializations in far-flung practices of colonial state formation, white settlement, and economic extraction, but also flourished in unofficial forms:

subaltern and demotic colonialisms among women, the working classes, and the petite bourgeoisie. This world of colonialism "from below," manifest in commercial amusements, in elusive forms of private reading and imagining, in grassroots associations and thwarted small-time colonial schemes, developed autonomously, but not without orientation either to the masculinist, bourgeois colonial movement, which both courted and disdained it, or to the potent, protracted anticolonialism of the Social Democratic Party (SPD). Antagonism was constitutive of German colonial discourse.

This book examines colonialism in its metropolitan context, in an environment of class conflict in which the colonial empire was itself bitterly contested. It argues that colonialism operated as a form of *knowledge* that both reproduced and dissolved class boundaries, and that it was out of this conflict that a modern image of the global emerged in Germany at the beginning of the twentieth century. What developed from the countervailing discourses of socialist critique and bourgeois colonialism was a rhetoric of colonial enlightenment, of *Kolonialaufklärung*, that took the uneducated masses as its object. The traditional public sphere, or better yet the idea of it—male, bourgeois, educated, insistently rationalist—was the template for colonial discourse, and the colonial movement emerged from the precincts of its associational life. Colonialists stood self-consciously aloof from the world of mass culture, where knowledge seemed to break down into sensation and distraction, and furiously opposed popular anticolonial mobilization by the Social Democrats. The working classes, and the broader masses of ordinary Germans in general, ostensibly required proper instruction to understand the German role in a world defined by resource extraction, commodity and labor flows, exchange and competition on a new, global scale. The "global," self-consciously staged first in the colonial public sphere, developed as an effect of capitalism and functioned to initiate Germans into a modern market worldview.[4]

The most intense phase of this process coincided with the founding and consolidation of the German colonial empire, the beginnings of which are celebrated in the Colonial Panorama. It was some year and a half before the panorama opened, on 14 July 1884, that Germany declared a protectorate in Cameroon, on the West African coast, when the famous African explorer and German consul at Tunis, Gustav Nachtigal, sailing across the Bight of Biafra, secured treaties from coastal chieftains. Here the flag followed trade: the substantial Hamburg houses of Woermann and Jantzen & Thormählen, well established in West Africa, had trading posts on the Cameroon coast, where Europeans sought palm oil and ivory. According to the press, the "natives . . . who had [already] concluded protection and trade agreements with the German trading posts had offered this step."[5] The violent scene depicted in the Berlin Colonial Panorama occurred only months later: journalists breathlessly reported on an "uprising" in the new colony in December 1884. German warships landed some three hundred men with artillery at

Hickory Town on the Cameroon River. As one popular magazine put it, "With a loud hurrah the steep bank, occupied by the rebels, was attacked and the natives, under the thunder of the German artillery, were driven pell-mell into flight."[6] A full-page illustration dramatized the battle as "The First Victory of the Germans in Africa." Sensation and adventure—the plain violence of colonial expansion—crowd out the original account of commercial enterprise and peaceful takeover.

The panorama itself re-creates the essential story, producing a scene—uncannily real—that transports Berliners far away:

> In the middle of the city . . . this massive round painting shows a tropical landscape beneath Africa's sultry sky, with the full, powerful vegetation of this region and the hazy, heavy atmosphere that almost always settles over the river that lends its name to our new protectorate of Cameroon. But a military action is likewise brought vividly into view here, the picture showing just that moment when our German navy attacks in order to punish the rebellious Negroes of the protectorate. . . . The panorama brings this moment into view with superb technique of depiction. The Negroes are put into furious flight through the tangle of plants; only scattered smaller groups stand their ground.[7]

The Battle of Hickory in Cameroon (1884). *ÜLuM* 53 (1885). Courtesy New York Public Library.

Painted in the pictorial idiom of the mass illustrated press, the panorama captures the interrelationships of media, eyewitness reality-effect, and the new colonial project in the 1880s. Media representation configures and amplifies the globalizing perspective integrated by the colonial movement, becoming accessory to colonization itself. The theme of war, like African adventure, is conventionally popular. The publicity is dramatic; advertising in "colossal colored letters" appears on buildings adjacent to the panorama, a confection of exotic polychrome ornament and waving palms. There are previews in the press and a two-page layout with substantial engravings in the *Leipziger Illustrierte Zeitung*. The colossal painting itself is the work principally of two men: Louis Braun, the well-known panoramist, painter of battle scenes, and one-time contributor to the *Illustrierte Zeitung*, reportedly already busy with yet another Cameroon view for a Leipzig panorama company, and Hans Petersen, an illustrator for the same paper, in whose employ he had actually witnessed the "battle of Hickory" as a correspondent in West Africa.[8] A multiform, ramified media linking diverse technologies of visual and print culture already flourishes in 1885.

Max Buchner—explorer, ethnologist, companion of Nachtigal and original "imperial commissioner" of Cameroon—was also at the battle, where he first encountered yet another member of the press, the unabashed colonialist Hugo Zöller, the "well known, widely traveled, and expert reporter" for the *Kölnische Zeitung* whose own books on Togo and Cameroon would rapidly appear in Germany. As Buchner remembered it, the "daring war correspondent" belonged right at the heart of this scene, the very "picture of the brutal conditions of war." "Writing this way I had never seen before," Buchner recalled. "It was a sight never to be forgotten, how he sat there at the corner of a table squeezed in between marines and weapons, steaming platters and baggage, the clashing of arms and heated conversation—and wrote and wrote and wrote. Numberless sheets already lay about, copies still damp . . . and Herr Zöller forced again and again to jump here and dive there as the din broke out anew of fresh troops arriving to alight next to him."[9] Zöller remembered editing his dispatch to Germany, "surrounded by jovial young officers, in the perfectly justified spirit of a hymn to the heroes of the German Navy and their bravery."[10] This is the primal scene that transforms Buchner himself into an ambitious writer, a professional and prolific publicist of empire.

Zöller, for his part, quickly makes a success of popularizing German colonialism—his name, according to an illustrated geographic magazine, becoming "generally known through the military events in Cameroon and his account of them."[11] Upon returning to Germany he undertakes an exhausting national lecture tour. He receives love letters. Even while he is "giving sometimes three to four lectures in a week," forced "to hurry from one German city to another," his editor urgently pushes for rapid publication.[12]

The German Colonial Panorama in Berlin (1886). *LIZ* 68, no. 2218 (January–June 1886). Courtesy Library of Congress.

Already a reporter for the Cologne paper, which sponsored his "research trip" to West Africa, he is now travel writer, hero, expert, and author of a very timely work on the "life and customs of the natives, the climate and cultural significance" of Cameroon, "an account of its commerce and German trading posts based on personal experience and study."[13] The rhetoric of "scientific" research, of authentic colonial "experience," and the authority of the eyewitness that attaches to Zöller pervade the public discourse—not least in the context of entertainment, the mass culture of panoramas and illustrated papers.

Of course, Buchner himself also observed the fighting in Cameroon, although feverish and weak from long illness. "The day of the big shoot-up was to me a bad dream," he recalled. "I was in the frame of mind of a drunk. In my brain, the hubbub of fever and quinine stupor."[14] But this hardly stops him from developing his own authoritative account in a mode of pronounced critical detachment. Buchner is a canny publicist of empire; he quickly makes a career of it, as journalist, lecturer, writer, scientist, expert. He has a subtle approach, contrasting his sober colonialism with that "disturbing new enemy of colonial policy," that "befuddlement of sound reason"—colonial enthusiasm—which had led to the point where "one cannot express oneself at all seriously on Africa without first having cleared away the confusion of talk" provoked by "this newest El Dorado."[15] Proclaiming the folly of colonial enthusiasm, he appears—everywhere. Once he returns, via Hamburg, where he recovers slowly from the many months of illness—from the fever dream of Cameroon—he cultivates a dour objectivity, an ostentatiously unsentimental, skeptical point of view predicated on hard experience, which serves to underscore his own authority. Like Zöller, Buchner goes on tour, delivering in January 1886 a lecture on "Colonial Policy" as part of a series of "popular scientific lectures" sponsored by the Munich Association for Popular Education. The following month, the "well-known Africa scholar" delivers a lecture on Cameroon at a geographical society in Frankfurt.[16] He writes for the Munich press.[17] He visits the colonial panorama in Berlin, where he sees—of course—himself, charging across the colossal canvas, pistol drawn, and certifies the true-to-life depiction of the African landscape.[18] In 1887, Buchner's book *Cameroon* appears.[19] Eschewing the techniques of the adventure story, it soberly describes geography, natural resources, peoples and cultures, the labor question, development potential, markets and trade, with appendices on rainfall, weather patterns, Cameroon English. The book is dry, but the market by now well prepared, earning it mention in the illustrated press: "Max Buchner reports on 'an inclination toward robbery and violence [among] the Duala, . . . the worst-developed half-savages known to this globe.'"[20] In the same year, Buchner becomes director of the Munich Museum of Ethnography, a site for the accumulation of colonial knowledge, of ethnographica from the whole colonized world.

Figures like Buchner, Nachtigal, and Zöller rise to new prominence on a great tide of public colonial discourse in the mid-1880s, which brings us back to Berlin, to the panorama. Germany is, for a moment, the colonial metropole par excellence, Berlin its imposing imperial capital. On 15 November 1884 the Congo Conference opens there. In just four months Germany has declared protectorates over Togoland and Cameroon, and over Angra Pequeña, on the distant southwestern coast of Africa. The European colonial powers are on the move, and they assemble in Berlin. The celebrated Henry Morton Stanley attends the Congo Conference, held in the German chancellor's palace in the Wilhelmstrasse, an event, he says, "of unparalleled munificence and grandeur of ideas." Stanley dines with Bismarck; delivers speeches and lectures in Berlin, Frankfurt, Wiesbaden; is formally recognized by the German Colonial Association; is honored and fêted wherever he goes.[21] It is already the age of publicity, notoriety, fame, and Stanley—newspaper man and explorer—is its avatar. He is "the man whose name is now on the lips of the whole educated world, . . . intellectual initiator of the conference, . . . the victorious commander in the service of science," celebrated among all men "called to the founding and promotion of a civilizing task that is among the noblest goals of human knowledge and civilization."[22] Publicity, science, and empire crystallize, once again, in bright constellation around the metaphor of the "Dark Continent" in the heyday of exploration and discovery, mapping and conquest.

When the conference concludes, in late February 1885, the colonial effervescence does not fade. The newly famous explorer Carl Peters returns to Berlin from East Africa in the same month, having secured imperial protection for a vast colony there. Some three months later, Kaiser Wilhelm I declares a German protectorate in New Guinea. In 1886, dioramas in Moabit, to the north of the Colonial Panorama in central Berlin, celebrate "the deeds and fates of famous modern African explorers and important moments of the new colonial actions of the German Reich": Stanley at the Congo Falls, Nachtigal's funeral, the fleet at Zanzibar, colonial pioneer Curt von François hunting elephant.[23] In December, the Ethnography Museum formally opens in Berlin, with Schliemann's dazzling Trojan artifacts and ethnological collections befitting a world-spanning power. Among the vitrines are wood figures and masks, weapons and idols from Nachtigal's last collection, and fetish, magic, and fortune-telling paraphernalia from German Southwest Africa.[24] The following year, 1887, Carl Peters launches the famous Emin Pasha relief expedition. Interest is "general, the sympathy everywhere so warm"—thanks no doubt to the great media fanfare and, perhaps above all, to the race against Stanley, at the head of a rival English expedition.[25] The explorer Wilhelm Junker returns to Berlin from his heroic travels among "little people," the "black dwarves" of Central Africa.[26] That same year the German Colonial Society is established in Berlin, unifying

Henry Morton Stanley in Germany (1885). *WIDM* 58 (April–September 1885). Courtesy Butler Library, Columbia University.

the movement nationally. In 1889, the "Cameroon Rooms" of the newly opened Passage-Panoptikum display wax figures in dioramas of the new West African protectorate.[27] Colonial fervor has only begun, perhaps, to ebb; and the strident anticolonialism of the SPD, which will provoke and renew it, to take faint shape.

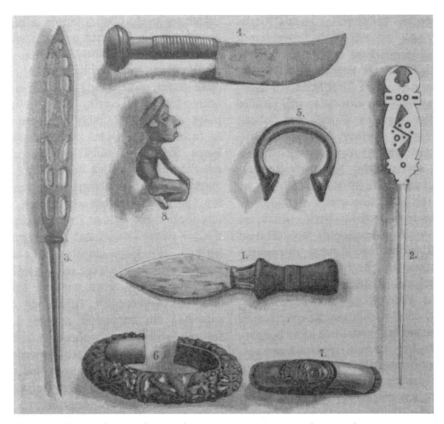

Mass-circulation ethnographica in the 1880s. *WIDM* 58 (April–September 1885).
Courtesy Butler Library, Columbia University.

"In modern times," says Hegel, "culture is essentially intellectual, and it immediately converts all events into reports for intellectual representation." The now-obscure Cameroon episode—in its combination of insignificance and media amplification it seems almost a made-for-media event—condenses many elements that would define colonial discourse in Germany: its foundations in tropes of highly specialized authority embodied in the eyewitness account, the travelogue, war reportage, official and scientific reports, expertise, personal experience "out there," on the colonial periphery. These were, so to speak, mirrored by the dense visual culture of the period—photography, the panorama, the diorama, the ethnographic show—typified by powerful effects of realism. Rhetorics and techniques of empirical, objective, and scientific authority shaped and sustained colonialism as the exuberance of the 1880s faded to boredom and indifference, or incomprehension, or was challenged by deep pessimism or vitriolic socialist critique. Empire appeared to constitute a vast field of knowledge, as of economic development, affording vital scope for the realization of German national advance in a world of dangerous

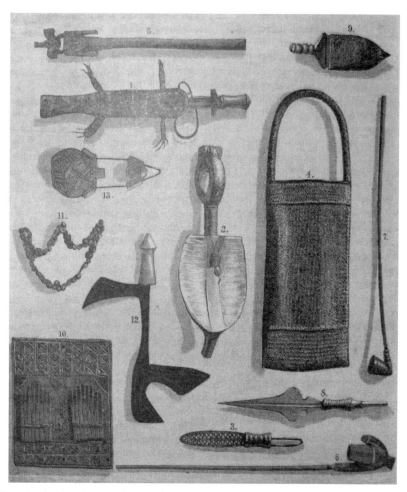

Mass-circulation ethnographica in the 1880s. *WIDM* 58 (April–September 1885).
Courtesy Butler Library, Columbia University.

rivalries. Colonial discourse unfolded powerfully and self-consciously, but
also jealously and defensively, as an ostensibly truthful description of modern
reality, and moreover, a hard reality of global competition to which only sober
facts were adequate. Colonialism was a form of social knowledge: a collective
way to know and describe the wide "global" world, knowledge by its own
claims rational, modern, scientific, universal, concerned with the common
good, but generated in the narrow milieu of the educated and propertied.[28]

Of course, error flourished in colonial discourse: error as rumor, as sensationalism, as propaganda, not least as the whole misconceived prospectus
of colonial political economy. This only made claims to truthful knowledge
all the more charged. The colonial movement from its beginnings approximated
the bourgeois public sphere, or rather vestiges of it. It reflected — and dis-

torted—the commercial logic of civil society and exemplified the public appeal to reason, the reproduction of discourse through "rational-critical public debate."[29] It first arose from the intermingled currents of scientific culture and bourgeois associational life. Or, as Stanley put it, observing the contemporary scene: "out of the most intelligent and enterprising of the sons of Germany"—he mentions Max Buchner—"twenty-four Geographical Societies had been formed, and a dozen Colonial Associations" by 1884, all signs of "the murmuring and latent passion" of the era.[30] The objective of the new colonial movement would be to crystallize and popularize that passion, to explain the overseas world to Germans and bind them together in colonial enthusiasm and resolve, and ultimately to disseminate a market worldview, an image of the global. What began in geographic, oriental, and natural history associations—and simultaneously in commercial and trade groups—developed in institutions of many kinds, in museums and universities, in an accumulating library and archive, in the emergent disciplines of African linguistics and anthropology, or more traditional ones such as geography, agronomy, zoology and botany, in commercial associations and exhibitions, congresses and seminars.[31]

What this meant was that colonialism—or rather, what the members of the institutionalized, organized, well-connected colonial movement understood by it—was the province of the few, those equipped for it through education and experience. Their shared forms of sociability, language, respectability, and knowledge—their banquets and scientific lectures and philanthropic noblesse, their stylizations of the officer, the explorer, the naturalist, the big-game hunter—excluded the great majority of German workers, the lower middle classes, women.[32] The broad and flourishing associational life from which the movement emerged was itself already long marked by its reproductions of these social and gender distinctions.[33] (More ordinary people formed now-forgotten "Cameroon Societies," but for conviviality and amusement.)[34] And yet it was the very purpose of, for example, the German Colonial Society, the central organ of the movement, founded in 1887, to advance "the national work of colonization" and "spread knowledge of its necessity among ever wider circles."[35] Colonialists appealed to reason, science, and urgent economic fact—to universals—and addressed themselves to the broad public. But of course, the public sphere, precisely in its general abstraction, its submergence of distinction, had historically concealed the constitutive privileging of bourgeois men, which defined the colonial movement.[36] Paradoxically, the movement reproduced precisely the social fissures it was meant to resolve.

And, indeed, the historical bourgeois public sphere, whose fleeting forms determined the outlines of German colonial discourse, was by the 1880s much transformed—or rather, survived as after-effect. Colonialists frankly sought to integrate state power and private industry around colonial projects of capital investment, infrastructure, and security—abandoning assumptions about privatized authority over exchange and labor, marking thereby a fundamental distinction from the idea of the classic bourgeois public sphere.[37] (One important dimension of the "new imperialism" of the late nineteenth century was, of course, a kind of free-trade panic.) At the same time, colonial discourse, proliferating along a spectrum from popular science to propaganda, became a tool in managing mass politics, if masked by its own self-presentation as pragmatic and scientific discussion. In effect, colonialism, even as it retraced the institutional and discursive outlines of the public sphere, seemed at the same time to trace its disintegration in late nineteenth-century capitalism: state intervention (in matters of capital investment, commodity flows, and colonial labor); the growing role of the state in regulating social conflict (in part through deploying colonial ideology in the sphere of mass politics); the rise of a commodified mass culture (in which colonial exoticism and adventure play a fundamental role, as in the panorama); perhaps even with the rise of monopoly capitalism (identical to colonialism in the view of contemporary anticolonialists like Rosa Luxemburg and Rudolf Hilferding).[38] Still, the colonial movement continued to ventriloquize the voices of the public sphere, while signifying its decomposition in a reality of grinding class conflict and dynamic economic change.

Certainly the rise of mass politics—of popular nationalism and, after 1890, of socialism—disclosed the limit of colonialism as it had originated in the intimate clubs and business groups of German bourgeois society, defining its internal contradictions but also new potentials. And the rapid growth of the SPD after the lapse of controversial antisocialist laws, confirmed by victory at the polls in 1903, also signified the elaboration of a sharp new critique of colonialism. The dissemination and popular reception of colonial discourse unfolded across a field of mass parties, media, and commercial culture, of contention and distraction, sensation and scandal. This tendency developed from the beginnings of the movement in the 1880s, through the relatively more diffuse, vegetative colonialism of the 1890s, to the apotheosis of propaganda during the German-Herero war in Southwest Africa from 1904 to 1906, and the so-called "Hottentot elections" that followed in 1907. Colonialists continued in the mode of self-consciously rational, critical discourse, of reasonable persuasion, characteristic of the public sphere, but in the period of its disintegration this concealed the reality of quickening manipulation.[39] Yet, if the implication of orchestration, of propagandism, is popular passivity, the social reality is considerably more complicated.

Colonial discourse did coalesce finally into a social form of knowledge, or ideology—into a collective and naturalized system of construing the world at a particular moment in the history of globalizing capitalism—and it operated within the fragmented, antagonistic, teeming sphere of mass culture and politics as a tool of manipulation. Colonialism appears, once again, as a form of power—within the metropole itself. It circulated above all as economic knowledge, as commodity propaganda designed to initiate the masses into the concept of globally sourced production and markets. And yet, at the same time, the movement hesitated in its encounter with the masses. It embodied and enacted countervailing impulses both to include and exclude. Not only did the colonial movement reproduce social division, excluding women and workers, shopkeepers and artisans, the uneducated and unpolished, but colonialists also frequently lacked the will, the experience, the temperament to engage the masses even as objects. They lamented constantly the indifference or hostility of the masses but could only with difficulty move to counteract these, and actually discouraged certain forms of colonial enthusiasm. They held female enthusiasts at arm's length; ridiculed lower-class ignorance; disdained grassroots colonial societies and self-made colonial publicists; denied irregular and spontaneous enthusiasms; left unacknowledged the colonial hopes and aspirations of uncounted ordinary Germans; responded sluggishly and ineptly to opportunities. And this was true even as their chief objective remained the broad popularization of colonial enthusiasm. Colonialism was the sign and enactment of a certain kind of power—encoded in language and expertise, materialized in institutions, wielded as propaganda—but it also marked the limit of that power.

In a strong sense, then, colonial discourse reveals the fractured and shifting nature of a post-public sphere in late nineteenth-century Germany. Most prominently, there is an enormous socialist "counterpublic," led by the SPD, which contests the colonial worldview. And there is another, forgotten, submerged colonial public; indeed, a whole other history of German colonialism—as, for that matter, of anticolonialism—from below, among the broad *Mittelstand* of artisans, shopkeepers, and white-collar workers, among women, among the proletariat. This grassroots colonial public amounts to a kind of "plebeian public sphere" formed from the lower middle and working classes and including countless women. In many ways, this alternate public was derivative of the bourgeois colonial movement, a submerged variant, a distorted—but recognizable—reflection of its discourse and aims.[40] It materialized in local colonial veterans' groups, small-time impresarios of travelling colonial shows, petit bourgeois colonial associations, the unfulfilled aspirations of colonizers without means. These were people without property or education, or without male entitlement, who wanted to be part of the colonial movement or empire. Their subaltern cosmopolitanism was surprising and vital. They aspired to a new start as settlers; imagined adventure and the exotic; celebrated their past colonial military service; cooked up small-time colonial exhibitions, in so many ways reflecting the discourse and practices of the colonial movement that excluded them. They were presumably the very fulfillment of colonialist aims—the "wider circles" so ardently dreamed of—and yet the colonial movement had no idea what to do with them. Nor with the even greater masses avidly curious about the colonies: the readers of dime novels, spectators at the wax museum and panorama.

This broad public was fickle, facile, credulous, complained the colonialists. The stern Max Buchner warned of this already in the first years of the new empire: "We begin to observe that in the field of colonial policy we still have awfully much to learn, and that one does not get very far in such a difficult, serious matter with the enthusiasm of the multitude. The more quickly and easily public opinion, that old childish nature, is roused to enthusiasm, the more rapidly it grows timid and disheartened whenever expectations of success are not met."[41] Public opinion, observed a contemporary analyst, was a powerful thing, but "always marked with prejudice, easily deceived" and too much driven by the mass imagination, the *Massenphantasie*.[42] Moreover, if the multitude wavers and frets, worse still is the ignorance and superstition that distorts empire in the popular mind: the empire of titillation, voyeurism, and idle excitements, of cannibals and crocodiles and Amazon warriors, of trash literature and fair booths. To colonialists, the suggestible, distracted multitude required education about flows of raw materials and the manufacturing sector, about global competition and labor. Especially the ceaseless circulation of colonial commodities, or their representations, would bring home their vital role in industrial production. And all of this so urgently necessary because ignorance and fancy together bred inattention, error and—worst of all—the recalcitrant anticolonialism of the socialists. Seen in the context of the social, colonialism appears, once again, as a problem of knowledge—knowledge that reflects and reproduces class difference. The knowledge of the multitude, in contemporary bourgeois discourse, appears as speculative, elusive, apocryphal, sensationalized, invented, fantastical. All the brute facts ostensibly generated by so many colonial congresses and clubs and expeditions, the careful object lessons in tropical commodities, and the persuasive voice of public reason seemed powerless to spread a defined and disciplined form of colonialism.

The sense of an idle popular curiosity, or a vulgar understanding of colonialism—colonialism as mass culture—reinscribes the problematic narrative of a decayed public sphere: its origins among men of property and education, among a literary public, where judgment was a matter of cultivation and rational-critical argument, but now debased, transformed into passive consumption by "the masses."[43] We can speak usefully here of a kind of popular "enchantment," or perhaps "reenchantment," in the stubborn fascination with fetishes and cannibals and idol worship and the ethnographic monsters of the freak show (pygmy, albino, the ritually scarred or tattooed). This is a late, mass-cultural form of the wonder aroused by Patagonian giants and mermaids, fantastic figures of the once unmastered, overseas exotic. Such dime-novel enchantment—produced not least by modern media technologies—is opposed here precisely to the rational-critical space of the public sphere, site of scientific knowledge and economic fact.[44] (The anxious contemporary impulse in ethnographic museums to supplant "curiosities" and "wonders" with "science" parallels the discourse of a sober, scientific colonialism.)[45]

Colonial discourse defined itself precisely *against* fantasy, against the "mass imagination." But that opposition is misleading. The anxieties and impatience evinced by colonialists confronting the ostensibly ignorant, vul-

garly curious, enchanted multitude conceal proximity as much as they express distinction or distance. The sharp divide masks underlying continuities. The bourgeois world of colonial, anthropological, and geographical
societies, that same world of scientific knowledge, technology, and cultivation, mirrors what it condemns.[46] Likewise the institutions of the socialist
"alternative culture." The "reenchantment of the world" in the form of
colonial knowledge cuts across classes and politics. By countless imitations
and imbrications, reciprocal influences and attractions, colonial knowledge
and colonial enchantment interact in a tense and intimate configuration.[47]

But, of course, what stands out here is not just the underlying, perhaps
deeper, continuity of "enchantment"; it is the fundamental intertwining of
that shared, suppressed impulse with sharp difference and conflict between
elite and mass. There *is* a gulf, socially and culturally, between upper-class
colonialist men and the broad masses of women or workers or petits bourgeois. Difference is expressed variously as disdain for mass culture or socialist critique of empire, or encoded in cultural markers of status. And it is
precisely the antagonism traced by colonialism as knowledge that accom-
plishes the fundamental work of disseminating colonialism. The discourse of
enchantment—of enchantment displaced onto the popular—produces both
the masses as object of "colonial enlightenment" and, reflexively, the very
measure and condition of bourgeois colonialist *rationality*, casting it into relief, reinforcing its claims to truth. The divide structures colonial discourse.

Still, hierarchical difference does not signify the historical (or conceptual)
flattening of the working classes, or the broader lower classes, or lower-
class women, into a passive mass. What apparent enchantment and ignorance reveal, in fact, are not only the concealed similarities between different classes *and* the lines dividing them but also the disharmony of plural
voices—and their sheer persistence. There is, as it turns out, no uniform
German "colonialism," but several, jostling and disturbing one another. The
colonialist bourgeoisie insists on a univocal, controlled, expert discourse
and thereby denies a reality of multiple voices that can be neither answered
nor contained by the institutionalized form. The contested rise of a *separate*
women's colonial movement—separate even though fundamentally aristocratic and bourgeois—points both to the exclusionary and dominating tendencies of masculinist bourgeois colonialism and to the reality of diffuse
power, to alternative assertions of agency.[48] Colonialism reveals a spectrum
of persistent, sometimes stubbornly "original," sometimes fantastic versions
of empire, versions that in turn suggest the limitations and complexities of
power—as education, manipulation, imposition, discipline, resistance—
across German society. If it functions substantially as a kind of social
knowledge, knowledge again and again predicated on a kind of rational
disenchantment, it reveals alternative knowledges constituted through error and wonder and naïveté. And an insistent working-class cosmopolitanism. The colonial public sphere is more heterogeneous and fractured, more
crowded and contested, than allowed by its own dominant terms.[49]

Of course, the outer limit defining public discourse on empire was the SPD and the many working-class and other Germans it inspired to anticolonial politics. The SPD exemplifies neither carnival enchantment nor the minor-key eccentricities of grassroots colonialists, but a whole rival public, institutionalized like the colonial movement but articulating a fierce, sustained "counterdiscourse."[50] Its powerful machinery of propaganda and vivid rhetoric castigating the colonial empire challenged the very idea of a "common good" subsuming class difference, an idea that underwrote both the public sphere and colonial ideology. Socialist writers and speakers poured scorn and derision on the futility, greed, violence, and corruption of the colonial empire, and their anticolonial discourse made its way into pubs and libraries, newspapers and political meetings across the country. The lasting grassroots effects of this propaganda counterbalanced the reformist impulse among sections of the SPD leadership. However, the social history of German colonialism is hardly a straightforward development of working-class or subaltern resistance to empire. Even the alternative world of the SPD, especially at the local level, was not entirely indifferent to the fascinations of empire, especially in the form of popular "scientific" knowledge. And the SPD was never simply identical to the working class, which counted resolute or hopeful colonialists in its ranks. But the SPD did produce a very powerful countervailing force that moved large numbers of people to oppose colonialism at the grassroots and that consistently shaped the production of colonial discourse in a protracted antagonism. The idea of a monolithically revisionist SPD, based on a superficial emphasis on the party leadership, belies the vigorous critical impulse of the more ordinary rank and file.

It is, then, precisely as *social* history—social history carefully synthesized with a cultural approach—that this book revisits some of the fundamental problems that have defined the study of German colonialism in its metropolitan form, problems that revolve principally around issues of class conflict and modernity. Social division and the politics that sprang from it lie at the heart of German colonial historiography, which privileges the political and social dynamic within Germany in explaining the impulse to imperial expansion. The essential, flawed concept of "social imperialism" emphasizes the role of colonialism in manipulating and distracting the lower classes to bolster ruling elites clinging to premodern forms of power against the threat of a new mass democratic politics.[51] However suggestive, the approach has lacked empirical foundation, an archive illuminating colonialism in everyday life, in the culture and politics of ordinary Germans: the ostensible site of manipulation. And its picture of passive masses and a thwarted German modernity effaces the ways that colonialism both expressed real—and heterogeneous—popular sentiment and exemplified precisely the globalizing modernity that Germany shared with its European rivals.[52] But the compelling counternarrative of a revolutionizing nationalist and colonialist Right animated "from below," while it restores a more complex historical reality, has not encouraged the degree of fine-grained socio-cultural analysis necessary to recover the currents and textures of colonialism in its most popular, ephemeral, and quotidian forms.[53]

To revisit that history of German colonialism in its metropolitan, sociopolitical context is not, of course, to see it once again as simply an effect, an epiphenomenal emanation of class antagonism. Rather, by restoring colonialism to its crucial place in the narrative of modern German history, we complicate that history, indeed showing how colonial discourse is not merely effect, but powerfully productive: of public, of nation, of globe. To construe colonialism as a kind of knowledge, and to observe it refracted and contested across lines of class and gender, points to the exclusions upon which the public sphere developed, certainly. But it also points beyond this, to the broader effacement of the colonized that emerges intertwined with the exclusions of the metropole, suggesting that an account of the public sphere must integrate the history of empire. Such exclusions underwrite the mapping of a German place in the world; its "place in the sun" throws long shadows. The public sphere, the site of bourgeois configurations of nation and empire, produced the staging of the global that effaced the broad masses, just as it did the colonized, even as it sought to initiate both into a particular version of market modernity. If this book does not substantially integrate the colonial situation in German Africa or the Pacific, it nevertheless turns on the centrality of a transnational logic drawing metropolitan and colonial labor into a common trajectory of global capitalism and class division.

Within Germany, this process unfolded across a highly charged field of conflict, a field marked by the ideological competition, party rivalry, cultural anxieties, and social distinctions expressive of German class society in the age of quickening mass politics and culture. All the more striking, therefore, that colonialism spread as extensively as it did. After three decades of indifference, skepticism, crisis, scandal, pessimism, and furious opposition, and *not* in spite of these, colonialism in Germany emerges as a growing consensus about the overseas world and its peoples, and about the German—and European—place in that world. It is precisely resistance and contestation that produce colonialism—and the powerful force field that emerges between the rhetorical poles of enchantment and knowledge. To foreground colonialism in German history is to illuminate the intimacy of their historical intertwinement. The stubbornly "idle" curiosity, the discordant aspirations, and the critical reflections of countless Germans of the lower classes represent—in precisely their tension with institutionalized colonialism—the conditions for the dissemination of a stronger, more supple, more sinuous, and pervasive colonialism: a way of viewing the wider world in terms of resources, commodity and labor flows, biological races, competition, rather than a particular set of policies for colonial East Africa or New Guinea. In this sense colonialism develops as a protracted initiation into the modern sense of the "global."

This is not to suggest that power was not hierarchical and unequal in Germany, or that colonial propaganda and manipulation played no part in the diffusion of colonial discourse. Colonialism was at one level an ideology

Logoization of the world: from the nameplate of *Globus* (1880s). Courtesy Butler Library, Columbia University.

wielded "from above"—by the state, capital, the dominant cultural and social institutions of the bourgeoisie—to integrate a recalcitrant German proletariat. But certainly these institutions themselves hardly existed outside of colonial discourse by the turn of the century. And, at the same time, the distribution of colonial discourse lay largely beyond the overlapping spheres of the state, capital, and bourgeois collective life. It was ordered, developed, enriched by all kinds of institutions, in all kinds of exchanges and transactions: national and local, bourgeois and proletarian, nationalist and socialist, commercial and scientific. Colonialism was, on many levels, *about* authority: colonial authority over the natives, but also the authority of scientific knowledge of the world, the unanswerable authority of economics—in the "tough" version of global competition—all of which buttressed *particular* claims to social and political authority in Germany.[54] And yet authority continuously challenged, as microhistories of the local and the everyday reveal: the sites of contestation, of surprising proximity, of stubborn difference, ambiguity, mutation.

Colonialism, then, was the form of consciousness in capitalism in which the *world* was remade as market, as exchange, as contested source of raw

Logoization of the world: knowledge astride the globe. Nameplate, *ÜLuM* (1880s).
Courtesy Butler Library, Columbia University.

materials. It was the social form of consciousness corresponding to processes of economic and scientific rationalization that took the globalizing world as their object and field. It initiated the broad masses into modernity, and indeed in fundamental ways produced them—laborers, servant girls, factory workers—alongside the colonized. That grassroots colonialism was substantially marked not as rational, but enchanted, appears paradoxical, but if there was an enchantment of myth and magic in mass culture, there was finally no less a fetishism of the colonial commodity and the colonial market in bourgeois economic discourse. Currents of knowledge and magic flowed, paradoxically, together. Resituating colonialism at the center of turn-of-the-century German society shows us how the very idea of bourgeois modernity was embedded in enchantment. The colonialists' discourse of enchantment produced the necessary object: the masses standing in need of *Kolonialaufklärung* and *Kolonialerziehung*, colonial enlightenment and education. And, reflexively, it produced—by contrast—the rationality of colonialism.

Neither the institutions of the state nor the colonialist parties and interest groups ultimately stood sufficiently "above" or "outside" the colonial worldview to imply manipulation of a distinct other. The margin beyond colonial discourse subtly contracted, so that there was finally no class or party that fully escaped the enchantment of colonialism, not even the Social Democrats. If bourgeois colonialist anxieties about plebeian enchantment—that mesmerism of snake worshipers and head hunters and witch doctors—concealed its reflection in the arena of formal colonial knowledge, then conversely it was often and precisely "science," and its corollaries of rationalization and progress, that drew socialists—workers *and* intellectuals—to colonialism. Difference both concealed and produced similarity: a fascination with the exotic; and with science, compounded by a shared sense of its authority; a common colonial library; the shared enticements of the panorama, of mass culture; an expanding world view.

CHAPTER ONE

Estrangement

Structures and Limits of the Colonial Public Sphere

IMPERIALISTS: *All respectable, polite, peaceable, distinguished people.*
—Gustave Flaubert, *Le dictionnaire des idées reçues*, 1870s

One by one, images appear in mechanical succession, silvered and luminous fragments: the vivid patterns of an Ovambo granary; serial portraits of mounted white officers; rows of Nama, San, or Herero posed for inspection; everyday life in a barracks; the forlorn isolation of the Rehoboth police station in a wilderness of dust and thorns. Altogether an unexceptional scene, a typical colonial magic lantern show in 1904, as the German-Herero War in Southwest Africa piqued public interest in the faraway colony. Unexceptional, that is, but for the lanternist himself.

Hermann Schlüter was hardly a typical travel photographer, explorer, or colonial propagandist of the turn of the century.[1] The son of a railroad conductor in Braunschweig, he was twenty when, in 1896, he went to Southwest Africa as a volunteer with the *Schutztruppe*, taking along a basic travel camera. This was an almost unimaginably distant, alien world, a true adventure for a young man of petit bourgeois origins from a provincial city with few prospects of travel. (But Schlüter's own story warns us against making too much of that stock character: the uneducated, parochial *Kleinbürger* who knows little of the world beyond hometown and *Heimat*. The vicissitudes of empire in the late nineteenth century set all sorts of people in motion and linked the remotest corners of the globe.) The adventurous Schlüter was in so many ways ordinary: lower middle-class, a common soldier, an amateur photographer. He was also surprisingly talented, and his superiors took him seriously enough to make him responsible for photographic documentation of an expedition northward into Ovamboland.

Five years later he returned to his native city and set up as a florist, continuing to collect images of Southwest Africa from books and magazines. When the Herero revolt erupted in 1904, Schlüter went so far as to produce a public lantern-slide lecture, his shows announced and enthusiastically reviewed in local Braunschweig papers. While it's not clear whether this was a commercial venture, he did sell tickets at least once, pledging part of the profit to the cause of the soldiers fighting in Southwest Africa. In this way,

Schlüter joined the ranks of itinerant lecturers—experts, explorers, colonial heroes, missionaries—who plied the circuit of local learned societies and voluntary associations with their magic lantern slides.

The German Colonial Society was, of course, a leading sponsor of such lectures, as well as a magnet for local colonial enthusiasts like Schlüter, but nothing suggests he had any link with the local chapter. He was certainly not a member. And given the ways that the fundamentally bourgeois colonial movement tended to reproduce the class divisions of Wilhelmine society, this is not surprising. Indeed, Schlüter's photograph collection and lantern-slide lectures mirrored bourgeois practice but belonged ultimately to a parallel world of grassroots colonialism, of travelling showmen and small-town veterans and would-be settlers. His trajectory as florist-propagandist suggests something of the ways that colonialism both crossed class boundaries and reconfirmed them. He could speak with authority and knowledge of Southwest Africa; but, although expert and enthusiast, and perfect model of colonialism reaching the "ordinary" man, he operated in a world separate from the colonial movement.

The most dedicated colonialists of Braunschweig—or Leipzig, or Bamberg, of cities and towns across Germany—took pride and pleasure in the emblems and trappings of empire. (That the promised abundance of German Africa and the South Seas proved illusory did little to temper this.) The leading men among them, together with a very few women and many "respectable" citizens of slightly lesser rank, gathered in influential political or scientific associations dedicated, like the Colonial Society, to the overseas empire. Here was an extensive interlocking machinery for diffusing colonial knowledge, information, propaganda. These forms of organized colonial enthusiasm became arenas of class sociability and solidarity, miniature theaters in which publishers and professors, industrialists and bankers enacted and celebrated the drama of empire building. Every two or three months they came together to smoke Cameroon cigars, pore over maps of Hereroland or Neu-Mecklenburg, and gaze at luminous magic lantern portraits of their Masai or Nama subjects, of cotton cultivation or missionaries under swaying palms. In all this, the working and lower middle classes, and for the most part women, had no share.

In Schlüter's case, no clear evidence survives of exclusion or aloofness on either side. The point is, rather, how it reflects and confirms a bold, broad pattern of class division, a pattern that seems to contradict everything the colonial movement stood for in the last decades of the Kaiserreich—and everything signified by interpretations of it, then and much later, as an agent of "social imperialism," of elite manipulation of the modern masses. If we attempt to reconstruct German colonialism as it existed for itself, in the form of the organized colonial movement, this is the pattern we observe universally. The dense network of associational life—colonial and national organizations, business groups, geographic societies—consistently reflected

"A Congenial Hour at the *Kolonialheim*": colonial conviviality in Berlin (1897). *DKZ* 10 (1897). Courtesy New York Public Library.

the participation of the educated and propertied bourgeoisie. The movement would not or could not assimilate colonialists from other strata of the population, precisely the "little people," as it sometimes called them, that it most sought.

We return here to the elusive idea of the "public sphere," to the tensions between universal claims—a broad public defined by rational-critical discourse, theoretically open to all, and materialized in communicative networks of civic engagement and sociability—and de facto exclusions of class and gender. Colonialists assembled the doubled civil society of private industry and stratified associational life into a late, vestigial form of bourgeois public sphere in which a particular colonial discourse claimed privileged status: as both a form of knowledge (current, rational, scientific) and a disinterested discussion of the common good. The colonial movement incarnated the contradictions inherent in the very concept of the "bourgeois public sphere": universalist intentions, exclusivist realities, the construction of "the masses" as object, the attempt to efface multiple voices.

The German Colonial Society (Deutsche Kolonialgesellschaft) formed the apex of the movement, the preeminent site of collective colonialist activism from its 1887 founding in Berlin to the wartime dissolution of the empire and beyond, into the 1920s.[2] Like its most important predecessor, the German Colonial Association (Deutscher Kolonialverein), the Colonial Society set out to publicize colonialism, excite popular enthusiasm, and win members and supporters. First among the "Objectives of the Society" listed in its original statutes was—once again—to further "the national work of colonization" and "spread knowledge of its necessity among ever wider circles" of the population.[3] This vision of colonialism rippling out across Germany presumably encompassed all sectors of society, from skeptical fellow bourgeois to factory workers and peasants. In the 1880s, however, envisioning broad public enthusiasm for colonialism meant something different from what it would come to mean in the later 1890s and after the turn of the century. The need to convince leading sectors of the educated and propertied bourgeoisie, of commerce and industry, and not least the government itself, of the urgent necessity of a German colonial empire focused colonialists' efforts on a narrower field. At the same time, the social origins and extremely limited democratic political tendencies among the aristocratic and upper middle-class founders of the Colonial Society restricted their ambitions to popularize colonialism. From the 1890s until the outbreak of war in 1914, colonialists grappled with the problems of opening their ranks to Germans of lower-class backgrounds and of how they might win the support of workers, artisans, and peasants. The evolving theory and practice of colonial propaganda reflected the transformation of Germany by mass culture and mass politics in the 1890s and after. But it did not ultimately transform the social limitations of the colonial movement.

From its beginnings in the 1870s, the organized colonial movement drew its leadership from the thin layers of the upper bourgeoisie in the cities and towns of Germany. Founders of the Kolonialverein in 1882, all men, included the prominent politicians Johannes Miquel, the lord mayor of Frankfurt, and Rudolf von Bennigsen, leader of the National Liberal Party, as well as literary and intellectual luminaries like Leopold von Ranke, Heinrich von Treitschke, Friedrich Ratzel, Gustav Freytag, the explorer Gerhard Rohlfs, and the archaeologist Heinrich Schliemann.[4] Many leaders of its successor, the Colonial Society, were also men of national reputation in industry, politics, banking, and commerce.[5] Locally, organized colonialism was the province of the *Honoratioren*, the notables, who formed branch associations and transmitted colonial ideology through the local political, cultural, and religious institutions they controlled. The social composition of the Colonial Society was almost entirely middle-class. Professors, doctors, lawyers, factory owners, officials, pharmacists, bankers, and editors paid dues, took the *Deutsche Kolonialzeitung*, and attended the occasional slide lecture or "gentlemen's evening." Officers, government officials, and businessmen comprised the great majority.[6] The society also included men of modest background—petty civil servants, innkeepers, clerks, small businessmen—but in disproportionately small numbers. There were no workers, artisans, or peasants to speak of, nor any attempt to attract them, which ensured sluggish growth and limited membership. By the turn of the century, the society had nearly thirty-five thousand members, climbing to over forty thousand by 1914, and preserved a remarkable degree of social and gender homogeneity.[7]

A somewhat alternative impulse found noisy but limited expression in a rival organization, the Society for German Colonization (Gesellschaft für Deutsche Kolonisation), formed by the "colonial pioneer" Carl Peters in 1884.[8] In contrast to the Kolonialverein, the passionate enthusiasts gathered around Peters demanded direct and immediate action: the foundation of overseas colonies for settlement by German emigrants. Their stated purpose was the "energetic furtherance of the colonial and German national movement" through the "founding of German national colonies," the "support of German colonization undertakings," the "direction of German emigration to suitable areas," and "promotion of German national interests" generally.[9] The Peters group rejected the cautious moderation of the Kolonialverein, and the carefully cultivated, deferential relationship to Bismarck's government that accompanied it. Late in 1884, Peters undertook his infamous expedition to Zanzibar and East Africa, where he set about extracting treaties from local rulers. The following year, the German government recognized Peters's dramatic fait accompli by establishing the colonial protectorate of German East Africa.[10]

This willingness to act decisively without securing either a broad consensus or Bismarck's approval, combined with brash criticism of the glacial drift of German colonization, exemplifies the more activist strand of "popular colonialism," or *Volkskolonialismus,* in the 1880s. Ideologically, the brand of popular colonialism promoted by the Peters faction consisted in recasting settlement colonialism in the radical nationalist discourse of the Kaiserreich.[11] The dream of white colonial settlement as a solution to the massive nineteenth-century German *Auswanderung*—as a means of keeping Germans from becoming American—had been since the 1840s the most popular aspect of German colonial ideology. The government, however, and most leading colonialists from the spheres of banking, industry, and Hanseatic commerce, were skeptical of the ideology of settlement. Peters nevertheless reworked it into a dynamic nationalist politics by associating settlement colonialism with lower middle-class fears and aspirations. Unlike the Kolonialverein, he appealed to petits bourgeois and peasants vulnerable to the demographic and economic forces that fueled successive waves of emigration, and to ardent nationalists anxious about the fate of Germandom abroad.[12] By emphasizing themes of emigration and settlement, and associating them with the vaguely anticapitalist resentments and longings of a lower middle-class public, the Peters group achieved limited success in articulating colonialism to broader popular currents in contemporary political life.

There was even a degree of correspondence between the GfDK's *Volkskolonialismus* and its social composition. Its membership did indeed represent a slightly broader spectrum of the middle class than the Kolonialverein— including lower officials, modest merchants, and tradesmen, although no workers or peasants. Yet, ironically, it remained much the smaller organization, boasting only forty-five hundred members by the end of 1887: the exception proved the rule.[13] When the Colonial Society finally formed in Berlin through the fusion of the two rival groups in 1887, the larger Kolonialverein essentially absorbed the Peters group.[14] *Volkskolonialismus*, with its brash, more radical style and emphasis on colonial settlement, took its place as an important but secondary current of thought and feeling within the broader movement.

Everywhere in Germany the movement—the Colonial Society at its center— reproduced the tradition of participation by bourgeois men. In the Rhineland, site of important early efforts since the 1870s, activist circles drawn from the male middle classes formed associations and propagandized.[15] In the Saxon industrial city of Leipzig, the colonial movement consisted of a dense network of influential men organized into several associations with overlapping membership: principally the Colonial Society, the Pan-German League (Alldeutscher Verband), and the Leipzig Geographical Association (Verein für Erdkunde zu Leipzig), but also perhaps the Association for Germandom Abroad (Verein für das Deutschtum im Auslande), or the large local branch of the Navy League (Flottenverein), though colonialism was a secondary element in its program and its large and relatively more diverse membership reflected a different approach to nationalist politics.[16] In 1899, the Colonial Society counted 808 members. In 1907 and again in 1910 there were 1,050, making it one of the largest in Germany.[17]

Industrialists, bankers, and merchants represented nearly half of the Leipzig section. The city and Saxon governments, the Leipzig-based Reich Supreme Court, and the local officer corps were also quite well represented. So were the ranks of educated professionals. In 1910, over 10 percent of members belonged to the medical and legal professions. Many important professors, together with the student fraternities Arminia, Dresdensia, Germania, and the Verein Deutscher Studenten, represented the university. The directors of the Ethnographic Museum, the Evangelical-Lutheran Missionary Society, and the Museum of Plastic Arts were also members. Probably most significant from the point of view of local political opinion was the membership of several Leipzig newspaper editors. These included the editor in chief of the ardently pro-colonial *Leipziger Neueste Nachrichten*, which in 1910 had the largest circulation among Leipzig's political dailies, and both the owner and the editor-in-chief of the National Liberal *Leipziger Tageblatt*.[18]

During this entire period, the Colonial Society in heavily industrialized Leipzig had not a single member from the working classes, and barely a handful from the traditional skilled trades and the new *Mittelstand* of white-collar workers.[19] Nor did the local Pan-German League have any workers among its members, though its membership was slightly more mixed than that of the Colonial Society.[20] There were also, of course, no workers among the cultivated audiences for "scientific" lectures at the Geographical Association. The objective of the Leipzig Colonial Society was to win workers for colonialism, not to draw them into its ranks. There was no parallel in the Colonial Society to the local Navy League's aspirations to mass membership.

The relationship between the local colonial veterans' association and the Colonial Society illustrates the paternalism of colonialists. The membership of these veterans' associations was generally much more heterogeneous, and much more reflective of the lower middle- and working-class majority, than was Colonial Society membership.[21] Tellingly, as was the case elsewhere in Germany, the head of the colonial veterans' association was not a member of the local Colonial Society, while the chair of the latter was, inevitably, an honorary member of the former. Pastor Johannes Wangemann, a member of the Pan-German League, the Geographical Association, and the Colonial Society board, and a frequent speaker on colonialism, was likewise an honorary member of the veterans' association. The veterans, on the other hand, were highly unlikely to find the Colonial Society affordable, familiar, or welcoming.

In the very different Kingdom of Bavaria most members of the Colonial Society—and the leadership in particular—were, once again, well educated, well connected, and well-to-do: the local notables of the bourgeoisie and the aristocracy. In June 1910, the Regensburg chapter counted 121 members, including no workers or artisans, but rather teachers, officials, pharmacists, officers, clerics, businessmen, factory owners, wholesale merchants, and professors.[22] The membership of the Bamberg chapter, which included the mayor as vice chairman, numbered 76 in 1895, and 57 in 1913.[23] In Nuremberg, most members hailed from manufacturing, commerce, banking, the officer corps, and the liberal professions. There were no workers and virtually no *Kleinbürger* with the exception of a few skilled tradesmen and small business owners.[24] Members included the mayor and prominent bankers and businessmen. The society held numerous lantern-slide lectures, organized a separate, junior branch for the less well-off, and helped to sponsor and publicize an important naval and colonial exhibition in 1898. In numbers, it was among the largest in Germany: just 212 in 1905, 349 by the end of 1913, and 367 by the end of 1914.[25] This was much smaller than the local Navy League, which counted 1,418 members in 1912.[26] But, of course, the Colonial Society's members—especially its leaders—were among the most influential men in the city.

Indeed, examined from the vantage point of the Bavarian elite—both Catholic and Protestant—colonialism appears to have occupied an extraordinarily privileged place. Many of the highest nobility, including Wittelsbach princes, and many more among the wealthiest and most distinguished of the bourgeoisie, were active in the movement. Prince Leopold von Bayern was honorary chair of the Colonial Society in Munich for almost twenty-five years. Notable colonialists from Bavaria included Count Julius Zech, the famously successful governor of Togo; Baron von Gravenreuth, a comrade of Carl Peters in East Africa; the explorer Max Buchner, first imperial commissioner of Cameroon and later director of the Munich Museum of Ethnography; Friedrich Fabri, the "father" of the colonial movement; the geographer and anthropologist Friedrich Ratzel; and Albert Hahl, governor of New Guinea. The major Bavarian newspapers supported colonialism, as did local business associations, private companies, chambers of commerce, and commercial high schools; museums, schools, and universities; and of course the churches and their corresponding missionary societies—one Catholic and one Protestant—based in Bavaria.[27]

The structure of the Colonial Society in Nuremberg demonstrates the striking way that class shaped the movement: in this case, in the construction of an intermediate social space where elite influence and popular colonialism combined. According to the *Kolonialzeitung*, in October 1907 the Nuremberg chapter of the Colonial Society established a *Zweigverband*, a "branch association of the chapter composed of members of the working class," that drew some 250 new men into the movement.[28] Emblematic of the hierarchical relationship between the main chapter and its affiliate, Christoph von Tucher and Heinrich Schrag served as chairman and treasurer, respectively, of both groups.[29] Even then, had the membership truly been "working-class," the *Zweigverband* would have been an unparalleled attempt to absorb workers into the organized movement. As it turned out, however, the new affiliate was not really made up of workers at all. In a later number, the *Kolonialzeitung* reported a membership of over 300 who, "through their professional activity as engineers, officials, and in commerce, brought the intention behind the establishment of the branch—disseminating as widely as possible the stimulation and instruction offered by the chapter's lectures, its library, and the contents of the *Kolonialzeitung*—substantially closer to fulfillment."[30] These were of course not working-class, but middle-class men, many of them professionals with some education.

The erroneous *Kolonialzeitung* report may simply have reflected the original, unrealized intentions of the Nuremberg Colonial Society to win working-class members, but it was more likely a case of mild confusion: if the new members were strictly middle-class, they were nevertheless—like workers—not the sort of people who normally joined the Colonial Society. That local colonialists praised the branch for "disseminating as widely as possible" the colonial idea is a telling example of their limited embrace of the "masses," even after the 1907 elections. On the other hand, evidence suggests that the branch really did accomplish a certain amount of popularization. Most members of the *Zweigverband* worked for a single company, the

Siemens-Schuckert Works, a giant Nuremberg manufacturer of electric rail-road and streetcars and builder of electric power plants.[31] The branch leadership attributed the "considerable" growth in membership—from 233 in 1911 to 285 in 1912—to the efforts of directors of the Schuckert company, 162 employees of which accounted for 60 percent of the membership.[32] And in the following years, Siemens-Schuckert employees consistently made up from 50 to 60 percent of the membership.[33]

In 1913, the boards of the *Zweigverband* and the main Nuremberg chapter continued to share a chairman, the manufacturer Julius Pabst, and now also a vice-chairman, Oskar von Petri (both of whom also served on the local board of the Navy League).[34] Petri was the general director of Schuckert, itself a longtime corporate member of the Colonial Society, and principally responsible for drawing its employees into the association.[35] The *Zweigverband* was a vehicle for the combined influence of local business—it was basically a company club—and the Colonial Society over middle- to lower middle-class men. Its minimum annual dues were two marks, which was "supposed to be occasion for the widest circles, those to whom the dues of ten marks for the main chapter were supposed to be too high, to join the *Zweigverband*." Indeed, the average dues paid in 1913 were 2.18 marks.[36] *Zweigverband* members were reminded that they were free to use the local society's library or attend its lectures, and strongly encouraged to do so, but separation was maintained. There were no efforts by the Colonial Society in Nuremberg to pursue any but the typical top-down approach to propaganda and dissemination.

And even among the more dynamic Pan-German and Navy Leagues, social class tended to determine membership. Although open to men of all backgrounds, and expected by its founders to become a mass organization, the Pan-German League remained much smaller than the Colonial Society. It was almost exclusively middle-class, finding members mainly among the Protestant *Bildungsbürgertum*.[37] And even the giant Navy League, many times larger than any of the other *nationale Verbände*, remained a middle-class association, although in a much broader, more inclusive, and differentiated sense. The navalists cast their net much, much wider than, say, the Colonial Society, and the great mass of members came from the petite bourgeoisie of artisans, shopkeepers, and small businessmen. Unlike the Colonial Society, the Navy League actively tried, as Geoff Eley put it, "to break away from the conventional model of the *Honoratiorenverein*," the society of notables. It also sought working-class members, but had little to show for it.[38] At least in terms of associational life, navalism, like colonialism, failed to take root in working-class culture.

Women, on the other hand—mostly upper-class women—were active in the colonial movement, but organized themselves separately from men, and often rather later. Some branches of the Colonial Society did accept women. In Leipzig, for example, the Colonial Society included 56 women in 1910, or about 5 percent of its membership.[39] Likewise in the Rhine-land, but in similarly tiny numbers.[40] Not surprising then, that colonialist women felt compelled to build organizations of their own, organizations that developed in some tension with the Colonial Society. By 1909, there were forty chapters of the Frauenbund der Deutschen Kolonialgesellschaft (the Women's Association of the German Colonial Society) in Germany.[41] In Bavaria there were only three, in Munich, Regensburg, and Kissingen, but much better established was the Deutscher Frauenverein für Krankenpflege in den Kolonien.[42] The Munich chapter, founded in May 1906, enjoyed the patronage of the Wittelsbach family, high-ranking officers, the Bavar-ian nobility, and luminaries among the local haute bourgeoisie. Women in nearby Augsburg established their own branch the following December.[43] At its 1910 annual meeting in the Munich *Palais* of Princess Elisabeth von Hohenlohe-Schillingsfürst, the Bavarian umbrella organization (Landesver-ein Bayern) was pleased to announce that membership had risen from 2,860 in the previous year to 3,278 women in 25 local branches.[44] Compare this with the all-male Colonial Society in Bavaria, which by the middle of 1913 had 2,618 members divided among 41 branches—some 660 fewer members than the Frauenverein für Krankenpflege in den Kolonien (the Women's Co-lonial Nursing Association) had had several years before. In this respect, at least, women played a more substantial role in the Bavarian movement than men did.

But this did not, of course, mean that colonialist women represented a broader cross-section of Bavarian—or German—society. The membership of the Frauenverein für Krankenpflege, the first women's patriotic-colonial organization in Germany, came disproportionately from the aristocracy and the propertied and educated bourgeoisie.[45] In rhetoric and style it tended to express the noblesse oblige of the upper classes.[46] Guests at a reception in the Munich villa of Rudolf Diesel, ardent colonialist and "famous inventor of the diesel engine," included Princess Elisabeth zu Hohenlohe, the Wit-telsbach Princes Georg and Konrad, Adjutant General Freiherr von Könitz, Lieutenant General von Keller, and Major General Nägelsbach, command-ing officer in Munich.[47] Less exclusive were the Frauenverein's public lec-tures, like the writer Margarethe von Eckenbrecher's Augsburg lantern-slide lecture on her "Fate in the Southwest Africa Revolt of 1904." But the ticket prices—the cheapest were one mark—almost certainly kept most workers and perhaps even the lower middle classes out.[48]

The leadership of the Frauenbund, which by 1910 counted seven thou-sand members nationally, came overwhelmingly from the upper reaches of the middle class.[49] They had to be "well-bred women from a higher station" since, "if for no other reason, the woman from the modest middle class, even when possessed of the requisite faculties, seldom has the time to regularly take an active part in public life."[50] The Frauenbund leadership appears to have emphasized opening the organization to participation by lower-class women. As Lora Wildenthal observes, the Frauenbund's "statutes expressed a kind of middle-class populism that contrasted with the social hierarchy of the Frauenverein." There were no noblewomen among the Frauenbund's founders, and the chairwoman Adda von Liliencron (if herself a baroness and supporter of the Conservative Party) displayed some dedication to opening the Frauenbund to people of modest means. Liliencron's "own particular social vision and energies made the Frauenbund quite different in tone than the Frauenverein. She combined political conservatism with a strong drive to involve herself personally across class lines."[51] But there is no further evidence to demonstrate that such aristocratic-conservative noblesse oblige—however colonialist women perceived their mission—actually amounted to "middle-class populism" or that the Frauenbund enrolled any workers, peasants, or artisans. As with the men of the Colonial Society, colonialist women's grasp exceeded their reach.

In the end, colonialists for the most part moved in narrow circles of their own kind, a milieu that served consistently to confirm their sense of identity and worldview. If class and gender distinction tended to exclude most Germans from organized colonialism, by the same token it operated to draw a constellation of political, commercial, and scientific associations into close, often overlapping relations. For example, if colonialism was but one of a series of burning radical-national issues for the Pan-German League, it was nevertheless an extremely significant one, and there were many ties linking the Pan-Germans to the colonial movement.[52] Prominent supporters of both organizations included, alongside Pan-German president Ernst Hasse, the famous Carl Peters, Colonial Society president the duke of Mecklenburg, Professor Johannes Wislicenus, Professor Friedrich Ratzel, and Eduard von Liebert, leader of the Imperial League against Social Democracy (Reichsverband gegen die Sozialdemokratie) and former governor of German East Africa.[53] At the local level, leaders and ordinary members frequently belonged to both groups, as well as to other patriotic associations like the General German School Association or the Navy League, and, in the larger cities, to colonialist geographical societies. Dense local networks of ardent bourgeois nationalists arose in the 1890s, linked by numerous overlapping political, cultural, and civic affiliations, and family and business ties.

Not only *nationale Verbände* like the Colonial Society and the Navy League but also religious and missionary societies like the Africa Association of German Catholics (Afrika-Verein Deutscher Katholiken) and Protestant Africa Association (Evangelischer Afrika-Verein), as well as geographical, anthropological, and oriental associations, and women's groups, connected colonialism to local patterns and forms of sociability, civic life, and patriotic feeling. But these several components of the colonial movement were not much more likely than the Colonial Society and the Navy League to draw members from the urban or rural laboring classes or even the lower reaches of the traditional *Mittelstand*. Rather, they tended to attract their members and supporters—certainly their leadership—from the same small pool as the Colonial Society, ultimately reinforcing the social tendencies dominant in the 1870s and early 1880s.

In the Rhineland, for example, there was substantial cooperation between the various associations—the Colonial Society and the Navy and Pan-German Leagues—and considerable overlap in membership.[54] The same was true of the dynamic, cosmopolitan industrial city of Nuremberg, where colonialism's roots in local associational life went back to 1879, when a local branch of the African Society formed to pursue the "scientific study of Africa and the opening up of this part of the world for commerce."[55] The Geographical Section of the Natural History Society was affiliated with the local Colonial Society, which also had many links with the local Navy League, not least through its chair, a local manufacturer and member of the Navy League, and its vice chair, again Oskar von Petri.[56] The previous local chairman of the Colonial Society, Christoph Freiherr von Tucher, served also on its national board, on the board of the local Navy League, and was chair of the German Emin Pasha Committee, sponsor of Carl Peters's notorious failed adventure in East Africa.

The Munich chapter of the Colonial Society similarly took its place among geographical, anthropological, and oriental societies that, together with the Navy League, the Pan-German League, and the Association for the Preservation of Germandom Abroad, formed the organizational backbone of the colonial movement in the Bavarian capital.[57] Close ties and numerous cross-affiliations linked many members of the Colonial Society to these other organizations: Professor Georg von Mayr, Bavarian undersecretary of state, was also president of the Munich Oriental Society. Royal Chamberlain Freiherr Baron von Pechmann, director of the Bavarian Commerce Bank, was a founder of the Society for German Colonization and member of the board of the German Protestant Missionary Aid (Deutsche Evangelische Missions-Hilfe). Friedrich Ratzel was a member of the Pan-German League, and the manufacturer Hermann Scholl, chair of the local Colonial Society, was a member of the Oriental Society. Royal Chamberlain Karl von Spies, an officer, was both a member of the Colonial Society and the leader of the Navy League in Bavaria, and Privy Councilor Carl Freiherr von Stengel, a university professor and expert on colonial law, was also prominent among the leadership of both groups. Professor Friedrich Freiherr von Stromer was a member of the Colonial Society board and of the Oriental Society.[58] For a few local enthusiasts, particularly among the leadership, colonialism demanded more than the occasional Colonial Society meeting or lantern-slide lecture; it was a central part of their public and civic lives.

In Leipzig, for a great many colonialists, the organized movement involved little more than a limited commitment of time and money to the Colonial Society. Many others, however, summoned extraordinary fervor for nationalist and colonialist activity, joining not only the Colonial Society but often the

Pan-German League, Navy League, Geographical Association or some combination of these as well. Among members of the Colonial Society in 1899, at least 14 percent also belonged to the Pan-Germans in the following year, and over 13 percent of Pan-Germans in 1900 had belonged to the Colonial Society in 1899.[59] The Leipzig Pan-German League was among the largest in Germany, with an extremely active membership of over one thousand by 1901.[60] Prominent colonialists like the "Anthropogeographer" Friedrich Ratzel, of the Ethnography Museum (having relocated from Munich), were also active in the Geographical Association, headed by Professor Hans Meyer.[61] Like the Colonial Society, the Geographical Association sponsored lectures on colonial themes, such as Ratzel's on Emin Pasha or future East African governor Graf von Götzen's on his travels in Central Africa.

A few Leipzigers, like Ernst Hasse or Theodor Habenicht, seemed a species of superpatriot. The founder and national chairman of the Pan-German League (1893–1908), Hasse was a professor of statistics and colonial policy at the university, where for over twenty years he delivered lectures on colonial themes. From 1893 until his defeat by the SPD in 1903, he was National Liberal Reichstag deputy for Old Leipzig, the city center. Founder and board member of the local Colonial Society, Hasse also sat on the national board, while finding time for membership in the Geographical Association, the General German School Association, and the Society for South American Colonization (Südamerikanische Colonisations-Gesellschaft). Habenicht, a factory owner, was chair of both the National Liberal Association and the Colonial Society, a Pan-German board member, a member of the Geographical Association, and honorary member of the Royal Saxon Military Association of "China and Africa Soldiers." Hans Meyer was not only a university professor and chairman of the Geographical Association, he also sat on the national boards of the Colonial Economic Committee and the Colonial Society, edited the series *Das Deutsche Kolonialreich: Eine Länderkunde der deutschen Schutzgebiete*, and addressed audiences across Germany on colonial topics.

These networks and affiliations defined the scope of the organized colonial movement and the fundamental limits of its ambitions. That it never became a mass movement—even approaching the relative mass appeal of the Navy League—is an emblem not of its failure but rather of its origins and composition. By design and temperament, the Colonial Society, its preeminent institution, remained restricted in numbers and essentially hierarchical.[62] The lower classes were not formally excluded, but also not encouraged, and obstacles to their participation were not removed.[63] Early advocates of a broadly based colonial movement—Friedrich Fabri among them—were frustrated by this prevailing indifference toward the masses.[64] And over the years, particularly during periods of stagnation, voices within the society were raised against the narrowness of its social base.[65] The leadership of the Women's Association of the Colonial Society, and the editors of the magazine *Kolonie und Heimat* (which became the official organ of the women's group) were prominent among critics of the Colonial Society's elitism—despite the ways their own membership tended to reproduce the same pattern.[66] The cost of membership in particular—six marks annually plus one or two marks for local membership—excluded workers, artisans, peasants, agricultural laborers, and others with limited means. On several occasions the society discussed and rejected proposals to lower membership fees in order to broaden its appeal among the lower classes.[67] Beginning about 1888, membership began to stagnate and remained sluggish, especially during the years of Leo von Caprivi's chancellorship, until about 1895. In 1894, the board even discussed cutting the dues by half, from six to three marks.[68] But the inclination to embrace all Germans in a national colonial movement never spread sufficiently to transform the Colonial Society, which at the local level merely reproduced the national culture of social deference, distinction, and hierarchy. As Karl Dove argued, without apparent irony, the purpose of the Colonial Society was the popularization of colonialism, not expansion of its membership.[69]

Colonialism, for these men, remained a matter of business, science, and German culture, and therefore the purview of those with education and property. Rather than popular agitation and dynamic expansion, they returned again and again to the formation of knowledge, the sphere of technical expertise and education: to agronomy, geography, tropical medicine, ethnography, the colonial labor question, and the dissemination of colonial knowledge in schools, universities, and commercial academies.[70] The powerful everyday experience of class and gender difference made it practically unthinkable that workers or artisans might attend a local "gentlemen's evening" to discuss the future of German business in Kiaochow or the national economic implications of rubber cultivation in Cameroon. That even "well-bred" women organized separately from their male peers suggests just how powerful the underlying impulse to exclusion remained. As late as 1907, the *Kolonialzeitung*, glancing back at the recent "Hottentot elections," could praise the Colonial Society for moving "beyond their exclusive, private circles and into the public sphere" while nevertheless taking for granted that "local chapters cannot be founded everywhere due, of course, to the membership fee and, not least, to the disinclination to expand the associations."[71] In 1913, in response to a proposal from the Rhineland to seek members among the working classes, Berlin demurred, suggesting that, if still only 43,000 out of some 66 million Germans were members, then they should first win the "educated and well-off circles of the population."[72] For the Colonial Society, a national colonial movement would carefully preserve the boundaries between men and women, and for the organized movement as a whole, between its cultivated, propertied leaders and the lower-class objects of their propaganda.

CHAPTER TWO

World of Work, World of Goods

Propaganda and the Formation of Its Object

> Nowadays, the yields flowing from abroad to the partners of a
> polity, including those of imperialist origin and those actually
> representing "tribute," do not result in a constellation of interests so
> comprehensible to the masses.
> — Max Weber, *Wirtschaft und Gesellschaft*, 1909–13

> Whatever be the ideas suggested to crowds they can only exercise
> effective influence on condition that they assume a very absolute,
> uncompromising, and simple shape. They present themselves then in
> the guise of images, and are only accessible to the masses under this
> form. These image-like ideas are not connected by any logical bond of
> analogy or succession, and may take each other's place like the slides
> of a magic lantern.
> — Gustave Le Bon, *Psychologie des foules*, 1895

What did the world look like from the vantage point of the organized colonial movement, from the perspective constructed through colonial knowledge? It was overlaid by far-flung markets, girded round by great streams of raw tropical commodities, animated by ceaseless and severe competition. The vast industrial production of the metropole depended, it was said, on these "hard facts"; and the livelihood of the working classes on the distant production of raw materials, the stuff of their labor. Ultimately, the "colonial education of the German people" was the metropolitan analogue to the colonial "education of the Negro to work."[1] In German Africa, colonialism introduced money, exchange relations, private property in land, and the appropriation of labor. In Germany itself, colonialism signified the initiation of the German lower classes, not unlike their distant African counterparts, into a view of the world understood as markets, abstract labor, and commodity flows. At the heart of the formation of this view lay the colonial commodity, which in infinite series anchored, visually and materially, the distant colonial periphery in everyday life.

In 1907, during the "Hottentot elections" to the Reichstag, the Social Democratic paper in Augsburg ran an article called "Kolonialkoller"—

"Colonial Fever"—ridiculing the opening of a "Deutsches Kolonial-Cafe" in nearby Munich:

> The "reichstreue" Hottentot Society [the Deutsche Kolonialgesellschaft] always takes great pains to cook up new attractions. . . . And so, in order to facilitate the exposure of wider circles to the "high quality of our German colonial products," a committee of young liberals of unknown origin has established . . . a German Colonial Cafe, where the obstinate, anticolonial, unpatriotic naysayers, who despite [Colonial Secretary] Dernburg and [Carl] Peters remain unconvinced of the superiority of our colonies, will be brought around to a new opinion through the enjoyment of German cocoa, German coffee, and German peanuts. An exhibition of other colonial products should further silt up the brains [*Gehirnversandung*] of visitors.[2]

For all the derision of the socialists, this form of publicity was neither new nor unusual in Germany by 1907. Indeed, among the peculiar characteristics of German colonialism was an apparently inexhaustible fascination for tropical commodities on display. Propagandists used such exhibits to instruct the masses in the utility of the colonies. Collections of colonial products—like rubber, coffee, and mahogany, and rather more exotic goods like rhinoceros horns, antelope hides, and mother-of-pearl—toured all parts of the country for a quarter of a century. These diverse fruits of colonial labor—commonly represented, however, as the stuff of metropolitan industry—bore great symbolic value. Popular science, mass consumption, patriotism, and commerce all intersected in the colonial commodity. In its simple materiality, it appeared as a self-evident, transparent fact; its use-value seemed to confirm the economic logic of colonialism. Displayed like scientific specimens in well-ordered, edifying series, sample imports illuminated the geography, botany, and zoology of the overseas empire in provincial hometowns across the country. Moreover, the practical, commercial aspect of colonial wares was fused with the vestiges of exotic wonder long associated with overseas trade. Colonial commodities projected the allure of strange novelties and historical luxuries like African ivory, spices, and ebony. They also promised physical pleasure: the mild stimulation induced by the consumption of the colonial semiluxuries like coffee, cocoa, tobacco, and tea.

This vitalizing effect was important, since the logic of commodity propaganda was inherently weak. It depended on suppressing and forgetting basic economic facts. In the 1870s and 1880s, the notion of colonies as markets for surplus industrial production had been an article of faith for German colonialists.[3] When the penetration of Africa revealed these great colonial markets to be chimerical, import largely supplanted export in colonial ideology. Propagandists began to emphasize the role of tropical commodities in domestic production and consumption. German manufacturing, they argued, depended on imported cotton, palm oil, copra, rubber, and many other raw materials. German workers would benefit doubly as the stream of colonial goods filled both factories and shops. The urgent demand for colonial *markets* to absorb excess commodity production had mutated into a demand for colonial *commodities* now described as essential to home production.

According to one propaganda pamphlet aimed at working people, "Jobs and wages depend on manufacturing costs, on how cheaply manufacturers can buy raw materials and sell their goods. . . . For this reason, we must see to it that the manufacturer can save on raw material costs: with what he saves on raw materials, he can increase wages."[4] The empire's propagandists conjured direct, vital connections between working-class livelihoods and colonization. To "support the economic development of the tropics and subtropics with all possible means" was "an urgent necessity, from precisely the standpoint of proletarian interests." Could Social Democracy, they asked, truly oppose the "vast, world-historical process" of European colonization, which amounted, after all, to a "gigantic cultural revolution"?[5]

Behind the rhetoric of economic self-sufficiency lurked the specter of rival powers controlling markets and materials. Without secure sources of tropical raw materials, German industry—and its millions of workers—would remain dangerously vulnerable to international competition. As Max Buchner put it, rather ominously, "Peoples and states isolate themselves from one another, new tariff barriers are erected, the struggle for national interest sharpens."[6] Germany needed African rubber for its electrical, bicycle, and automobile industries and palm oil for soap manufacture. Its textile industry, with about one million workers, could truly prosper only with secure supplies of German colonial cotton.[7] Colonialists downplayed the fact that Germany imported almost no cotton from its own colonies. If, of the seventeen million bales of cotton produced worldwide in 1902, German East Africa produced only one and a half bales, then so much greater the need for colonial development.[8] Indeed, the German colonies produced very little of what German industry required. Most of the tropical commodities imported before 1914 flowed freely from Central and South America or from other European colonies, not from German Africa or the Pacific.[9]

These included the sundry articles of mass consumption like coffee, tea, and chocolate that Germans tellingly called *Kolonialwaren*, "colonial wares"—a category that overlapped with *Genußmittel*, "means of enjoyment." These ubiquitous products furnished the most direct, quotidian commodity link between consumers and the European overseas empires. Propagandists highlighted their colonial origins in order to show the masses—and workers in particular—how the colonies made a difference in their lives. A 1907 election pamphlet printed by the Colonial Society insisted that "if our colonies can supply us with the *Kolonialwaren* that the worker needs more cheaply than foreign countries," then "the worker can, for the same money as before, buy more food and live better than before."[10] Propagandists had only to "direct the worker's glance from his humdrum, everyday work to the faraway world, to stimulate his imagination, to put before his eyes the origins . . . of the raw materials with which he works every day" in order to make it clear that "for the German working class, it is not all the same whether Germany, with its growing need for raw materials and semiluxury goods is dependent on foreign countries or on its own colonies."[11] Colonial commodity charts, simply illustrated pictograms printed for mass distribution, made plain even to the semiliterate the worth of the colonies.[12] Orderly series of iconic colonial commodities—miniature coffee cups, cigars, ostrich plumes, and two-pfennig coins of African copper—represented the place of tropical goods in the burgeoning world of metropolitan consumption. Imperial tribute belonged to everyone.

From the mid-nineteenth century, both the diversity and the volume of German food consumption had increased dramatically, eventuating a revolution in the way most Germans ate and drank.[13] The consumption of *Genußmittel*—most significantly alcohol but also colonial goods like coffee, tea, cocoa, sugar, and spices—was an important element of the new patterns.[14] Yet, colonial propaganda notwithstanding, these changes did not always signify links between colonialism, consumption, and the German masses. One of the most far-reaching transformations in food consumption actually produced the opposite effect, as cheaper beet sugar supplanted tropical and subtropical cane sugar on the German market.[15] Other colonial goods found greater success, though often varying by social class. Contemporaries calculated an increase of 17 percent in German coffee consumption in the colonial period.[16] By 1914, the share of expenditures on *Genußmittel* devoted to coffee had risen from 6 to 8 percent per capita, or by about 2 percent annually.[17] Even among the working class, coffee was becoming a part of everyday life, although rarely in pure form.[18] Cocoa consumption grew by an average annual rate of 8 percent but was still less than 1.5 percent of total expenditures on *Genußmittel* by 1914.[19] In working-class households in particular, cocoa, like tea, was insignificant.[20]

Their tonic properties notwithstanding, hawking colonial commodities—and the colonial empire itself—presented propagandists with a challenge. Though the provisioning of the great industrial cities was accelerating, *Kolonialwaren* remained largely middle-class luxuries. If German colonial products were critical to the economy, as maintained in the propaganda, they nevertheless remained only a small part of the market at a time when most tropical commodities came from the Americas or other European colonies. In 1890, the African section of the Trade Hall at the Northwest German Commerce and Industry Exhibition in Bremen, intended to showcase colonial commodities, could barely muster any, an embarrassment that had to be masked by a profusion of ethnographica.[21] Rather than domestic requirements for colonial products justifying the need for a colonial empire, support for the empire became the rationale for buying colonial goods. "Imperialism," as Hannah Arendt wrote, "the product of superfluous money

"All that can be gained from the German Colonies": commodity propaganda for the masses (1907). "Deutschland halte fest an deinen Kolonien!" BA, DKG, R8023/509, Bl. 441. Courtesy Bundesarchiv Berlin.

and superfluous men, began its startling career by producing the most superfluous and unreal goods."[22] What the market could not support, exhortations to patriotism perhaps could: the patriotic pleas to "buy colonial" that characterized the limited advertising of German colonial goods in Wilhelmine Germany, particularly before 1900. Even as, from the later 1890s, a burgeoning commodity culture began to develop vivid advertising in which racialized exoticism figured powerfully, it seemed to be detached from the movement for German colonialism, oriented more toward iconographies circulating transnationally.[23]

Nevertheless, by the constant repetition of words, images, and exotic samples, propagandists sought to compensate ideologically for the statistical and empirical gaps in the realm of consumption. Keen to convince workers and the lower middle classes that the empire promised concrete advantage, they developed a particular technique and aesthetics of display. Exhibitions combined the natural history vitrine with the department store window. Endless series of tropical goods arranged in glass cabinets evoked the scientific, the exotic, and the commercial all at the same time. Lists, catalogues, collections, and massed objects insisted on a limitless abundance of valuable tropical commodities. And those not fortunate enough to see the exhibitions could always read about them. Long, narcotic columns in newspapers, pamphlets, catalogs, and magazines reproduced Rabelaisian inventories of goods: ivory, sisal, sorghum, ebony, spices and aromatics, tropical hardwoods, mangrove bark, ramie, jute, gutta-percha, copal, copra, cotton, mica, india rubber, cocoa beans, peanuts, Cameroon tobacco, palm nuts, tortoiseshell, trepang, coffee, East African rubies, garnets, titaniferous ironstone, copper, cola nuts, bananas, mother-of-pearl, peanut oil, rice, tea, mahogany, palm oil, vanilla, sesame, corals, millet, and on and on.

Beginning in the mid-1890s, colonial commodities linked the spheres of propaganda and consumption. Limited commercial advertising and display reflected the contents and style of the new colonial exhibitions and traveling commodity collections. Patriots could buy merchandise like "Togoland Underwear," made from "*guaranteed German colonial cotton*, smooth and light, the most comfortable and lasting, and also recommended in the national-economic interest." Other ads recommended "German Colonial Cigars" from Cameroon, "not just to friends of the colonies, but to all lovers of fine, extraordinarily low-priced cigars." In late 1895, the Berlin merchant Bruno Antelmann approached the Colonial Society with the idea of opening a store devoted exclusively to the sale of German colonial goods. The store's extracommercial purpose was to "demonstrate the practical use of the colonies and inspire interest in them among ever wider circles."[24] All merchandise would bear a special colonial trademark guaranteeing authentic German-colonial origins. The society responded favorably and proceeded to solicit its members for investments in the scheme.[25] But after encountering strong opposition from potential competitors like chocolate manufacturers, whose own brands might suffer from the competition, and who were likewise members of the Colonial Society, the plan was dropped.[26]

Rejected by the Colonial Society, Antelmann proceeded independently to establish his Deutsches Kolonialhaus, a fantastic, quasi-oriental emporium stuffed with tropical commodities, ethnographica, and handicrafts made by the proprietor's own African craftspeople. From its headquarters in the capital, it was to "make propaganda for colonial products across the entire German Empire." New "friends" would be won, "not through the political significance of colonialism but rather through the actual intrinsic value of the colonial products" themselves.[27] The new four-story facade, which resembled nothing quite so much as an early picture palace, combined a vaguely Moorish aspect with the popular visual style of colonialism: Alhambraesque crenellation, a dome flanked by minarets, orientalizing arches and vegetal ornament, palms in relief, and a pair of elephants with ivory tusks.[28] Dried palm leaves, stuffed parrots and cockatoos, and real African clerks adorned the interior. Antelmann's Kolonialhaus epitomized the mingling of spectacle, pleasure, and consumption that developed into a principal element of colonial propaganda in the 1890s.[29]

In the summer of 1896, the Berlin factory owner Karl Supf founded a Committee for the Importation of Products from the German Colonies. Supf had been a principal supporter of Antelmann's planned colonial emporium, and the foundation of his committee occurred just weeks after the Colonial Society's disappointing abandonment of the project.[30] Supf's committee was neither an import firm nor any sort of commercial venture but rather an association dedicated to promoting the colonial empire. It was an expression of his ardent colonial enthusiasm, and of the particular conviction that firsthand knowledge of tropical commodities would translate into popular colonialist sentiment. The committee's principal objective was therefore to "promote the importation of products from the German colonies, and thereby to awaken interest for our colonies among wide sections of the people."[31] By centralizing and coordinating the circulation and display of German colonial goods, the committee hoped to intensify the effects of a kind of colonial exhibition endlessly replicated throughout the Reich. Such exhibitions materialized the otherwise distant, unknown colonies through direct experience—visual, tactile, and olfactory—with a series of tropical products. The expectation was that the transmission of this kind of knowledge tended to make self-evident the practical value of the colonies, and therefore colonialism. The committee accumulated collections of popular, mass-consumption stimulants and semiluxuries, and raw materials for modern industrial production, and offered them for public display.

In 1897, Supf's association became the Colonial Economic Committee, which in 1902 formally joined the Colonial Society and emerged as an influential source of colonial economic expertise and propaganda. It published both a specialist journal— "The Tropical Planter" (*Der Tropenpflanzer*)—and

Deutsches Kolonialhaus: colonial department store in Berlin (c.1900). BA, DKG,
R8023/56, Bl. 212. Courtesy Bundesarchiv Berlin.

pamphlets for mass distribution, and participated in the Berlin colonial congresses and in numerous exhibitions. The 1898 Marine and Colonial Exhibition in Nuremberg, for example, included a small display of German colonial products provided partly by the committee, and by Antelmann's Kolonialhaus in Berlin. Visitors encountered a range of goods, including "Cameroon cocoa, Cameroon chocolate, Usambara coffee, vanilla, cola nut liqueur, massoy liqueur, New Guinea and Cameroon cigars, peanut oil, Kiaochow cigarettes from our Chinese colonial acquisition, and the first German tea from the Shantung region," all "clearly arranged in a series of glass cases."[32] By 1908, through an agreement with the Colonial Office and the Prussian Ministry of Education, some six hundred of the committee's commodity collections appeared in Prussian schools.[33] Many hundreds of thousands of Prussian schoolchildren encountered ivory, cotton, sisal, coffee, cocoa, peanuts, copra, palm kernels, rice, sorghum (also called *Negerkorn* or *Kaffernkorn*), rubber, gutta-percha, ebony, and mahogany from the colonies.[34]

In the spring of 1896, just as Supf was establishing his Committee for the Importation of Products from the German Colonies, and Antelmann his Deutsches Kolonialhaus, the first great German Colonial Exhibition threw open its gates in the capital. It marked a new phase in the effort to reach the masses and make colonialism popular. The Colonial Society, an important participant, had envisioned the exhibition as "an outstanding attraction within the framework of the Berlin Trade Exhibition," a kaleidoscopic display of Berlin manufactures. To this end, the society proposed a series of lantern-slide lectures styled as travel accounts, as well as giving out 30,000 free colonial atlases. It also planned a reading pavilion, the eventual *Kolonialheim*, with decorative paintings of colonial scenes by Rudolf Hellgrewe and a collection of albums, maps, and magazines.[35] The exhibition would also include a series of re-created African and Pacific island villages.

The display of colonial commodities played a leading role in the overall scheme. If, as Walter Benjamin later put it, "world exhibitions were places of pilgrimage to the fetish Commodity," then the colonial exhibition amounted to a virtual temple of tropical goods.[36] Limited commodity collections had already appeared at a number of smaller colonial exhibitions, including Hamburg in 1889 and Bremen in 1890. In 1895, the Colonial Society had lent its set of 324 samples for a show in Lübeck.[37] At Berlin, however, we see the culmination of the colonial commodity exhibition as a form of spectacle combining propaganda, commerce, and an aesthetic of abundance. The exhibition, as Georg Simmel observed, highlighted the "shop window quality of things."[38] Organizers presented a bewildering range of both exotic and more ordinary tropical goods from across the colonized world—if not, alas, from the German colonial empire itself.[39] A partial inventory of items on display in the exhibition's Tropical House includes:

> sorghum, rice and maize, assorted beans, sugarcane, sugar and molasses, Usambara coffee, Cameroon and Togo coffee, cocoa beans and powder, cola nuts,

vanilla, red pepper, ginger, cloves, tobacco, hippopotamus and rhinoceros hides, sesame and peanuts, coconuts, palm nuts and oil, gum arabic, copal, india rubber, Cameroon mahogany and ebony, calophyllum wood, ivory, rhinoceros horns, the hides of cattle, sheep, goat, and antelope, wild Southwest African ostrich feathers, guano, trepang, Polynesian ivory nuts, and shark fins.[40]

The plumage of wild Southwest African ostriches was "extraordinarily prized" just then for the manufacture of "splendid boas, fans, etc.," while so-called "vegetable ivory," the Polynesian ivory nuts that formed "an important export article of the Solomon Islands," were popular as "large buttons for ladies' coats and fashions."[41] Adding to the formal commodity display was a "true-to-life reed hut" among the imitation "Negro villages" where Antelmann's newly established Kolonialhaus offered Usambara coffee, Cameroon chocolate, and cigars to the hundreds of thousands of visitors.[42]

The position of the colonial exhibition within the larger Berlin Trade Exhibition was ultimately somewhat paradoxical. The extraordinary profusion of manufactured goods formed a perfect backdrop for the tropical commodities that propagandists were attempting to convert into signifiers of imperial power and riches. The organizers crammed every imaginable object of modern consumption into a series of pavilions built expressly for this purpose. Lace, optical instruments, cameras, porcelain, and pianos commingled with glasswares, hats, fabrics, stationery and paper goods, with saddles, rope, construction materials, sewing machines, wallpaper, and scientific instruments, with pumps, carriages, drills, borers, presses, lathes, and much else.[43] Yet this exuberant, miniaturized simulacrum of modern superabundance, along the margins of which the colonial exhibition formed a kind of exotic satellite, announced precisely the failures and limits of colonialism. The origins of the trade exhibition lay in part in the realization that the colonies would be unable to supply markets for German goods, and that other alternatives would need to be found. As officials of the trade exhibition reiterated, recent colonial history had meant

the opening up of new areas, little or not at all developed economically, for the industrial exports of the civilized peoples [*Kulturvölker*] who, as a result of repeated, almost universally enforced, reciprocal economic closure [of markets] through often truly Chinese tariff walls, were all the more pressed to expand exports to both fully and half-barbaric lands. These efforts found their limits at first in the inadequate capacity for consumption, and later in the development of the economically backward countries themselves. The result had to be renewed zeal for maintaining the position of the domestic market. To this end, reduced production costs through technological improvements and the adoption of all the advantages of the foreign competition were required. For this, too, exhibitions proved suitable means.[44]

Moreover, even commodities from the German colonies proved hard to come by.[45] Ironically, the setting and occasion for the first great German colonial exhibition grew out of the recognition that the fabled colonial markets had proved illusory, and out of the barely concealed scarcity of German colonial goods. All the fanfare was meant to open up the domestic market to homemade manufactures and to nonexistent colonial goods.

Not that this made any real difference to colonial propagandists, who—as we have seen—required neither logic nor truth for their reality-confections. Commodity displays, for all their facticity, belonged substantially to the world of consumption and amusement—the world of the Berlin Trade Exhibition. Contemporary observations on the trade exhibition by Georg Simmel suggest a way of thinking about colonial commodity propaganda within this particular context. In a review of the exhibition, Simmel wrote that the sheer number and variety of goods exerted a powerful, yet intellectually superficial attraction ultimately equivalent to the manufactured thrills of popular entertainment. In the pavilions of the trade exhibition, he wrote,

> the abundance and diversity of the offerings ultimately permit as the sole focus and distinguishing characteristic only amusement. The narrow proximity in which the most heterogeneous products of industry are shown produces a paralysis of the perceptive faculty, a true hypnosis, in which the individual impression impinges only upon the outermost layers of consciousness. Finally only the most frequently repeated idea . . . is retained in the memory: the idea that one should find amusement here.

Such experiences supplied exactly the hyperstimulation and distraction demanded by modern urban life. "Every refined sensibility feels violated and deranged by the mass impact of what is offered here," he observed. Yet, "on the other hand it cannot be denied that this colorful abundance of rushing impressions quite meets the need for excitement of overstrained and exhausted nerves."[46]

Among colonialists themselves, at least, the amusement and excitement of the spectacle alternated with pessimism, frustration, and awkward fumbling in their encounter with the broad masses of German society. They found it consistently difficult to translate their image of the globe, of commodity and labor flows and overseas exploitation, into a lasting popular idiom. For all their efforts, the suggestible multitude nevertheless seemed stubbornly ignorant, distracted, sensitive only to cheap thrills. Colonialists' strong sense of a public malaise, of widespread pessimism and indifference to the colonial empire, only magnified the giant task of propaganda. The euphoria of the 1880s—the heroic period of colonial exploration, acquisition, and the consolidation of the colonial movement itself—had begun to fade by the close of the decade. Carl Peters's Emin Pasha expedition of 1887 was the last great source of colonial publicity in this period. The early 1890s were inauspicious for inspiring mass enthusiasm. Despite all the work of commodity propagandism, as the promise of new markets and settlement colonies evaporated, investment barely trickled into the new protectorates, and administrative difficulties mounted. A skeptical Bismarck had soon soured on colonialism, and friction grew between him and the movement.[47] Nor was his successor, Caprivi, any better disposed to the colonial empire. The Helgoland-Zanzibar Treaty of 1890, which ceded potential territorial claims in East Africa to England in return for the North Sea island of Helgoland, enraged colonialists, sparking the founding of the Pan-German League the following year.

For years after the colonial movement reemerged from the doldrums of the early 1890s, the perception of broad disaffection and resistance persisted, even among its most ardent supporters. In 1902, Carl Peters lamented the "colonial weariness" — the *Kolonialmüdigkeit* — hampering overseas endeavors. "The German colonial movement gives a truly melancholy impression," he observed. A "deep resignation has set in . . . a paralyzing pessimism dominates the outlook of so many men."[48] In 1904, a speaker in Berlin posed to his Pan-German audience the bitter question, "What will save us from *Kolonialmüdigkeit*?" "What do we care for the weariness of the eternally weary!" he thundered. "We have no time to be weary of the colonies!"[49] The well-known colonial publicist Karl Dove, a forceful critic of "colonial pessimism," was still addressing the sense of inferiority and failure even after the great colonial victory in the elections of 1907. "If we ask about the causes of such a desolate mood among even the thoroughly national-minded," he wrote, it becomes clear that the note of despair "rings faintly in our own souls too."[50]

The kaiser's January 1896 *Weltreich* speech, followed that summer by the German Colonial Exhibition, then the naval agitation of 1897–1900, the seizure of Kiaochow, the Boer War, and the Boxer Rebellion all contributed to a more positive new climate for colonial propaganda. Yet the sense of a movement sapped of vitality and riddled with self-doubt persisted, and colonialists were extremely sensitive to the constant criticism of German colonial policy. Ubiquitous *Kolonialfeinde* — the hated "enemies" of colonialism — included Social Democrats, the Catholic Center Party, humanitarians, and skeptics of every stripe. The successful anticolonial propaganda of the SPD enraged colonialists, whose efforts among workers were dwarfed by the much larger and more sophisticated machinery of Social Democracy. The substantial gains made by the SPD in the Reichstag elections of 1903 seemed only to confirm the victory of socialism among workers. The ranks of "enemies," class division, vast popular ignorance, and indifference all complicated winning the lower orders for the great "national task" of empire building. The masses seemed forever out of reach.

In 1908, a propagandist for the Colonial Society described his journey to a small village in the Odenwald, capturing the pessimistic assumptions underlying every effort by the movement. The local Committee for Popular Education had invited him to deliver a "popular lecture on the products of our German colonies and their use by industry"—the standard theme of tropical commodities and industrial production. The author shapes his account of the experience around the conceit of an uncertain adventure into unknown territory, in this case a remote village of laborers and peasants. This is a journey of exploration and discovery, from which the author ultimately returns enlightened by the positive response to colonialism among such strange and distant beings. Some indication of local "interest in colonial matters" had already persuaded him that "to further awaken and increase" it would be "a rewarding task." But he approaches the village with pessimism and doubt: it is self-evident that few villagers will attend such a lecture. When the locals arrive—late, barely trickling in—the author's gloom deepens. But at last, as he begins, "the room fills up more and more and is eventually as crowded as one could wish." A sense of redemption as villagers "of every age and both sexes, and—alongside those from the worker and peasant estates—teachers, officials, and doctors" filled the room. "A more attentive and thankful audience is hardly ever to be found," he writes, "although the lecture lasted two hours."[51]

A story of low expectations happily exceeded, it presupposes, but finally overcomes, grinding doubts and disillusionment about rural colonial propaganda among ordinary Germans. In this—its picture of the gulf between colonialists and any popular and rural constituency—and in its pessimism, it was typical. Rhetorically, it assumes readers deeply skeptical of converting the countryside to colonialism. Indeed, peasants, villagers, agricultural laborers, and small-town people rarely ever appeared as targets of colonial propaganda. "They are mostly people who live far from the intercourse of the big city and thus know little of the circumstances in the colonies, the more so because the agricultural newspapers only very seldom print appropriate articles about this topic." The general impression was of a countryside rife with misinformation and distortion. "Today the view still frequently prevails in the country that, if someone emigrates to Africa, he never comes back, but rather goes miserably to ruin."[52] Worse, the colonies were supposed to threaten competition in the befuddled minds of peasant farmers who could not grasp that colonial cocoa and rubber threatened no competition against homegrown wheat and rye. According to the *Kolonialzeitung*, "People are still frequently inclined in agricultural circles to imagine an unbridgeable opposition between homeland and colonies." The propagandists' task was to correct such distortions and spread enlightenment to rural pockets of ignorance, suspicion, and indifference. All that was required was "better knowledge of our colonies" to "awaken a lively interest in the advancement of our colonial policy."[53]

Publicists and propagandists had a kind of faith in such knowledge, even if plagued always by doubt, and worked uncertainly to make colonialism

"popular": "to spread knowledge of its necessity among ever wider circles."
It had to be comprehensible and appealing to vast numbers of Germans pre-
sumed to be uneducated, parochial, and often hostile, both rural and urban,
Catholic and Protestant, from every region of the Reich. The objective was
not to absorb the lower classes into the organized colonial movement itself
but to secure their acquiescence in a policy of colonial expansion. This in
turn involved the development of a whole worldview in which colonies, as
markets and suppliers of commodities, were integral to modern production.
The social backgrounds and narrow experience of the bourgeois propagandists meant that a psychological, political, and cultural gulf separated them
from the masses, whom they regarded as indifferent or ignorant—and elusive. The colonialists remained for a long time naïve and tentative in their
approach, especially toward the peasantry and the working class. It never
became entirely clear how to win the workers and, until 1914, traces of
hesitation, bewilderment, and surprise continued to mark discussions about
strategy. Nor did the countryside seem to offer a readier, more receptive
audience. Peasants appeared rather seldom in the discussions, often as un-
fathomable, almost exotic beings dwelling in obscure, faraway places. Colonialists seem to have had only the murkiest, most general, even stereotypical
idea of the men and women they hoped to influence.

They made much of the deep ignorance of the "masses" and ridiculed
their preference for sensational accounts of cannibalism or "white slavery"
over the sober facts of colonial political economy. The Colonial Society had

> never indulged in illusions about the participation, or rather lack of participa-
> tion, of the masses in the colonial efforts of the German Empire. German co-
> lonial policy, which arose out of purely economic and political considerations,
> appeared to the people initially as foreign and incomprehensible. The exotic
> and adventurous, which acted upon the imagination, indeed made some im-
> pression on many people, although at the same time it filled their heads with
> false views. However, a deeper interest among the masses of the people was not
> to be discovered.[54]

Such interest had instead to be implanted and cultivated by the Colonial Society's central Propaganda Commission, and by its active branches around
the country. At the heart of the disinterested masses, according to this view,
lay the working class, sunk in dime-novel fantasy or maddening socialist delusion. Workers presented by far the greatest challenge to the propagandists.
But despite the many difficulties, and the widespread disinclination to draw
workers into the movement, securing their support was an integral part of
colonialist strategy.

A long-term, lively discussion about the purpose and practicalities of
working-class propaganda unfolded at all levels of the movement. Assem-
blies and publications debated the movement's prospects among workers,

and itinerant speakers took the discussion to the local chapters.[55] According to the standard account, originated by Richard Pierard, the Colonial Society did not really attempt to approach workers until the very end of the colonial period. Pierard attributes the outlines of a specific working-class strategy to the executive committee in Berlin in 1913.[56] In fact, though, the Colonial Society had turned its attention to the working class by the turn of the century, coinciding with a period of enormous growth of the SPD. This was a period of intense naval agitation and the elaboration of German *Weltpolitik*, when other *nationale Verbände* were turning to the masses for support. In the case of the Colonial Society, the impetus seems to have come not so much from the national leadership as from the local chapters at the periphery. In October 1903, the Bochum chapter, in the heavily industrialized Ruhr, proposed that "the interest of the working class in the further development of the protectorates be explained in popular articles suitable for mass circulation" in the form of pamphlets.[57] The simple proposal generated a substantial discussion of "propaganda among workers" in the following meeting a month later. It appeared to some on the committee that the cost of producing and distributing so many pamphlets would far exceed the results. It was suggested that the society provide "articles on colonial questions written in a popular style to newspapers read especially by workers—in the provinces for the most part the so-called 'General Gazette'—rather than daily political papers." Calendars and simple colonial wall maps were also suggested, and the proposal was tabled for further consideration.[58]

Incredibly, the proposal only came before the full board two years later, in November 1905. There was apparently not much urgency about converting the working-class masses to colonialism, except of course that there *was*—pointing to the contradictory impulses at the heart of the colonial movement. During the interval, the Bochum chapter had suggested that the Propaganda Commission prepare statistics on the relationships between individual industrial areas and the colonies, and work began on a pamphlet suitable for workers.[59] The final vote, however, engendered another lively discussion about how best to reach the workers. A Bochum city councilor introduced the proposal—from the city's "industrial circles"—for "approaching the working class" and inspiring "whole masses with enthusiasm for colonial policy." In certain regions, he argued, and "especially in the Rhenish-Westphalian industrial area, where there are many relatively educated workers," it was only reasonable to show "what great advantages our workers had from colonialism."

Still the proposal seemed too expensive and risky to the executive committee. Success would come only if the pamphlets were "distributed in millions of copies several times a year; the printing and shipping costs would naturally be very high; and there is no [realistic] thought of [Colonial Society] members from working-class circles." The solution was to insert articles into cheap, popular calendars and "press read mainly by workers. . . . Purely agitational writings distributed in pamphlets frequently encounter a certain mistrust and very easily provoke the criticism and resistance of the anticolonial press. . . . If one publishes articles in daily papers, these could be absolutely unobtrusive and factual, but yet convincing, and arouse the reader's interest, as it were, unconsciously." Karl Dove spoke of his numerous experiences giving popular lectures before audiences made up mostly of Social Democratic workers who "followed the presentation with the strongest interest and showed themselves able to speak easily and sensibly about these things." In public lectures at the Jena Geographical Society, Dove noticed that workers eagerly read newspapers actually published in the colonies. A Berlin member assured the assembly that the "workers are an extremely thankful public" at colonial lectures.[60]

The debate surrounding the proposed distribution of leaflets among workers, while it reveals something of the colonialists' social naïveté and isolation vis-à-vis the working class, nevertheless belies the actually extensive propaganda network that was already in place. By the turn of the century, the Colonial Society had already developed an arsenal of techniques and devices. The 1896 Colonial Exhibition in Berlin, for example, attracted over a million visitors during its nearly six months of operation.[61] The relatively successful exhibition gave rise to a German East Africa Exhibition in Leipzig the following year and the eventual establishment of a colonial museum in the capital. And this brand of popularization reached beyond the metropolis into smaller cities and towns. More modest colonial exhibitions took place in Regensburg, Nuremberg, Hamburg, Aachen, and elsewhere. Some six thousand people reportedly visited the small, "popular" colonial exhibition mounted by the Lippstadt chapter of the Colonial Society, which some colonialists hoped to transform into a permanent traveling exhibition at the disposal of the society and other associations.[62]

Among the earliest measures to reach into the countryside was a plan approved by the Colonial society's Propaganda Commission in 1901.[63] The commission agreed that, for effective rural propaganda, "a great knowledge of local conditions is necessary and the central administration is little suited to this." Individual chapters would be urged to dispatch suitable members to the local environs to spread the colonialist message. Indeed, rural propaganda would be an extremely local phenomenon, without much apparent coordination or impetus from Berlin. It precluded mass meetings, great exhibitions, colonial lending libraries, and other common instruments of propaganda in Wilhelmine Germany.[64] In the countryside, "the actual preconditions for mass meetings—large assembly-rooms and electric lighting—are mostly lacking," and the widely dispersed population meant that one would "therefore have to content oneself for the time being with smaller conventicles."[65]

Still, the peasants were not entirely unapproachable. Many colonialists argued that Germany's farmers, more so than any others among their countrymen, had a natural affinity for colonization:

> Many a younger son who cannot take over the paternal farm, who is not in a position to acquire his own property in his homeland, but who doesn't want to eat foreign bread his whole life long, can become an independent planter or cattle-breeder in the colonies. The young farmer, the market-gardener, or the forester makes the best employee for the plantation companies. Likewise as an officer, or as a government official, and especially in newly developing colonies, the son of the countryside is superior to his cousin from the city.[66]

For many, propaganda was simply a matter of appealing to rural Germans from a particular perspective, by stressing farmer life in Southwest Africa.[67] The Colonial Society proposed "that itinerant lecturers on colonial policy travel the countryside and be paid a fee by the Colonial Society" and that they "be equipped with appropriate wall maps, photographic views (not lantern slides), and a small collection of colonial products."[68] "Simple world maps" depicting the German colonies were to be hung in "inns in smaller cities and towns (in the common rooms and club rooms) and in pubs in suitable villages."[69]

In 1908, the German Agricultural Society reached agreement with the Colonial Society to establish a colonial section that, through annual touring exhibitions, exposed thousands of farmers to colonial propaganda. The Agricultural Society became, according to the *Kolonialzeitung*, a "champion of the union of agricultural and colonial questions."[70] Its exhibitions offered an opportunity to "show the great masses of the population, and especially the agricultural population, the importance of colonial-economic efforts for our national economy."[71] Visiting colonial farmers delivered lectures in order "to win disciples for their work and to acquaint our people with the work of our pioneers."[72] By 1914, the Colonial Society was occasionally reporting the growing popularity of its lectures in rural, provincial Germany.[73]

In the contest for working-class support, colonialists worked with the antisocialist, sometimes Christian, often employer-organized so-called "yellow" trade unions.[74] The Central Association of Christian Textile Workers, based in Düsseldorf, actively supported colonialism, even joining the Colonial Economic Committee. As part of its "educational work," the association cooperated with the committee, and with the Colonial Society, which offered lantern-slide projectors with pictures and accompanying text.[75] Local branches sometimes arranged joint lectures with Christian Workers Associations. Ultimately, though, colonialist agitation among the "yellow" unions failed to translate into much influence among workers, not least because there were relatively few Christian textile workers in the first place. In its peak year, 1907, the central association claimed 41,916 members nationally. By 1913, the number had dropped to 37,109, divided among some 300 branches.[76] There were, for example, only 180 members in the textile center of Augsburg by 1912.[77] In Upper Franconia, where the cotton industry employed nearly 20,000 spinners and weavers, from 1912 to 1914 the association counted on average only 178 and 38 members respectively in Bamberg and Bayreuth.[78]

Other forms of propaganda among the "masses" included diverse publications, lectures, circulating tropical commodity collections, colonial maps and atlases, newspaper articles, and the introduction of colonial topics into the school curriculum.[79] (Of course, most of what was published by the society—congress proceedings, the journal *Der Tropenpflanzer*, and the *Kolonialzeitung* itself—was written for special business interests or educated bourgeois readers. Only the Frauenbund's magazine, *Kolonie und Heimat*, with its serialized literature, puzzles, and pictures, aimed at a popular readership.)[80] Propaganda reached a high point during the "Hottentot elections," with rallies, lectures, and the distribution of millions of pamphlets designed for the lower classes.[81] For example, the Colonial Society inserted over a million copies of the leaflet "Deutschland halte fest an deinen Kolonien!" ("Germany, Hold On to Your Colonies!") into newspapers and still could not meet the demand.[82] And it encouraged the production of short patriotic-colonial plays—"living pictures from army life in Southwest Africa"—in "theaters, circuses, and similar institutions" across the country.[83] The great propaganda and electoral achievements of 1907 marked an unanticipated reversal in the fortunes of colonialist publicity among the masses.

In the spring of 1913, an omnipresent Captain von Amelunxen was delivering his lecture, "The Importance of the German Colonies for Industry and the Working Class," accompanied by an exhibition of pictures and colonial commodities, at meetings across Bavaria—although only to the bourgeois audiences of the Colonial Society.[84] At the general meeting of the society in June of that year in Breslau, the Harburg chapter introduced another proposal regarding the "education of the working class." The colonial enthusiasts of Harburg rather vaguely hoped that "the German working class would be better informed than heretofore about the value of [Germany's] colonial efforts," that "suitable measures" would be taken, and the "necessary funds" provided.[85] Dr. Busse, the delegate from Harburg, declared that the Colonial Society had "not yet approached as such the task of interesting the German working class in the colonies." The society had "rather until now directed its efforts predominantly toward winning over the educated and well-to-do among our people." The Harburg chapter, on the other hand, was "convinced that here lay an extraordinarily rich and rewarding field for the operation of colonial propaganda."[86] In Berlin, for example, it was reported that the Association of Berlin Street Cleaners came together twice a year for colonial lectures. Indeed, what better evidence of interest among the common people could there be—and moreover a source of sneering amusement to the assembly: "Commoner people than the street sweepers," joked the speaker, "one cannot approach."[87]

Once again, as in 1902, the simple proposal had excited a flurry of discussion, both during and after the Breslau meeting.[88] Much of the response was resoundingly positive, though the secretary of the society reminded Dr. Busse that the initiative lay with the local chapters and not in Berlin. A worker who had read the published proceedings of the meeting wrote a letter actually admonishing the society for its failure to approach the working class. "From my standpoint as a worker I must say that the German public, and above all the German worker, is very poorly served." The workers, he argued, were not enemies of colonialism, but "simply indifferent" to it, and among colonialists only "two of every hundred can speak to the worker and do so in a way that the worker grasps and understands."[89] The *Kolonialzeitung* pointed out that, given the society's charter, the proposal was "actually superfluous, though welcomed on all sides with pleasure and gratitude." The paper insisted the society had done a lot to appeal to workers, and reiterated the simple impossibility of directing such efforts from the central headquarters in Berlin.[90]

For his part, Dr. Busse undertook to hold a popular colonial lecture in Harburg, "India Rubber: Its Production, Processing, and Economic Significance." To entice local workers, the Colonial Society made tickets available at a reduced price to owners of rubber factories, who then provided free tickets to their workers and salaried staff. This proved attractive enough to fill "the great hall almost to the last place." Three-quarters of the audience were thought to be workers from local rubber factories, five hundred of them from a single establishment.[91] The Greiz chapter held eleven lectures accompanied by colored slides. Local associations of veterans, workers, tradesmen, and gymnasts all displayed a "lively interest" in the colonies, and the success prompted an appeal to Berlin for one thousand marks for further propaganda efforts.[92]

The limitless appetite for such magic lantern slide lectures was striking. As late as 1913, colonial propagandists confidently predicted that the "main means to education will always be lectures and, in connection with them, the showing of slides that illustrate the landscape, life, and activities in the colonies."[93] In this the Colonial Society resembled the generally much more ambitious Navy League, which sponsored its own collections of lantern slides for an extensive series of illustrated lectures.[94] The ubiquitous lantern-slide lecture appealed to all classes and every type of audience. Itinerant lanternists had traveled the European countryside since the eighteenth century, entertaining audiences with the luminous wonders of the wider world. The Colonial Society had begun in the 1880s to hold lectures for its members and gradually expanded these to include a wider public. As the organization grew, its speakers traveled around the country projecting images of "savage peoples" and "exotic" landscapes from changing series of photographic transparencies. The illustrated lectures eventually attracted rather large numbers and became effective as colonial propaganda. The Colonial Society in Rostock, for instance, counted twelve hundred people at a lantern-slide lecture in 1901.[95] Ten years later, the Mannheim Verein für Volksbildung and the local chapter of the Colonial Society together sponsored a public lecture series entitled "Our Colonies." The ten "popular" lectures attracted "around one thousand listeners each, or about ten thousand altogether, drawn from all circles of the population."[96] In Essen, a member of the Colonial Society exhibited commodities and gave a lecture—"What Do the German Colonies Already Today Supply for the Households of the German People?"—five times over a few weeks in 1907 to "national and working-class associations."[97]

The universal appeal of the lantern-slide lecture did not, however, signify the submergence of class. The Colonial Society remained keenly aware of the cultural and linguistic effects of class difference and their implications for disseminating colonialism. Lectures were effective as working-class propaganda only so long as the "right speaker" could be found. "How many are there who can speak to a worker and be generally understood?" asked the *Kolonialzeitung*. "What's the use of a lecture that is recognized as something outstanding by the educated, but that the worker does not—cannot—understand at all?"[98] The Colonial Society could take particular satisfaction in "the favorable news from the firm Lenz & Co. that a Charlottenburg bricklayer's foreman called Werner, who had worked on the Togo railroad, was offering to undertake lectures to workers."[99] And the slide show itself was just right for workers because it both entertained and instructed visually. Pictures were generally considered a necessary alternative to words because of the low level of working-class education.

The Colonial Society, which furnished speakers, slide collections, and projectors for its own local branches, gradually got into the business of "popular" slide shows as well.[100] Local chapters began to sponsor public lectures at little or no cost to the spectators, often securing a working-class audience by selling blocks of tickets to factory owners. Speakers also visited workers' organizations—the Evangelical Workers Associations in particular, which were among the few organized groups of workers to propagandize for empire. Their declared loyalty to "king, fatherland, Kaiser, and Reich" blossomed into corporate membership in the Navy League and enthusiastic support of colonialism.[101] The associations were on the national circuit traveled by colonialist speakers, with their small ethnographic or tropical commodity collections or true-to-life stories.[102] A veteran of the Boxer Rebellion, for example, on his "War Experiences in China" before the youth group of a Leipzig branch."[103] Or Friedrich Naumann, influential leader of the National Social movement, who argued passionately for the role of colonialism in social reform and harmonious class integration.[104] Or Pan-German leader Ernst Hasse.[105] In the Rhineland, the society approached evangelical workers' associations in Elberfeld and Mühlheim.[106]

In Dessau, according to local enthusiast General von Kracht, lectures for workers were "frequently given" in a "large pub with a huge hall in the middle of the workers' quarter." The workers were "of course mostly Social Democrats" and one had "first to overcome a certain antipathy." Furthermore, workers "really wanted to come to the lectures" but were terrified of being seen. "The Social Democrats always had their messengers on the lookout at such lectures. Whoever is seen there is later on in his factory so abused [*verhagelt*], that he forgets about ever coming back."[107] In 1910–11, the Propaganda Commission produced 398 lectures. In Berlin, "the presentation of free colonial lectures to attract . . . such circles of the population as are not approachable for membership in the German Colonial Society was successfully continued." Twenty-four lectures "in merchant and trade associations, guilds, patriotic and Hirsch-Duncker workers' associations, and provincial and veterans' associations proved particularly effective." In the year before the war, the Propaganda Commission sponsored 483 lectures nationally. The Berlin chapter sponsored 50 lectures that winter among "the most diverse associations, whose members had until then been total strangers to our efforts."[108]

The colonialist perspective still teemed with "strangers" some thirty-five years after its first beginnings: those great masses of the uninitiated, the misled, the feverishly imaginative. They belonged broadly to a kind of ignorant and distant underclass, to Gustave Le Bon's crowd. In the best of circumstances, they were the passive and receptive objects of colonial propaganda; in the worst, alien objects of anxiety and derision. But perceived always as *objects* of colonialism, of the colonial movement, without autonomy or volition or legible ideas. The propagandists remained ambivalent, slow to expand the scope of their efforts, responding with awkward confusion and hesitation to the prospect of real cooperation with the working and lower middle classes. Colonialists demonstrated nothing like the Navy League's dynamic embrace of the new mass culture medium of film, whose propaganda use they pioneered already by the turn of the century.[109] Numberless commodity samples continued their circulation; thousands of successive lantern slides slid into and out of their grooves; and colonialists lamented the masses insensible to knowledge. Which is all the more striking to the extent that we consider the reality of subaltern and grassroots colonialisms that flourished in Germany, unacknowledged or dismissed by the movement. These formed alternative worlds of idiosyncratic colonial enthusiasm: sometimes eccentric, sometimes obstinate, but for all that no more or less reasonable than the flights of fancy underpinning the colonialist picture of the world.

CHAPTER THREE

No Place in the Sun

The People's Empire

> *Could one but dispel the idea of human happiness which during the*
> *last decade our Social Democrats have been sedulously building into*
> *their imaginings, reveal to them the secret of contentment, and arouse*
> *in them hopes of a new kind, then our Social Democratic crisis would*
> *be largely resolved, that is to say, an atmosphere would have been*
> *created in which the economic reforms and measures of support to*
> *which our working class are fully entitled could be successfully carried*
> *out. . . . Ought not the question of colonies . . . have an important*
> *effect in this direction too?*
> —Friedrich Fabri, *Bedarf Deutschland der Colonien?* 1879

What does it look like when we peer into that other world, into the everyday life of the lower classes? As it turns out, it looks strangely familiar. "I do not," writes Lucie Böttcher, a twenty-six-year-old Berliner living at home with her parents, "intend to settle in Africa out of romantic overexcitement—as, perhaps, many other young women do—rather for me it is a serious thing."[1] Emil Zeiller, a machinist in Mönchengladbach, is terse: "My trade is fitter (cylinder engraver) but could also work as mechanic or for the railroad. But best of all I'd like to devote my work to the Fatherland."[2] Likewise Magda Henck: "I have the lively wish to go" to Southwest Africa "and place my modest strength in the service of the beloved German fatherland."[3] In Darmstadt, young Apollonia May and Johanna Demmel are "absolutely determined to come to Africa."[4] Ida Hofter of Breslau, twenty-two, is undisturbed by doubts or fears: "A sure desire draws me to distant lands."[5] Richard Thier, a Leipzig stenographer, has "long had the wish to settle in the German colonies."[6]

Perhaps Germans had a "colonizing vocation" after all, that historic "colonisatorischer Beruf" that the colonial publicist Friedrich Fabri exhorted them to fulfill. These ordinary Germans, men and women from the laboring classes, from the lower middle classes, from all parts of the country, look to the colonies with interest and enthusiasm, sometimes patriotism, often with a kind of longing. Their surviving letters—addressed to the Colonial Society, the Foreign Office, even the Kaiser—envision striking itineraries reflecting a broad diffusion of popular colonialism that disturbs notions of empire as a purely bourgeois formation. Even among the most parochial, the most stationary, the most traditional Germans a cosmopolitanism flourished, an imagined geography encompassing far-flung places. These elusive objects of colonial discourse, these shop girls and maids and mechanics, emerge — fleetingly — as subjects of empire.

How strange, then, their coexistence, precisely as prospective colonists, as enthusiasts of the first order, with a colonial movement predicated on their nonexistence, indeed on the pressing need to *produce* them. Of course, we might understand them as objects of propaganda, as signifiers of its success: the pale effects of a dominant colonial discourse. But, paradoxically, we observe flashes of their status as subjects, as agents, precisely in their isolation, futility, impossibility, their inadmissibility. If they seem to reflect the diffusion of a shared colonialist mentality, what they bring to colonialism nevertheless sets them apart. They offer only their labor: tailoring, ironing, mining, farm work, hairdressing, typing, laundering — not capital. They cannot be assimilated to the colonial project because they have no capital and because their labor is superfluous in the colony. The "colonial labor question" is omnipresent in German colonial discourse. However, the answer to it is not the German working classes, but the "Erziehung des Negers zur Arbeit," "educating the negro to work." Cheap black labor set in motion by German capital.

Max Buchner, the pessimistic publicist, compresses this truth in his warning against "illusions" about life in colonial Africa. "It is no small thing standing around day after day in the hot storerooms stinking of palm oil, palm kernels, and Negroes."[7] The conflation of black labor and tropical commodities that constitutes "factory life in Cameroon" fuses deep racism and capitalist production with the exclusion of subaltern whites. The only European is, after all, the owner of capital, or his overseer, "standing around day after day" supervising African labor. The logic of colonialism recognizes the German worker only in the metropolitan factory, destination of tropical goods — palm oil, sisal, rubber — commodities that in turn *provide him labor*. But working-class colonialists do not understand this, for if they have no access to material resources, to capital, they likewise have little access to symbolic resources, to colonial knowledge.

From the perspective of that congeries of discourse and institution that was the bourgeois colonial movement, strange ideas and crank schemes flourished among the untutored. Their letters are naïve, hopeful, often abject. They suggest again and again a remoteness from power, as from knowledge. Minne Gotzen goes straight to the top, addressing herself to Kaiser Wilhelm — "All-highest most gracious Emperor and Lord!" she begins breathlessly — before going on to explain that she is "here in Riesenburg (West Prussia) at a shoe company and would very much like to go to Southwest Africa, but [hasn't] the means to do it."[8] A down-on-his-luck Leipziger sought to put his failed marriage and business behind him by appealing for a position in the colonies: "Since March 1912, I've worked independently as a salesman but haven't achieved the success I hoped for. Beyond that, I've had little luck in marriage . . . so that I've now applied for a divorce. All of this leads me to look for a position abroad, so that a lot of work will make me able to forget what unpleasantness I've experienced here."[9] Or Eugenie Beez, of Haselbrunn: "Like I learned in the paper, German girls are being sought for German Southwest Africa, I would certainly be willing if it's not too bad there." Please let me know, she asks, "how things are": "if one comes as a slave, I certainly don't want that, or whether one can do women's work, like what is customary with us, for example tailoring, ironing and so on, I also know something of farming. Where I am now . . . I do right and fear no one and God our father is everywhere, but slavery or among savages I don't do."[10] Her understanding of the colony seems compounded of official "information" and the dime-novel fantasy of "white slavery," or perhaps "Die Weisse Sklavin in Afrika" films of the cinematograph.

Ironically, the aim of making colonialism "popular" entailed the denial or suppression of popular colonialism, or *Volkskolonialismus*. These marginal, grassroots colonialists are disowned, nearly invisible, separate in their enthusiasms and longings, contemptible in their abjection, laughable in their illusions. They have no future in the colonies or role in the colonial movement. They are inadmissible to the public sphere. And yet, if their ideas were perhaps strange and naïve, stranger still was the similarity of these ideas to the hegemonic public discourse of colonialism, their mirroring, however indistinctly, of official colonial ideas. Let us consider, for example, the fantastic plans of Joseph Dietze, a handloom weaver and textile designer in Hamburg, as revealed in his letter to the Imperial Colonial Office:

Hamburg, July 3, 1914

> The undersigned tradesman in hand weaving requests from the Imperial Colonial Office assistance so that we can settle in Africa. Weaver and designer by profession have completed training etc. . . .
>
> Have got patent on my mechanical handloom, which makes it possible to compete somewhat with mechanical loom system.
>
> Unfortunately have had no more business recently.
>
> The textile trade has fallen on hard times. . . . The hand weaving trade, dependent on assistance, has a hard struggle keeping our fine old art of hand weaving from dying out. Assistance is lacking.
>
> For hand weaving, *waterless* regions come into consideration. Africa—our colonies are the land for this!
>
> We could teach the blacks over there, the Negro women too, and that way establish this industry over there and gain back some lost ground. The cheap black labor would receive wages and hand weaving would profit.

Our fatherland would also reap advantage—in that the industry would be preserved because steam power needs water, which is lacking there, while the handloom needs no water power.

We need only the assistance and permission of the Imperial Colonial Office to be able to settle there, so that the black population can be trained.[11]

Dietze included a photograph of himself surrounded by his family and looms. It depicts a scene of extremely modest respectability, domestic order, and industry in which the paterfamilias, reading to his children, carefully projects an image of cultivation belied by the awkwardness and confused ideas of his letter.

Dietze's ingenious, cockeyed scheme to save handloom weaving by substituting cheap black labor in waterless Southwest Africa for Hamburg's steam-powered factories is a reflection—however distorted—of the received colonial ideology of the day. Confronted by mechanized mass production, he hoped to avert ruin by settling in Africa. In the colonies, he would preserve traditional handloom weaving and his own dignified independence as an artisan. This corresponded to the idea, widespread but not actually dominant in colonialist circles, that the colonies should provide refuge for those "traditional" elements of German society threatened by industrialization, and thereby relieve pauperization and social unrest. But the empire promised much more in Dietze's mind: the strange prospect of a capitalist handloom mass production, a system both traditional and modern, made possible precisely by the *lack* of water—and therefore steam—coupled with the exploitation of indigenous labor and a subvention from the government. Dietze presents a micro-image of popular colonialism in Germany; his willful suspension of realistic economic calculation—indeed of reality—in favor of dreams of far-flung colonial success had its counterpart in bourgeois colonialist ideology.[12]

The plan was, of course, stillborn. The German government declined to finance the colonizing schemes of penurious artisans, and, in any case, the outbreak of war a month later put an end to German overseas colonization. But, however confused and ingenuous the proposal—and indeed because of just these qualities—Dietze's letter is significant: rare evidence of the circulation of colonial discourse and the formation of colonial knowledge and aspirations among the urban lower classes, in this case the vanishing remnant of independent artisans engaged in handloom weaving. It represents a kind of popular colonialism: not an alternative to the official, institutional, and scientific knowledge disseminated by, for example, Hamburg's new Colonial Institute or the local Colonial Society, but a slight corruption and reconfiguration of it.

How common was this sort of knowledge or intention among lower-class Germans? How many in Hamburg, not to mention others living far from the bustling port city, could be considered "colonialists" in some sense?

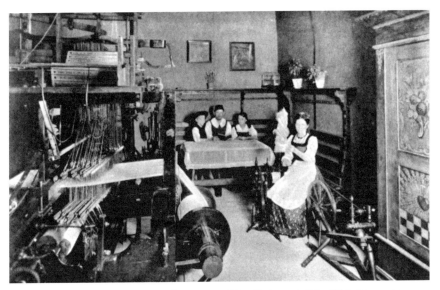

Hamburg handloom weaver Joseph Dietze and family (1914). BA, RKA, R1001/6244, Bl. 145. Courtesy Bundesarchiv Berlin.

That a poor urban weaver from northern Europe should look to the deserts of southwestern Africa for his salvation may, of course, have had a lot to do with the city he lived in. Dietze's Hamburg was filled with the signs and wonders of the European colonial empires: sailors from distant ports, ships loaded with tropical commodities, Carl Hagenbeck's famous ethnographic shows, shops selling *Kolonialwaren*, ethnographic displays. A wealthy entrepôt of world commerce, it maintained dense connections to the scores of European colonies, protectorates, and spheres of influence created by the "new imperialism" of the late nineteenth century. Already since the 1830s, long before the colonial movement of the 1870s, Hanseatic merchants had been part of the West African maritime trade, selling tobacco, linen, and spirits and buying tropical hardwoods, animal skins, ivory, and coconuts.[13] From the 1840s, they traded in Zanzibar and along the East African coast. By 1914, after thirty years of German overseas empire, Hamburg had become the center of the German colonial trade, and a chief point of departure for its explorers and settlers, and for soldiers shipping out to China or Southwest Africa.[14]

So much activity may even have concealed the relative worthlessness of Germany's colonial empire, which provided but a small fraction of Hamburg's business. Indeed, the local mercantile bourgeoisie, with its strong free-trade convictions, had originally, in the 1870s and 1880s, been skeptical of colonialism.[15] Their longstanding commercial penetration of the West

African littoral and Zanzibar had by no means implied a predisposition toward formal colonization. But by the turn of the century, the Hamburg-America Line, the Woermann Line, and the German East Africa Line all provided regular transport between Hamburg and the colonies. Jantzen & Thormählen, Woermann, and O'Swald were only the best known Hamburg firms plying the African coast—firms celebrated "not only as pioneers of German trade but also for spreading culture among the savage peoples of Africa."[16] The German Trading and Plantation Company of the Pacific Islands, active in Samoa, was based in Hamburg, as was the Jaluit Company, holder of commercial privileges in the Marshall and Caroline Islands.[17]

More importantly, the colonial trade crystallized in the everyday life of the working classes. Hamburg's dock workers unloaded exotic shipments of antelope horn, ostrich feathers, and "curiosities" (presumably ethnographic) from Southwest Africa, and india rubber, palm nuts, ebony, cocoa, and elephant tusks from West Africa. Its warehouses stored East African coffee, wax, hardwoods, vanilla, and especially rubber. From the South Pacific came copra, ivory nuts, and mother-of-pearl. Local factory workers rolled Cameroon tobacco into "Bibundi Cigars" sold under the names of famous German explorers: Zintgraff, Wissmann, Nachtigal, and Gravenreuth. Not only the city's show business impresarios, publishers, scholars, journalists, and writers but also its sailors, merchants, dock workers, printers, postcard makers, and shipping clerks had a hand in the everyday business of empire.

Dietze's cosmopolitan outlook, his interest in the distant, colonized lands of Africa, may not have been particularly out of place in this context. The volume of trade, the commercial popularity of "exoticism," and the profusion of tropical commodities, of colonial artifacts and images—of an everyday colonial material culture—meant that even the poorest, least educated, and parochial among Hamburg's lower classes encountered the colonial empire—however fantastic or mediated—as quotidian reality. And yet, if the bright thread of colonialism wound its way through everyday life in Hamburg, this did not necessarily amount to the transmission, or broad assimilation, of colonialist ideology or politics or racism. A range of responses was possible: indifference or hostility, dim awareness, spectatorship, enthusiasm, even imagining oneself a settler, an explorer, a soldier. Not least among these was the strong Social Democratic critique of colonialism. For someone who most likely had little education, free time, or money, and limited access to books, Dietze developed a rather substantial grasp of colonization, knowledge that he adapted to his own predicament.

Compare the weaver Dietze to his fellow Hamburg colonialist, the lawyer and writer Wilhelm Hübbe-Schleiden. The poor artisan, with his basic education, represented the last of a dying class of skilled workers supplanted by an international, mechanized, capitalist textile industry. Hübbe-Schleiden, on the other hand, was extremely articulate, well educated, a lawyer and colonial merchant, but—after three years in West Africa, significantly—a *failed* merchant, who by the early 1880s had become a leader of the colonial movement. A radical nationalist and one of the most influential colonial publicists in Germany, he warned vehemently against the perils of overpopulation and industrialization, which he saw leading inexorably to revolution, but also against extracolonial mass emigration, which signified cultural loss and national weakness. In a series of books published in the late 1870s and early 1880s, he envisioned German colonies as traditional, agrarian societies, a refuge where pure forms of German artisan and peasant culture might once more flourish.[18] For both Dietze and Hübbe-Schleiden—each from a very different perspective—colonialism seemed to promise a solution to the tensions and problems of a society in rapid transition to urban, industrial modernity.

Yet the relationship between these two men—or, rather, between their respective ideas of colonial empire—is something of a puzzle. The hyperarticulate publicist's enthusiasm concealed his own colonial failure. A failure that contrasted with the privileging of his discourse on empire, even as it reflected the poor weaver's own deepening failure, which of course marked the invisibility of his own colonial aspirations, their futility, even though he was almost a perfect illustration of Hübbe-Schleiden's thesis. Status is key. More than twenty years after Hübbe-Schleiden's great burst of publicity, his ideas—and those of many like-minded colonialists—appear to have filtered down to the struggling traditional classes, urban or rural, he had originally described.

Certainly it is possible to read Dietze's letter as a debased, popular mutation of colonial discourse, a version in which only faint outlines of received, official colonialism remain visible. Such a reading already assumes a movement of ideology in a sense "downward," from an aggressive, bourgeois vanguard of colonialism at the top of German society to a relatively passive, lower-class public. In this scenario, colonial knowledge or ideas filter "down," from "above," or radiate "outward," from a "center," implying a prior, privileged site of authority, authorship, and persuasion. Dietze and Hübbe-Schleiden seem to converge, the down-on-his-luck weaver almost conjured by the publicist, purest affirmation of his vision of empire at once popularized and peopled. But Dietze's own colonial idea is finally impossible, a mark of his estrangement from capitalist and colonialist "reality." There is neither simple reproduction of the dominant discourse here, nor a negation of it, but a kind of stubbornly naïve appropriation. His letter, or its fate, suggests not a convergence of masses and movement, but a paradoxical gulf between them.

And the same is true for the thousands of Germans just like Dietze, for whom colonial enthusiasm culminated in the wish to leave their homeland for a new life in the colonies. Surviving letters to the Imperial Colonial Office in Berlin reveal the broad diffusion of colonizing ambition among young, mostly unmarried men with rudimentary education and few prospects.[19]

Most struggled as artisans or workers, or described themselves vaguely as merchants. For these men without means, the costs and hardships of settlement presented basically insurmountable obstacles. There was almost no chance that any of them would ever reach Africa or the South Seas. Nevertheless, a compound of desperation, boredom, hope, and curiosity drove them to contemplate emigration to German Southwest Africa, Cameroon, or Samoa.

In the spring of 1902, the Colonial Society finally opened a Central Information Bureau for Emigrants, a site for the continuous rehearsal of unattainable objectives.[20] In its first year, 509 artisans, 107 workers, 14 miners, and 501 farmers and farm laborers were among the 3,376 who contacted the bureau, 2,315 of whom were specifically interested in the German colonies.[21] The figures for the following year 1903–4 showed little change, while the number of requests in 1905–6 actually dropped to below the level of the first year.[22] As actual German emigration, mostly to the Americas, slowed to a trickle—only 28,000 in 1905—and the colonies became mired in war and revolt, the new bureau failed to catch on.[23] In 1906–7, however, the number climbed dramatically, though workers and artisans accounted for a much smaller share of the 9,547 queries than farmers and merchants.[24] In 1910–11, inquiries arrived from 264 mechanics and electrical workers, 107 machine builders, 119 smiths, 249 masons, 108 fitters, 618 locksmiths, 350 joiners, and 148 metalworkers among artisans and skilled workers, as well as 390 miners and 876 unskilled laborers.[25] Of 19,714 queries in 1911–12, some 3,722 come from skilled industrial workers and artisans, 1,753 from unskilled workers, 2,307 from farmers and farm laborers, as compared to 4,106 from merchants.[26] By this time, economic change had transformed the source and nature of the emigration impulse. Up to about 1895, the typical German emigrant sought to own a farm, usually in America, where his family could settle and begin a new life. By the turn of the century, however, the dwindling *Auswanderung* counted mostly industrial workers seeking temporary work.[27] And there was no place for these restless metalworkers, bricklayers, and lathe operators in Southwest Africa. By the time the war came in 1914, the seventy-year-old dream of German overseas settlement colonies had become merely the stuff of propaganda and colonial romance—and an extensive grassroots enthusiasm.

Many of the correspondents were unused to writing and virtually mute on their motivations. Georg Biebrach of Leipzig, probably an unskilled or casual laborer, was typically laconic:

To the Colonial Office for German Colonies in Berlin.

I the undersigned am German, born on 17 August 1882 in Magdeburg. Thoroughly healthy, big, strong, and unmarried, and would like to immigrate to

German East Africa but lack the means for the journey. Allow me therefore the humble request . . .[28]

Others had a somewhat more elaborate style and occasionally included some autobiography with their requests. The younger men frequently expressed the desire to fulfill their military obligations by joining the colonial military force, sometimes a bridge to settlement in Southwest Africa. Among the few writers who revealed their hopes in any detail, most sought unspecified positions with the state or in commercial firms. They appear to have shared a vague sense that some distant, lucrative, maritime trade in tropical goods promised success far beyond what they might dream of in Germany. The impression of hardship, scarcity, and thwarted ambitions pervades nearly all of the letters:

> At present, I am in Breslau at the Royal School of Mechanical Engineering. Due to my financial circumstances, it is unfortunately no longer possible to continue attending the school. . . . My father, a pastor living in Görlitz who is already past seventy-four, can unfortunately give me no allowance, since I have five sisters and five stepsiblings. My only stepbrother died several years ago of fever in Cameroon, where he was employed on the plantation of a Berlin company. . . . Since my greatest wish was always to go into the service of our German colonies, I trust in His Excellency to give me any advice as to a position for the colonies. . . . In January I turned 21.
>
> Your most obedient servant,
>
> Stephan Broske[29]

The colonies appeared to be a way out of the straightened circumstances, déclassement, bankruptcy, professional obsolescence, or failure that beset many Germans in a period of economic change and inflexible social hierarchy.[30]

Colonial settlement also promised a form of escape from the boredom of modern life. The impersonal, repetitive, and exhausting nature of modern factory labor or white-collar office jobs alienated many from their everyday work. The letters are never so explicit, but they imply restlessness, a simple desire for change: "Since it is my greatest wish to get to learn commerce in the colonies, I approach you with the request whether you can perhaps do something for me. . . . Until my fourteenth year I attended elementary school, learned baking for three years but then gave it up again for reasons of health and came to the Bremen Besigheimer oil factory, where I am in my fourth year and hold the position of registrar."[31] A young white-collar worker from Leipzig gives a similar impression of apparent dissatisfaction with clerical work in a law office:

I Friedrich Richard Thier was born on 9 July 1889 in Leipzig-Reudnitz the son of the . . . lithographer Friedrich Ernst Thier. . . . I attended first the twelfth district school in Leipzig-Reudnitz, after that the third municipal school for continuing education and after leaving school began as apprentice in the office of the attorney Hofmann in Leipzig. . . . After the complete term of apprenticeship, I took a service position in the law office of Dr. Wohrizek in Leipzig . . . where I am still employed. Here I am engaged as stenographer and typist and with all the work that is to be met with in an office.[32]

Some vocational training and an apprenticeship have carried him from the laborer's life of his father, but modern, urban, white-collar work does not seem to satisfy him. Explaining that he has "already long had the wish to settle in the German colonies," he "most humbly begs" for assistance in finding a position with the colonial authorities or a private firm. A young woman simply has nothing better to do: "Since nothing in particular ties me to the old homeland and I came of age a few months ago I have a huge desire to go" to Southwest Africa.[33] At the very least, the colonies offered an exotic change of scenery, novelty, perhaps even a kind of freedom.

In the end, the appeal of colonialism crossed lines of social class and geographical region. Most of those who actually wished to leave for the colonies belonged to a heterogeneous mass of stenographers, clerks, mechanics, metalworkers, traveling salesmen, and artisans. They shared a common predicament more often than a common social class. Whether shopkeepers and artisans threatened by economic transformation, or factory and white-collar workers created and absorbed by it, they were women and men without property or prospects, who lacked sentimental or professional bonds strong enough to tie them to local communities. At loose ends, they concocted fantasy itineraries leading from the shop floor, the kitchen, or the vocational school to Dar es Salaam, Togo, and the Southwest African frontier.

And their fantasies had deep roots by the 1890s. An outstanding current in colonial discourse was settlement, the idea that Germany must acquire territories for colonization by its surplus population.[34] The figure of the impoverished, displaced German was already intertwined with the image of the settlement colony in the earliest colonial discourse. German colonialism had from the 1840s been bound up with the whole problem of emigration, particularly in the minds of the many bourgeois nationalists who perceived the protracted loss as an emblem of German disunity and weakness. And indeed, the great nineteenth-century *Auswanderung*, the massive emigration during which over five million Germans left behind homeland and countrymen, lived on in colonialist propaganda long after the last giant wave of departures had crested in the mid-1880s.[35] By about 1890, industrialization had advanced sufficiently to absorb impoverished migrants from the countryside, and the vanishing American frontier no longer offered the possibility of agricultural settlement.[36] Yet a vestigial urgency about the future of

Auslandsdeutschtum—of Germandom abroad—and the need for settlement colonies survived and flourished in language and imagery. Many colonialists and Pan-German nationalists remained fixated on the dream of a new German *Heimat* overseas, bound to the fatherland by strong ties of language, custom, and sentiment. Because emigration affected such large numbers, the settlement strand of colonialism seemed to promise a natural appeal to the broader public.

In 1886, Carl Peters's Gesellschaft für Deutsche Kolonisation organized a General German Congress in Berlin. Just two years before, annual emigration had peaked at 203,000.[37] The Peters group were fierce and flamboyant advocates of settlement colonialism, and the rhetoric of the congress reflected the sense of endemic crisis:

> For centuries, a heavy stream of German emigration flowed across the borders of the empire into foreign lands. In every land and among all peoples it was the Germans, who have, in outstanding numbers, taken part in the great cultural task of civilizing and cultivating our earth. Generations of our countrymen [leaving] unimpeded from the common homeland in Europe are permanently lost. The great national achievements of the last decades have put an end to this process. Germandom across the whole world begins once more to think seriously of its great common fatherland, and the urge for a closer union with their countrymen at home comes everywhere to life.[38]

The group spoke for many colonialists and nationalists who lamented that Germans had for decades colonized on behalf of other peoples, "civilizing and cultivating our earth" for America, and for Anglo-Saxon culture in general. Moreover, the healthier elements of German society were leaving, not radicals or the unemployed: "We may no longer bear with indifference the great loss of labor and national strength. . . . The emigration does not free us of bad elements, but robs us much more of the better workers."[39] National unification and the seizure of vast African territories—the "great national achievements of the last decades"—meant that Germany could finally put an end to this loss by diverting the flow of emigrants to its own colonies.

The fiery nationalists at the General German Congress could not know that the emigration had just run its course. Even long afterward, colonialists and Pan-Germans continued to speak and write as if moved by the great magnitude and immediacy of a persistent crisis, although year after year only small numbers left, mostly for America, and increasingly as single industrial workers (more and more women among them) looking for jobs, rather than peasants seeking farmland.[40] The propagandists conjured images of dramatic loss and the rise of a "new Germany overseas." The "ethical-national significance" of colonialism lay in settlement colonies.[41] As late as 1907, election propaganda argued that Germany should send its "surplus people not only to foreign lands, where emigrants of German origin and language are lost, but rather also give them in their new fatherland the possibility of holding on to their motherland for all time."[42] "All over Germany," they claimed, "are able young people who want badly to go abroad, . . . whose adventurous spirit dwells within, matched by joy in work and production and the serious inclination to establish a proper existence and become useful people." "Even when abroad," these virtuous, industrious people, untainted by socialism, would "remain German citizens within the extended, overseas German fatherland."[43]

Yet, for all the vague promises of a bright future overseas, the place of lower-class working people in this scheme was far from clear. The history of colonial propaganda reveals a discursive mutation over the course of the nineteenth century representing a fundamental shift in the relationship between the colonial movement and Germany's working classes. Colonialists moved from talking about the politically menacing masses to addressing them, however ineptly or indirectly. Originally, from the 1840s, theorists and publicists had looked to emigration and colonialism as solutions to the social question.[44] The inability of the German economy to keep pace with population growth had produced impoverished, unemployed, landless masses who threatened to undermine stability. The organized colonial movement really took shape in the 1870s, against a background of fear and uncertainty intensified by the crash of 1873, the formation of the Social Democratic Party in 1875, and the fiercely contested antisocialist law of 1878. By the early 1880s, Wilhelm Hübbe-Schleiden was calling for a colonial safety valve, a *Sicherheits-Ventil*, for the diversion of dangerously dissatisfied elements. "Every ruined man," he warned, "is but one more dangerous fellow citizen!"[45] The Saxon colonialist Ernst von Weber warned of the need for the "mass export of revolutionary tinder" (*Massenexport des revolutionären Zündstoffes*).[46] There were "approximately forty million proletarians living in Germany" whose "titanic spiritual and physical forces threaten the normal development of human culture here in Europe."[47] Friedrich Fabri, the leading colonialist voice of the 1870s and 1880s, argued that, while the repressive antisocialist law of 1878 had "broken up the public organization and . . . suppressed the whole of the agitatory activity of our anarchists," this was not by itself sufficient. "No intelligent person . . . will believe that this has dispelled all danger, or removed for all time the possibility of an attempt at the forcible overthrow of the existing order." Indeed, the spread of radicalism, "particularly among the working masses," would eventually require the transportation of criminal elements to penal colonies.

> Supposing, then, that . . . violent attempts at revolution might take place in Germany, too, like those undertaken by the Commune in the spring of 1871, and that, after a possibly bloody struggle, thousands and tens of thousands . . . would suddenly have to be brought to justice, would not such a sad eventuality confront the Reich Government with an insoluble dilemma? What to do with

the thousands under sentence, given our already quite inadequate and over-crowded prisons? There would simply be no other alternative than that which France adopted with her deportations to New Caledonia. With well-intentioned generosity, a suitable island—called, perhaps, Utopia—could be allotted to the Communards . . . so that their program of universal happiness could for once somewhere be put into practice, and to the test. But in order to be able to take such a course, Germany would already have had to have acquired appropriately situated colonial possessions.[48]

This extreme vision of revolutionary violence, mass exile, and penal colonies evolved over time into the idea that colonies offered workers the hope of a better life, rather than punishment for political crimes. The sense of colonialism as a promising solution to the social question resurfaced in recognizable forms in propaganda. One widely circulated pamphlet warned that

> An outsized population produces an army of proletarians, which gradually be-comes a burden on the fatherland.
> **Fewer proletarians, more colonists:**
> that's the solution. Emigration is only a healthy bloodletting to the nation if the emigrants remain bound to their people and nationality.[49]

Here "proletarians" include the working class and the poor more generally—men and women without education or property who, though still a "bur-den" on the country, might expect to share in the advantages of organized colonial settlement. But the lower classes emerged only gradually as a true public—an audience, readers—and after any real sense of a colonial future for them had faded.

By the 1890s, working-class and other readers of SPD papers would have encountered strident criticism of the settlement idea. There was no end to at-tacks on the false claims, sterile pretensions, and dead ends associated with settlement. For socialists, the very fact of emigration became an implicit in-dictment of prevailing conditions in Wilhelmine Germany. SPD newspapers reported stories like "Flight from the Homeland," about a factory worker's family "fleeing their homeland" for South America because "the future in the old one looked so critical," or a local pair of journeyman mechanics leaving to "seek their fortune in the land of the Boers."[50] Who, they asked, would escape Germany only to wind up in a German colony, a reconfig-ured capitalist police state overseas? The basic idea of settlement colonies as re-creations of Germany abroad was precisely what made them unac-ceptable to emigrants who sought to leave Germany behind: "The German who shakes the dust of the fatherland from his shoes because the double yoke of capitalist and police rule becomes too heavy for him will not turn to the deserts of Damaraland or the swamps of Lake Tanganyika, where he encounters the same police director and the same state prosecutor whom he has just happily escaped at home. Rather, he will search for a freer land."[51]

There was an occasional Social Democratic voice in favor of settlement colonies, but it most likely never reached the ears of SPD workers. The revisionist Eduard Bernstein, for example, argued that the "proletariat, too, has an interest in a reasonable geographical expansion of the nation. We have not only the present interests, but the future interests of humanity to protect, and on the question of settlement we stand in competition with other peoples, with the civilized peoples of Europe."[52] Most Social Democrats, though, continued to cast settlement colonialism as mere illusion, and a distraction from more urgent questions. As Wilhelm Liebknecht insisted before the Reichstag in 1885, the colonialists were "simply exporting the social question. They conjure before the eyes of the people a type of fata morgana in the sands and the swamps of Africa. . . . The social question can be resolved only at home, never through colonial policy abroad."[53]

The colonial movement tended, ironically, to agree—if in rather different terms. The Colonial Society continued to entertain the settlement question up to 1914, but only half-heartedly. It advocated the ongoing development of white farming in Southwest Africa and funded research on carving a second settlement colony out of East Africa, particularly the highlands of West Usambara.[54] Yet, contrary to the elaborate ideological and propaganda programs, German colonies would never provide settlement opportunities for the lower classes of the metropole. In the first place, most experts thought the African colonies unsuitable for Europeans of any class because of altitude and climate. The miasmal tropics, they said, bred fever, madness, and degeneration.[55] As Max Buchner put it, "For our worrisome surplus population, for actual emigrants, there is nothing in tropical Africa. Those newspaper articles that recommended even the Niger and Congo territories . . . were nothing else but stupidity attempting mass murder."[56] Nor was there any market for a German labor force where the exploitation of cheap local labor was possible. As Walther Rathenau observed following his 1908 trip to Southwest Africa, "We have no right, nor is it in our interests, to . . . induce part of our home population to expatriate itself for the purpose of forming a white proletariat in a protectorate to do that work which normally falls to the lot of the natives in other colonies and for which they, for climatic and ethnic reasons, are better qualified."[57] There was a miniscule white working class in Southwest Africa, Germany's only true settlement colony, but it was the exception.[58] The value of the colonies was quite simply commercial, they were "suitable for . . . trading stations, and some of them, perhaps eventually, . . . for plantation agriculture with native labor, but none of them, as is now and again erroneously suggested, for the absorption of the surplus German population, which is to say as a destination for mass emigration. Climatic conditions stand almost everywhere in the way of that."[59]

Already at the founding meeting of the Deutscher Kolonialverein in 1882, Hermann von Maltzan observed that "among the adherents of coloniza-tion," there were "two main schools of thought." One sought "great settle-ment colonies to compensate for the large German emigration to America and to preserve an intimate connection with the motherland," while the other thought only of "erecting trading posts and settlements for the pur-pose of cultivation [plantations] in unclaimed territories." The association's founders, he concluded, "are of the opinion that a direct, practical handling of colonization is possible only through the last-named course."[60] The Co-lonial Society and its affiliates ultimately tended to focus much more on economic development—trading and plantation colonies—than on a settle-ment colonialism (*Siedlungskolonialismus*) marked by failure and delusion: the impractical, unrealistic ideology of the lower classes who had no place in the movement, no voice in the public sphere.

Indeed, echoing the intertwinement of settlement discourse and the social question from the 1840s, the discourse of German settlement continued to be charged with powerful class anxieties and confusions. The brief history of settlement in Southwest Africa in particular was mired in scandal and failure that was often coded in the language of class. In the spring of 1892, the Colonial Society established the Syndicate for Southwest African Settle-ment (Syndikat für Südwestafrikanische Siedlung), the first organized effort to resettle Germans on the colonial frontier.[61] A nearly indiscernible trickle of settlement in the Windhoek area began, only to end in a string of failures and lawsuits and a dire tale of proletarianization. Accusations in the press ridiculed the scheme, and the whole dream of settlement colonialism. It was reported that, among the settlers who actually arrived at Windhoek, one sold liquor, one opened a bar, and one's daughter went into prostitution, while his wife took in laundry from colonial soldiers. Only one had been able to free himself from the "Windhoekmisere," while yet another poi-soned himself "when he saw that founding an existence in Southwest Africa was unthinkable." The image of a downward social spiral on the colonial frontier was vivid, although the Colonial Society and the Syndicate denied the reports as outrageous fabrication.[62]

Fifteen years later, the colony's reputation had not much improved. Images of a debased settler population prone to violence, alcoholism, and crime per-sisted.[63] Most disturbing was settler miscegenation: interracial concubinage, or even marriage, and the emergence of a half-caste underclass. The coding of colonial society as déclassé here assumes its biological aspect; markers of race and status become exchangeable. Race dramatically transformed and amplified the problem of class in colonial discourse, which by the turn of the century was rife with descriptions of a racial order undermined by uncon-tainable sexual desire. The language of the Protestant Africa Association in Berlin was typical of warnings against the social and cultural degeneration threatened by racial mixing. The "moral dangers" of marriage were thought to be

> twice as great for our countrymen over there. They [the indigenous people] have a corrupting effect on colonial as well as missionary work: the white man, like the colored women, becomes wild down there far too easily. The former become brutalized in temperament, devoid of all that is noble—even national feeling—and the latter become insensible to the influence of the mission and to all culture. Even a marriage between a white man and colored woman is harmful, for it pulls the man down to a lower level and leaves on the mixed marriage no imprint of the originality of the higher European culture, as the experience of history has taught all mixed races.[64]

The popular press, too, warned that the "formation of a mixed race" in Southwest Africa, "and in the South Seas, too—namely on Samoa—makes frightening progress."[65] According to the head of the Colonial Society's Frauenbund, Adda von Liliencron, the whole southern part of Southwest Africa faced the twin dangers of "going Kaffir" and "going Boer" ("verkaffern" and "verburen").[66] Many colonialists, of course, imagined Southwest Africa as a place to create and control a particular version of "Germanness" that was respectable, enterprising, and traditional.[67] But miscegenation cast doubt on whether and how the colony could ever really be transformed into a German homeland.[68] The dream of preserving threatened Germandom, "bedrängtes Deutschtum," in a New Germany overseas had instead given rise to a shocking, hybridized frontier culture of mixed alliances and social decay that threatened to contaminate and undermine the whole colonial order. The urgency of race powerfully recast the question of class.

The prospects of settlement for the working classes were never very good, even before the miscegenation debate. People without means were by and large excluded, and efforts made to limit unsuitable settlers.[69] There were exceptions: according to Leutwein, a number of former soldiers, lent capital by the state, had "done well, in any case better than in the homeland, where they would have belonged almost without exception to the propertyless classes."[70] But most land was held and sold by large concession companies like the Southwest Africa Company or the Deutsche Colonial-Gesellschaft für Südwestafrika, and was beyond the reach of those without means.[71] The 1903 Reichstag appropriation for loans to prospective settlers recognized only those with their own capital of at least ten thousand marks as eligible, expressing a general hope of raising the social status of settlers.[72] Following the war, the colonial administration instituted capital requirements, suggesting that failed settlers would become an agricultural proletariat possibly even capable of radicalization.[73]

It was in this context that the discursive articulation of moral, social, and racial "degeneration" through the apparent links between miscegenation and the decay of bourgeois respectability and sexual mores made the social class of prospective settlers an even more urgent matter.[74] The director of the Colonial School at Witzenhausen called "young men, especially from the educated and leading circles" to a "difficult but beautiful life's work as champions of Germandom, pioneers of culture abroad."[75] Governor Lindequist recognized the school for producing prospective colonists from the more educated middle classes, lamenting however the few opportunities for them in the colony. According to Director Fabarius of the Colonial School, students from a more educated, middling background would "know better what awaits them out there than the simple land folk and craftsmen or even the urban factory population, and . . . are also capable of subsequently assuming economic and intellectual leadership."[76] But male settlement remained largely unplanned, not infrequently a consequence of colonial military service, and there was ultimately little opportunity for settlers of any class.

On the other hand, the rhetoric of class might actually shape women's emigration, which was more organized, and might therefore transform future social, racial, and sexual relations in the colony. In 1898, the Colonial Society established a female emigration program, administrative responsibility for which it handed over to the auxiliary Frauenbund in 1908.[77] Once again, the racial and sexual problems of the colony appeared substantially as a question of social class, of bourgeois respectability. The selection of women socially and culturally suitable to reproduce *Auslandsdeutschtum* spurred a lively discussion about emigration and social class on the colonial periphery. Initially, the lack of sufficiently cultivated women in Southwest Africa aroused concern in the women of the Frauenbund, who foresaw a general social disequilibrium and déclassement as middle-class men were forced to marry below their station.[78] Immigration by "girls of a higher station" was "of the greatest importance for the colony" since "only the educated woman can serve as a proper bearer of culture [*Kulturträgerin*]."[79]

Actual conditions in the colony, however, tended to dampen these ambitions. In 1912, a Colonial Society board member, disturbed by the specter of a mixed race, a *Mischlingsrasse,* in Southwest Africa, called for sending more "educated young girls there, so that German family life can rise to a somewhat higher level." But another objected that "for the present, the level of the male population is not very high," and he considered "extraordinarily dangerous" the idea of sending educated girls.[80] As early as 1897, Governor Theodor Leutwein had informed the Colonial Society that the colony needed "the working woman, simple burgher-artisans' daughters and servant girls," women accustomed to work and the hardships of farm life, rather than more educated, cultivated women.[81] Best were women "from the peasantry and working class" who would go over as servants and later become wives who could "set up a household with [their] own hands."[82] And, indeed, though Southwest Africa, like the other German colonies, was beyond the grasp of nearly all working-class Germans, the particular ethnic, social, and sexual situation called for a steady trickle of minimally respectable, hardworking, single women without means. Most of them came from working- or lower-class backgrounds and hoped to escape misfortune and hardship in Germany by exchanging their labor and reproductive power for a new life on the colonial frontier.[83]

Hardship and labor and dreams of the future marked not just those few who made it to the colony, but the many thousands who wanted to and never would. Lucie Böttcher, for example, experienced in all sorts of household work, is "hardworking, healthy and modest." She explains in her letter that "I have led a quiet life in my parent's house, have had very few pleasures, and have the intention to emigrate only for the reason that here in Germany there is a lack of good positions because all trades are over full." Her father owned a brickworks but lost all his money, so she hasn't the means to settle in Africa.[84] Twenty-one-year-old Berlin dressmaker Hedwig Standte likewise lacks the means to travel and hopes for help from the Colonial Society, which she promises to repay: "I have the intention to work as a maid in the first years, in order to come to know local circumstances, but then later to establish a dressmaking shop."[85] These women are deliberate, careful, sober in their straightened circumstances and powerlessness. Ida Hofter, perhaps nervous about the purposes of women's settlement and averse to the terrible risk an extramarital liaison posed for women in her world, makes clear that an "affair with some male person is not a possibility for me."[86]

So much evidence of women's colonial aspirations, in highlighting the oppressive sense of their economic and sexual vulnerability, serves to magnify our picture of the deep fissures, social and gendered, that both shaped and reflected the hierarchical nature of colonialism in the period. There was no unified colonial mass movement, even on the level of German navalism, but several strands of popular colonialism, or *Volkskolonialismus*, developed outside of the organized enthusiasm of the upper classes. *Volkskolonialismus* embraced the hairdressers, saddlers, and machinists who belonged to colonial veterans' associations, would-be settlers from the traditional *Mittelstand*, local *Kolonialwarenhändler*, small-town missionary supporters, spectators at the Colonial Panorama, and fantasists and patriots of all kinds.[87] Nationally, a handful of smaller colonial associations like the German Colonial League (Deutscher Kolonialbund) and the German Popular Colonial Association (Deutschvolklicher Kolonialverein) expressed the interests and attitudes of the less well-off and less educated.[88] The latter group published *Aus fernen Landen und deutschen Kolonien*, a "richly illustrated, popular-scientific, colonial magazine" aimed at a popular audience.[89] The Frauenbund likewise sought with limited success to appeal to a broad public with its magazine *Kolonie und Heimat*. It published serialized novels, pictures, and humor that stood out next to the rather dull scientific, political, and business articles in the *Deutsche Kolonialzeitung*, which never targeted a broad public. But popular colonialism was never just an effect of organized propaganda "from above."

Since the 1840s, ordinary people had banded together in numerous grass-roots "colonial societies" across Germany. By the turn of the century, their numbers and significance had dwindled dramatically, but had not disappeared. In 1904, for example, an obscure Association of German Colonists was founded in Nuremberg for the purpose of mutual assistance in the overseas settlement of its members.[90] In November of the same year, Franz Fiala, an innkeeper in Munich, wrote to the imperial government in Berlin for information regarding possible government assistance for a Verein für Auswanderer nach Deutsch-Südwestafrika, which he said had recently been founded at his suggestion. The new association counted twenty "honest businessmen" and hoped for about eighty more. Concerned, perhaps, that this might be some kind of fraudulent settlement scheme, the government opened a brief inquiry. The investigation, involving the Colonial Society, the Munich police, and two state ministries, determined that Fiala, the "ostensible founder" of the association, was a "married master joiner and innkeeper" with "a good reputation," and furthermore that, beyond preliminary discussions, the association did not yet really exist.[91]

Incredibly, when unmistakable signs of popular colonialism actually emerged, the whole apparatus of the state and the colonial movement combined to investigate and neutralize the unanticipated activity. That Fiala's association aroused the suspicion of the Colonial Society and the state—that he became an object of official investigation—highlights the divide between elite and popular colonialism. Despite the constant circulation of settlement propaganda, this kind of initiative was ultimately discouraged. The episode shows once more the restricted class basis of the organized movement. The colonial establishment preferred more carefully coordinated forms of association whose membership, no matter how small, reflected the upper middle-class origins of the Colonial Society.

The colonial veterans' associations were among the most important arenas for the *Volkskolonialismus* of the lower middle and working classes.[92] There was much local variety in the development of these associations, which tended to change over time to accommodate soldiers from successive conflicts. Earlier groups, like the Association of Veterans of the China Volunteers in Augsburg, or the Nuremberg Union of Veterans of the East Asian Expedition of 1900–1901, reflected the first great colonial military expedition, the suppression of the Boxer Rebellion in China. Over time, such associations changed their names and expanded their membership to reflect later conflicts, above all the German war against the Herero and Nama in Southwest Africa, the Bamberg Union of Former Members of the East Asian Expedition Corps becoming, for example, the Association of Veterans of China and Africa. These local groups belonged to the combined national Union of Associations of Veterans of China and Africa (Vereinigung der Veteranen- und Krieger-Vereine ehemaliger China- und Afrikakämpfer Deutschlands).

Varying combinations of agricultural laborers, skilled and unskilled workers, and the lower middle class of artisans, lower officials, and small property owners formed the basic membership of most Kriegervereine across Germany. The nobility, the propertied bourgeoisie, peasantry, and white-collar workers were generally underrepresented.[93] Workers ordinarily made up about one-third of the membership, although occasionally, in the larger industrial cities, the proportion rose to over three-quarters.[94] Generally, members tended to fall lower in the social hierarchy than members of the Colonial Society. Although the nobility was overrepresented in the German officer corps, it had virtually no presence among the rank-and-file members of veterans associations. If involved at all, noblemen and upper bourgeois usually sat on the board or accepted the title of honorary member.[95] For example, the membership of the Veterans Association in Munich in 1907 included a factory worker, a machinist, an innkeeper, a master saddler, a letter carrier, a tram conductor, and a mechanic; its honorary members, on the other hand, included the university professor and prominent colonialist Dr. Carl Freiherr von Stengel.[96] In Leipzig, while prominent colonialists and other local notables served as honorary or board members of veterans' associations, lower-class veterans of colonial wars virtually never joined the Colonial Society, even as regular members. In Nuremberg, the local Kriegerbund was a corporate member of the Colonial Society, while its individual members did not join.[97] A figure like Adda von Liliencron, chairwoman of the Women's Association of the Colonial Society, was exceptional in her efforts to open her organization up to people of modest means, veterans in particular.[98] (And when the Colonial Society in Nuremberg rebuffed requests to help found a chapter of the Women's Association, she turned to the local colonial veterans for help.)[99]

Local veterans founded the Nuremberg Union of Veterans of the East Asian Expedition in 1901. By 1913, membership cost three marks plus monthly dues of sixty pfennigs, evidently cheap enough for workers to join.[100] The seventy active members included a hairdresser, merchants, machinists, a day laborer, soldiers, mechanics, a glove maker, innkeepers, a shoemaker, a lacquerer, a glazier, a bookkeeper, a painter, and a policeman.[101] Andreas Kroher, a court assistant, was chair—and treasurer of the Colonial Veterans Associations of Germany—but neither he nor the other board members belonged to the robust, rather large local branch of the Colonial Society.[102] Mayor Georg von Schuh, a member of the Colonial Society, was an honorary member. The Bamberg Union of Former Members of the East Asian Expedition Corps, founded in 1904, cost only one mark thirty pfennigs (later two marks) to join and thirty pfennigs a month thereafter. Its chairman, Hans Gerber, was some type of merchant, while other board members included a railroad worker, a brewer, and an office assistant.[103] (The board of the local Colonial Society, by contrast, included a noble landowner, a rentier, the mayor, a state prosecutor, a physician, manufacturers, and officers.)

Through regular meetings, celebrations, and collective observance of national holidays, the associations helped structure local everyday life and a lower- to lower middle-class public sphere.[104] Typical of such groups, the Nuremberg association devoted itself to fraternity, sociability, and mutual assistance—as well as patriotic celebrations of past colonial wars. Its members met on the first Saturday of the month and received the *Kolonialpost*, the journal of the colonial veterans' associations, in the mail.[105] In Munich, the Association of *Schutztruppe* Veterans celebrated Christmas in 1907 with a lantern-slide lecture and a raffle to support ill or needy members.[106] In 1909, the Bamberg veterans—now called the Association of Veterans of China and Africa—organized a local "colonial exhibition," a modest, grassroots imitation of the grander affairs that had been so popular in larger cities. In preparation, they wrote to "most humbly request from the highly esteemed city magistrate kind permission" to hold a two-week exhibition at the White Dove (presumably an inn or tavern) in midsummer, and to charge twenty pfennigs admission in order to raise money for the relief fund.[107] The Colonial Society publicized it as a "Naval and Colonial Exhibition, the proceeds . . . intended to support needy colonial soldiers." It was to "display all possible articles: hunting trophies, insect and butterfly collections, model ships, silk and silk embroidery from our colonies, etc."[108] Local memorials quickly became another important goal of many associations around Germany. In 1912, the Munich Association of German Overseas Veterans decided to erect a memorial to German soldiers of Bavarian citizenship who had died or been injured in battle in overseas territories.[109] In Leipzig, too, there were substantial efforts by the 120 organized colonial veterans to construct a victory memorial in the city.[110]

Such examples complicate our picture of colonialism's function in senses both political and social in the Kaiserreich. There is available no straightforward theory of elite manipulation, nor any simple picture of mass indifference to empire. What kind of "manipulated masses" are these ordinary men and women, unassimilated to the colonial movement, their colonialism weirdly, stubbornly irreconcilable with it? Taken together, the mass of evidence on colonialism and the lower classes, on their many points of intersection, produces a confusing picture. The colonial phantasmagoria of working-class figures—ruined settlers overseas, or anarchists and revolutionary workers at home—was constitutive of colonial discourse from its origins. Fundamental anxieties persisted, along with the insurmountable distance between bourgeois and grassroots colonialists, even when and where they seemed on the point of convergence. Lower-class colonialists remained elusive, remote objects even as they came into reach.

This early bourgeois perspective resurfaces in later scholarship—highly critical, Marxist-inflected scholarship—on German colonialism, suggesting something of the sinuous durability, the sheer adaptability, of colonial discourse.

Local colonial enthusiasm in Nuremberg: "Association of Veterans of the East Asian Expedition 1900–1901" (1904). SAN, E6 292, Nr. 1. Courtesy Stadtarchiv Nürnberg.

Hannah Arendt's *Origins of Totalitarianism* accounts for imperialism at least partly in socioeconomic terms, as an "alliance between capital and mob." What she calls the "mob" is a "by-product of capitalist production," a novel social formation "begotten by the monstrous accumulation of capital" and by recurrent industrial crises. It is not the industrial working class, but the "refuse of all classes," the "scum of the big cities," the ruined, uprooted "human debris" of the modern industrial age.[111] The idiosyncratic Marxist George Hallgarten is more specific, calling colonialism a "palliative for the German *Mittelstand*," that wretched flotsam of artisans, shopkeepers, and peasants who were "struggling against the forces of capitalism and the powers of rationalization."[112] Imperialism represents a form of bitter, escapist longing among anachronistic, dying social groups. And according to the postwar East German Marxist Müller, the "urban, petit bourgeois intermediate classes [*Zwischenschichten*] merit considerable attention in the history of imperialism," supplying its "mass basis." "Condemned to destruction" by capitalist industry, reeling from the crash of 1873 and the crisis of 1882, "each man saw himself threatened with falling into the proletariat." Imperialism was the "medicine" prescribed by the "Finanzoligarchie" to the *Kleinbürgertum*. "The patient gulped it down eagerly," for, in the "ecstasy of chauvinism, the German subject [*Untertan*] was supposed to, and wished to forget his own misery."[113]

There is obviously no room in this discourse—still!—for the agency or autonomous experience of lower-class colonialists. Colonialism appears under the sign of capitalist modernity, rationalization; the manipulated masses as retrograde, anachronistic, naïve. But, as the weaver Dietze's letter, and much else, suggests, the motives and fantasies of lower-class colonialists could defy easy categorization. He was a struggling artisan, but also a kind of budding capitalist, eager to exploit the profit potential in cheap African labor. Many would-be colonizers came from the so-called "new *Mittelstand*" of white-collar workers—office clerks and registrars—and others were factory workers fleeing boredom, crushing hierarchy, or the lack of opportunity. Many were women, doubly vulnerable to systems of production and reproduction beyond their control. Many Germans facing hardship seemed to believe the promise of empire and looked to the colonies as a panacea. These were hardly, or simply, the "traditional elements" that somehow continuously reappear in accounts. The "logic" of contemporary capitalism, grafted onto deep-rooted traditions of social hierarchy and interacting with discourses of science and modernity, of course *produced* its other, both economically— through dislocation, impoverishment—and culturally—as error, enchantment, strange ideas. The whole discursive formation of colonial knowledge and its other produced in turn the foundation of colonial rationality, and was the source of its constant replenishment. Enchantment, as it turned out, embraced both bourgeois colonialists and their subaltern others: the enchantment of empire itself.

CHAPTER FOUR

Carnival Knowledge

Enlightenment and Distraction in the Cultural Field

> *Colonization nowadays is truly no longer a fantastical experience of adventure; it demands more than the surging energy of the past. It is work, true hard work in the highest sense of the word: colonization is cultural work.*
>
> —Wilhelm Hübbe-Schleiden, *Deutsche Colonisation*, 1881

> *Over against this, let us consider . . . a culture . . . condemned to exhaust all possibilities and feed miserably and parasitically on every culture under the sun.*
>
> —Friedrich Nietzsche, *The Birth of Tragedy*, 1872

> *It is abducting magic without compare, . . . this life pushed forward with the air of a host who knows all about kitsch and horror, the shock of anatomy and lecherousness of appearance, or at least all about superfluity. So is the fair, so does its cheap, its overflowing dream ship moor on the dusty squares.*
>
> —Ernst Bloch, *Heritage of Our Times*, 1935

Bourgeois colonialists encountered the broad lower classes uncertainly in the sphere of popular and mass culture, unsure of what to make of them and their amusements. This was preeminently the field of colonial enchantment—of cannibals and Amazons and fetish priests—and it therefore substantially represented the antithesis of "colonial enlightenment," of the public sphere. But the insistent polarity of colonial knowledge and mass distraction was misleading, concealing the more complicated reality of the interpenetration of knowledge and fantasy. For this was also the field of popular science, the hegemonic code linking—and legitimizing— disparate cultural forms. The masses came to the fair or the panopticon to gawk at savages and crocodiles and talismanic objects, but so too did the bourgeois, in pursuit of anthropology, natural history, or geography. The anxiety provoked by popular forms registers precisely this proximity. And the proximity in turn suggests a more subtle and pervasive enchantment running beneath the deep distinctions of class and transcending them.[1]

German culture in the Second Empire was layered, heterogeneous, and fractured; it both reproduced and effaced the deep fissures running through German society. Elites insisted on the divide between high culture and low, between the purity of academic art or the importance of science and the crassness of commercial entertainment, even as the dominant social and economic system ineluctably transformed the cultural field through the rise of mass culture.[2] The dynamic industrial economy of the late nineteenth century created unprecedented mass markets, supplied capital to cultural industries like publishing, cinema, and the ubiquitous stereoptical Kaiser-Panorama, and produced successive waves of technological innovation in the mechanical reproduction and projection of aesthetic forms. It plastered cities with new forms of advertising that drew on the exotic iconography of overseas empire.[3] It drew millions of factory and white-collar workers into the great cities and manufacturing zones, and divided their time ever more neatly between labor and leisure. The gradual rise in real wages, the expansion of free time, and rising literacy rates turned these new urban masses into consumers of cultural goods and commodity excitements.[4] The illustrated papers, zoological gardens, amusement parks, and picture palaces of the modern industrial city sprang up to meet the burgeoning demand.

This new mass culture took shape in the 1880s and 1890s, just as the European powers embarked on their last great frenzy of colonial expansion. Whatever its political or economic fortunes, the German colonial empire, which by 1900 spanned Africa, China, and the South Pacific, attracted an immense, heterogeneous *audience*. As a spectacle of adventure and exoticism, it sold books, and tickets to the panorama, the cinema, and the wax museum. Millions of readers and spectators consumed numberless pictures and stories of the colonies in their free time. Newspapers popularized the heroic explorers and military expeditions of the "scramble for Africa" and glamorized empire building. The convergence of the "age of imperialism" with both a nascent mass culture and German mass politics produced an unprecedented encounter—however mediated—between even the most parochial Germans and the foreign cultures of the colonized world.

Germans' deepening engagement with their own—and others'—African and Pacific colonies supplied the unending series of novelties, curiosities, and sensations with which the prolific new entertainment industries competed for audiences. Already by the time Germany established its first protectorates in 1884, mass-circulation colportage novels and traveling troupes of authentically "savage" Africans were bringing a sensationalized "Dark Continent" to the German public.[5] Fresh technological advances and rising income multiplied the effect, even as elements of the new mass culture fused with vestiges of an older commercial popular culture surviving in the form of local fairs and traveling showmen. By 1914, colonial battles, adventures, and primitive peoples commonly appeared in dime novels, photographs, panoramas, and magic lantern shows; in dioramas, peep shows, stereopticons, and waxworks; in magazines, picture postcards, the cinematograph, and ethnographic exhibitions.

The relationship between these amusements and colonial politics was for the most part ambiguous. Many commercial amusements were not even German, their colonial content reflecting a pan-European rather than a national development. It was not, for the most part, German politics, or even national borders, that determined what was seen by mass audiences, but rather extrapolitical, international factors like technology, markets, and flows of capital. Impresarios of ethnographic shows might be English, most colonial films were French, and nearly all European colonial postcards were made in Germany. Nor were adventure and exoticism ever simply reducible to colonial ideology. They did not straightforwardly approximate a politics. Indeed, the concepts of propaganda and ideology lose their precise applications in the sphere of popular culture, where distinctions between distraction and pleasure, on the one hand, and manipulation, on the other, tended to blur, and where reception was contested and unpredictable. Colonial propaganda was most often calculated, targeted, explicitly political, and deployed by powerful agents like the German Colonial Society and the state. In the field of commercial entertainment, however, any sense of unified agency or political intention disintegrated into a mass of show business entrepreneurs, publishers, photographers, painters, writers, and impresarios. Profit, not politics, was most often their chief incentive. The forms and venues of mass culture became in some cases political instruments, vehicles for the dissemination of colonial knowledge and enthusiasm, but they also tended simply to reflect broad social and political developments, and appetites for cheap novelty.

Looking at popular and mass culture reveals the diffusion of colonial knowledge, its near ubiquity, but also its instability—its escape from the sober, insistent discourse of the bourgeois public sphere, and yet its orientation to those same claims and codes of science and authenticity. Colonial discourse was refracted—and fractured—through popular entertainment. It was indirect, mediated, filtered, but also palpable. Exhibitions and wax museums transmitted colonial knowledge—however flimsy or debased—in the mode of popular science, as object lessons in anthropology, geography, or natural history. Their benign educational claims, intended to elevate them above the much-criticized vulgarity and trash (*Schund*) of mass culture, rehearsed the scientific and racist justifications of empire. Showmen, peddling distraction, took freely from the colonialists. But the reverse was just as true: it was often the propagandists who imitated the impresarios, by borrowing forms of popular amusement to sell colonialism to the masses. Nor was it rare for the two spheres of propaganda and culture to merge seamlessly into one. As the following account of an exhibition in Augsburg demonstrates, colonial popular culture—examined here in its most local, quotidian form—combined strands of entertainment, propaganda, distraction, education, and commerce that were not easily unraveled. Moreover, it suggests once again the anxieties and limitations that marked the German colonial movement; forces that challenge any simple model of manipulation of the masses.

It was early in July 1911, in the week following the appearance of a German gunboat at the Moroccan port of Agadir, that newspapers in Augsburg began to advertise a coming attraction: "Captain Köster's Traveling Naval and Colonial Exhibition," then touring Bavaria. It was hardly unusual for traveling shows to visit the city in those days, but neither was it so common that the prospect aroused no excitement. Augsburg was a small industrial city with no ethnography museum of its own and the news stirred generally enthusiastic anticipation. The exhibition would reportedly include "a number of true-to-life models of warships, artillery pieces, and nautical instruments, as well as extensive collections of ethnographic artifacts and colonial products." Advertisements promised a "valuable collection of nautical instruments, an 8-mm Maxim machine gun . . . a 7.5-cm landing gun captured in the great Arab uprising, rich and valuable collections of ethnographic artifacts and products from our colonies, over 300 of the most vibrantly colored and rarest butterflies and beetles from the tropical lands, among them specimens with twenty-six-centimeter wingspans, etc." In addition, " 'Consul Peter' and his black friend 'Mucky,' representatives of the African animal world," promised "humor and entertainment for young and old."[6] The exhibition was to run for ten days in a hall belonging to the local infantry regiment.

Captain Köster, impresario of the traveling show, wrote in advance to the city government to explain the nature and purpose of his exhibition. His main objective, he wrote, was "to awaken and promote interest and appreciation for our colonies, and for the Christian missionary organization closely connected to them."[7] This seemed, on the face of it, respectable, even welcome, and the city eagerly anticipated Captain Köster's arrival. Having apparently just "enjoyed a lively visit" in Bad Tölz and among "the country population of Upper Bavaria," the "remarkable, most highly instructive exhibition" was expected to meet with "great interest" in the small Swabian city. Advance tickets for 768 officials and workers from the postal service had been requested, and the local branch of the Deutsche Gewerkvereine—the antisocialist, integrationist, so-called "yellow" trade unions—had reserved a private evening tour. Visits by the local garrison, as well as the higher grades of the local elementary schools, were also arranged.[8] The captain offered special prices and lectures on the colonies for these group visits.

It therefore might not have seemed especially remarkable when Captain Köster requested that the city government waive local taxes in favor of disseminating colonial and naval knowledge. He pleaded the high costs of the traveling exhibition, insisted on its broadly educational purpose, and claimed that equivalent taxes had been waived elsewhere in Bavaria. Traveling shows and fair booth amusements ordinarily paid a *Lustbarkeitsabgabe*, the tax on public entertainment. Köster, however, his request denied, refused to pay, since his exhibition was, he claimed, educational rather than entertaining, and, despite the demands of the Augsburg authorities, he eventually left town without surrendering a pfennig. This was legitimate scientific education—entomological, ethnographic, economic. The city, on the other hand, insisted that the exhibition was a form of commercial amusement. The resulting lawsuit brought by the Augsburg city government presented local judicial authorities with the thorny problem of identifying the basic nature and purpose of the colonial and naval exhibition. Separating and evaluating the intertwined threads of propaganda, instruction, amusement, and business required some investigation.

Of course, whatever the merits of his case, as the proprietor of a traveling exhibition Captain Köster would inevitably have been the object of inquiries by skeptical local authorities. In the years before 1914, as during the whole of the nineteenth century, cities and towns like Augsburg drew all types of itinerant attractions, from Siamese twins and magic lanternists to troupes of acrobats, Amazons, and Ashanti warriors. All such shows had to register with the local government, and the vague menace of confidence men, mountebanks, and purveyors of erotic titillation occasioned frequent police surveillance and the scrutiny of moral reformers.[9] It was therefore not at all unusual for the authorities to make inquiries in this case. Who, indeed, *was* this "Captain Köster" and what, if anything, had he ever been "captain" of? A self-described "seaman by profession, a marine noncommissioned officer of long standing in the navy and holder of a sailor's commission," he had "come to know the colonies himself."[10] Such credentials, if vague, were nevertheless extremely important. Wilhelmine society attached great weight to titles in general, and the claim to authentic experiences in the colonies in particular gave lecturers and writers a certain undeniable authority when describing Germany's exotic, faraway possessions. (Sometimes, indeed, impostors were exposed.[11]) Köster also claimed to be exhibiting in Bavaria "with the support of the Imperial Naval Office."[12] Yet, in response to a query from Augsburg, the Naval Office in Berlin contradicted Köster's claim, declaring the exhibition a "purely private undertaking."[13] The captain was not altogether who he said he was.

Nor, on the other hand, were the "politics" of Köster's exhibition—its "propaganda value," so to speak—any more easily identified. What exactly was it that made someone a legitimate naval or colonial propagandist, as opposed to a showman or just a fraud? Even the name of the exhibition was uncertain, appearing variously over time as a traveling colonial exhibition, "Kapitän Kösters Kolonial-Wander-Ausstellung," the "Marine-und Kolonial-Ausstellung," and an ethnographic and entomological exhibition, "Kapitän Kösters völkerkundliche und entomologische Ausstellung."

Carl Gabriel's Tripoli Caravanserai (1912), SAM, Zeitgeschichtliche Sammlung/Historiches Bildarchiv: Chronik 1912/70 (Plakatsammlung 17997 1912 401214). Courtesy Stadtarchiv München.

"Our New Countrymen": Samoa Exhibition (1910). Courtesy Museum für Völkerkunde, Hamburg, Nachlass Adrian Jacobsen.

Stanley, Emin Pasha, and the Wakamba Negro Warriors of East Africa (1893). SAM, Zeitgeschichtliche Sammlung/Historiches Bildarchiv: Chronik 1893/69 (Plakatsammlung 18354 1893 121191). Courtesy Stadtarchiv München.

"The Amazon Corps": ethnographic show (ca. 1890). Courtesy
Museum für Völkerkunde, Hamburg, Nachlass Adrian Jacobsen.

Köster seems to have had no official connections, he represented no association, and he lacked the academic or honorific titles of the respectable bourgeoisie. He had no apparent ties to the Navy League, and the Naval Office had just disavowed him. A few months earlier, the Propaganda Commission of the German Colonial Society had refused him a loan of five hundred marks for what he then billed as his "Wander-Kolonial-Ausstellung."[14] (At the end of 1911, he renewed his request, again stubbornly claiming the support of the Naval Office and the Colonial Economic Committee.)[15] It is not clear whether Köster had sought the legitimacy of an association with the Colonial Society, whether he hoped to take advantage of its naïveté and largesse, or was simply in need of some cash. From the Naval Office he at least received the loan of some model warships, which he did indeed display in Augsburg. But whatever his motives, Köster was certainly no agent of the government, big capital, or the influential bourgeois *nationale Verbände*.

A final decision in the matter of the Naval and Colonial Exhibition, issued by the court of the Royal Government of Swabia and Neuburg in the name of His Majesty the King of Bavaria, ruled that the exhibition had in fact appeared before the public as an entertainment. The court therefore levied the *Lustbarkeitsabgabe* and a further fine.[16] It based its decision on several aspects of the exhibition. First of all, "in assessing the tax, the high attendance at the exhibition and its character as a private undertaking are taken into account." That Köster had sold many tickets, and therefore stood, theoretically at least, to gain a profit, was undeniable. The local press had reported favorably on the instant success of the exhibition. According to the city papers, visitors from all social classes and many local institutions flocked to see it. The "round of visitors" began at eight o'clock in the morning on opening day with whole classes of schoolchildren, followed that evening by a battalion of the local infantry regiment.[17] The exhibition "enjoyed immediately, on the first day, a brisk business among those interested in the navy and colonies from almost every class of the local inhabitants, especially military circles, the schools, the clergy, the local Augsburg chapter of the German Colonial Society," and others.[18] The court conceded that "the popular-educational value of the show should not be underestimated" but concluded that such instruction nevertheless served "not only this purpose, but also the business interests of the promoter."[19] Profit and pedagogy, while not indistinguishable, were nevertheless inseparable in this case. Although the press reported that any "later surplus from the exhibition" would be "devoted to the missions" overseas, the court found no "proof of the said use of any net proceeds for the benefit of German missions."

There was, on the other hand, evidence that the contents of the exhibition resembled displays of a sort then common in public amusements. According to the court, "Senior assistant teacher Hösle visited the exhibition on behalf of the magistrate and stated that it is indeed instructive but, apart from several model ships, no different from what is ordinarily shown at fairs

[*Jahrmarktausstellungen*]." According to the inventory in Köster's own guide to the collection, the exhibition included, among other items:

> colonial rubber, cotton, and ivory, Cameroon and New Guinea tobacco, a rhinoceros horn, coconuts, copra, peanuts, cocoa, mahogany, a live monkey— "Mucky, the little East African," photos of "Samoan beauties," spears, dance masks from the South Seas, idols from Cameroon, diverse specimens preserved in formaldehyde, including the egg of a giant snake, a horned chameleon, and an "abnormality," as well as knives, bows, three zebra hoofs, ebony, coffee, arrows from the Bismarck Archipelago, a Chinese soldier's raincoat, and a complete mandarin suit.[20]

A motley collection, certainly. This traveling *Wunderkammer*, with its accumulation of insects, colonial commodities, ethnographica, and miscellaneous oddities, was judged to be just another variety of itinerant entertainment, the stuff of the fair booth, and Köster himself a showman. For the city authorities, the educational-propagandistic element was secondary, and the court concurred. Nevertheless, the court stopped short of dispelling the ambiguity surrounding the exhibition. In the end, it left open the "question of whether the show serves a higher interest of art and science," as it was "of no consequence for the obligation to pay the entertainment tax according to the local statute." Whatever else it was, the naval and colonial exhibition was amusing, popular, and taxable.

Just a few weeks earlier, in the middle of June, a different Naval Exhibition had opened in nearby Munich, the Bavarian capital. Like Köster's Naval and Colonial Exhibition, it was a traveling show established "to spread interest and understanding of our navy throughout the whole of Germany."[21] Like Köster's, it displayed model warships and a collection of colonial artifacts, the conventional object lessons in empire. "Along with a rich collection of minerals from German East and Southwest Africa, and an ethnographic collection from the German colonies in Africa and the South Seas, the Kiaochow Territory—subordinate, as everyone knows, to the Imperial Naval Office—is really especially well represented with collections of every sort." Here again was a sort of curiosity cabinet assembled for the instruction of the masses. But unlike Köster's travels through the backwoods of Bavaria— with stops in Ingolstadt, Sulzbach, Bad Tölz, and other small towns—the naval exhibition planned only a "circular tour of Germany's larger cities." And it enjoyed the support of powerful industrial interests, influential patriotic notables, the Imperial Navy, and—locally—the royal Wittelsbach Prince Georg, "protector" of the German Navy League in Bavaria.[22]

Köster ultimately represented propaganda of a different order, confusingly bound up with flimflam popular science, profit, and amusement, and the ambiguity of his roving bricolage exhibition brushed up against the system of police surveillance and control of commercial popular culture. He lacked

precisely the connections, the bourgeois respectability, and the aura of of-
ficialdom associated with the Munich exhibition. Strikingly, the German
Colonial Society, constantly frustrated in its efforts to reach beyond its own
precincts, showed no interest in him. Yet it was Köster who fulfilled the most
elusive aim of the bourgeois colonial and naval movements: the dissemination of knowledge—colonial ethnography, geography, economics, natural
history—with whatever fanfare he could muster, among ordinary people in
out-of-the-way places. Even more, perhaps, than Social Democratic workers, the German countryside appeared almost entirely unreachable, making
Köster's efforts remarkable. Indeed, the Naval Office had lent him "some
ship models and some other objects," believing "that the undertaking is
suitable for spreading knowledge . . . among the inland population."[23] The
Augsburg press agreed, reporting that the exhibition, during its tour of
small-town Bavaria, served "the promotion of interest and understanding
of our colonies, and the missionary efforts closely connected with them."[24]

The available evidence suggests that Köster self-consciously sought to
reach a broad—and in particular a working-class—audience. Both his advertising and his exhibition guides mention workers, and he offered reduced
prices for groups of workers from individual factories. A brief series of "Testimonials from Employers and Workers," for example, praised the exhibition. The management of the Amberg Enamel- and Metal-Stamp Works
in northern Bavaria enthusiastically suggested that the sale of one thousand tickets in its factories "shows that our salaried staff and workers, too,
are keenly interested in your exhibition."[25] Other ostensibly grateful audiences included an Evangelical Workers Association and a trade association
in Dresden. And Köster's propaganda was calculated to appeal directly to
workers, both organized and unorganized, particularly with its unusual calls
for government aid for impecunious working-class colonizers:

> Also the German worker, who cannot find sufficient use for his capacity for
> work here at home, can settle his own piece of ground there [in Southwest
> Africa], if our government grants the necessary assistance. Taken from an eco-
> nomic perspective, that is the main goal of colonization, namely to settle, with
> state aid, surplus domestic workers where they have hope of making a sufficient
> livelihood. Instead of thousands of German workers and peasants settling in
> foreign lands (Brazil and North America) with the help of foreign governments,
> aid and support are granted so that they can settle in the single protectorate
> suitable for colonization by German citizens.[26]

How thoroughly he misunderstood the aims of colonialism in 1911! There
was no realistic chance, of course, for "surplus" workers to settle in the
colonies, and the implicit demand for state subsidies was precisely the opposite of what the government and the organized colonial movement sought.
In the end, Köster's brand of colonial propaganda—the quasi-official, mildly

unorthodox, commercially successful and bricolage nature of his exhibition—defied conventional categorization as either politics, education, business, or amusement. It crystallized the broader ambiguities and anxieties around colonialism in commercial popular culture.

By the time Captain Köster arrived in Augsburg in 1911, public amusements with colonial themes had been appearing in the city for some thirty years. The cinematograph, traveling panoramas, and many other types of popular entertainment brought the faraway colonies to local audiences. Most were much less explicitly propagandistic than Köster's exhibition. Their relationship to colonialism was more indirect and contextual. But most of them reflected, or attempted to reflect, the singular status of science in German society. Among the most celebrated were the so-called *Völkerschauen*, ethnographic exhibitions featuring performers from Africa, Asia, and the Americas.[27] These shows were ubiquitous, not only in Germany but across Europe. They were run by show business entrepreneurs, figures like Carl Gabriel in Munich and Carl Hagenbeck in Hamburg: innovative, successful, sometimes famous impresarios of wax museums, menageries, and cinematographs. They were big operations, profitable, mounted only with substantial capital. Hagenbeck's famous *Tierpark*, opening in 1907, marked the culmination of their development.[28] How popular audiences experienced the ethnographic shows, how they made sense of them—and whether the shows actually operated within a specifically colonialist framework of signification—have been difficult to determine because so little evidence of their reception survives.[29] They appeared occasionally at colonial exhibitions, but operated mostly in the arenas of commercial and mass culture: the fair, zoo, or some other *Vergnügungslokal*.[30] Like Captain Köster's exhibition, they were for the most part ambiguous, combining entertainment, business, science, and politics.

A rare exception was the traveling "Togo Troupe." Under the direction of the impresario Albert Urbach, who had brought a "Negro Caravan" to Augsburg in 1888, the troupe from German Togo arrived in 1898. Urbach billed it as "Togoland and its inhabitants from German West Africa, the only traveling troupe from the German colonies."[31] The explicit connection with German colonialism in Africa was entirely uncharacteristic of ethnographic exhibitions. Urbach emphasized that his performers were the "first and only troupe" of Togolese, "fellow-countrymen from our German colonies."[32] In the long history—some seventy years—of *Völkerschauen*, very few troupes came from those parts of Africa or the South Seas that would come under German "protection" in the 1880s and after. Carl Hagenbeck, the most successful impresario of ethnographic shows, produced only three out of about thirty-nine during the three decades of German colonial rule: the Duala of Cameroon in 1886 and Samoans in 1889 and 1910.[33] To be sure, the Somalis, Egyptians, Sinhalese, Zulu, Bedouins, and hundreds of others who toured Germany and Europe hailed from colonies, but not from German colonies, and the relationship to colonialism was not usually as explicit as in the case of the Togo Troupe.

Urbach's advertisements promised "thirty-five Togo girls" — "fetish-priestesses, singers, and dancers from the royal palace of Togo." The exhibition opened every morning at ten o'clock for twelve hours, with special performances four times daily. For fifty pfennigs, spectators could see "displays of African conditions and customs, war dances, and national dances."[34] Advertisements, reviews, and handbills all described the show as a presentation of African life as it really was. Typically, one newspaper proclaimed the "unhindered daily and family life of the troupe in a corner of the garden" at least as interesting as the "national dance of the fetish-girls" and other "numbers on the program." Such authenticity was more important than mere performance: the promise of unmediated, up-close ethnographic knowledge. The press urged readers not to miss a rare chance to observe the real, everyday life of colonial Togo. "A visit to these people from the Dark Continent will certainly not be regretted; there appears here a characteristic picture of culture from far off Africa that one does not too often have the opportunity to see."[35]

The documentary virtues of the show, such as they were, were inseparable from other, more sensational aspects. Reviews referred to "human sacrifice"

Samoa in Munich: colonial *Völkerschau* (1910). SAM, Zeitgeschichtliche Sammlung/ Historiches Bildarchiv: Chronik 1910b/10/9. Courtesy Stadtarchiv München.

and "idol worship" in precolonial Togo, and described the appealing phy-
siques of the performers. The troupe's chief, "a Herculean figure fully symmetrical in body," was "supposed to be a full-blooded king's son." The
"other members of the troupe, too, present well-shaped forms, especially the
girls [who have] mostly slender, graceful figures."[36] With thirty-five "court
dancers" and rumors of royal birth, idolatry, and human sacrifice, the show
promised something of the cheap, scandalous pleasure of colportage literature. No less than other *Völkerschauen*, it functioned substantially as performance, as commercial spectacle. And yet it also made a special appearance,
several years later, before the scientific membership of the Munich Society
of Anthropology.[37]

In its exoticism, the show resembled fin de siècle theater in Augsburg.
The local public had already developed a certain taste for theatrical representations of the "Dark Continent" by the time Urbach's dancers arrived.
A month earlier, a local theater staged Suppé's operetta *Die Afrikareise*.
The *Augsburger Abendzeitung* recommended it—his "most melodious"
work—and the presumably African "décor of the costumes and scenery" in
particular, which was "worth seeing in and of itself."[38] Three months later,
a work called *Die Afrikanerin* enjoyed a "positive reception" on the Augsburg stage. Its realization of the "kingdom of Queen Selica" was reportedly
"an ethnographic wonderland," in which the "pallid European faces" of
the actors "presented the mugs of the 'savage' Africans in every nuance
of color from darkest brown to brightest white."[39] The notices made no
connection between the theater and the larger "ethnographic wonderlands"
of the *Völkerschauen*—or, for that matter, the African colonies themselves.
But the theatricality, spectatorial pleasure, and exotic sensibility common to
both suggested just how closely colonialism, entertainment, and edification
could be intertwined.

The Bavarian impresario Carl Gabriel, based in nearby Munich, was one
of the great entrepreneurs in the business of producing *Völkerschauen*. His
entertainments, in contrast to the Togo Troupe, displayed not German but
other European colonies. In 1912, he presented one of his many shows, a
spectacular "Arab city of Tripoli," at the Oktoberfest, the mammoth annual
fair in Munich.[40] A local newspaper anticipated "a true picture of the Orient" conjured by Gabriel and his staff of "artists and specialists." "In the
different streets . . . will be found mosques, minarets, cafés, bazaars, and real
Arab houses and workshops." Colorful posters promised the exciting spectacle of North African horsemen performing behind the great façade, with
its vaguely Egyptian statues and giant oriental mural. Thanks in large part
precisely to its fetishized realism, its cultural authenticity, Gabriel's show
undeniably belonged to the world of commercial popular amusement, the
mass consumption of ephemeral, fifty-pfennig thrills. The fabricated Arab
city offered something "new and original," just as the "fairytale city Lilliput had the year before."[41] Gabriel simultaneously displayed midgets and
acrobats in his Circus-Cabaret "Lilliput." His Hall of Phenomena revealed

the wonders of "Miss Lucie Volta, the Electric Riddle—the electric Fire and Flame Queen" and the "Man with Revolving Limbs."

Viewed in this broader commercial context, the Oktoberfest Tripolitans belonged to an endlessly recurring series of novelties and oddities, much of which had apparently little to do with popular ethnography or European colonialism. Although increasingly elaborate and well financed, the exhibitions—as Gabriel's wide-ranging endeavors suggest—still bore traces of their origins in the traditional annual fair, the *Jahrmarkt*, which remained an important site of popular amusement in Wilhelmine Germany. (Indeed, most of Gabriel's shows still appeared at an annual fair, the Oktoberfest, while Carl Hagenbeck, although proud of his father's origins as fairground entertainer, was careful to distinguish his shows from traditions of hucksterism and cheap illusionism.)[42] The fairs had long attracted all sorts of itinerant performers, among them "savages" and the human "curiosities," "abnormalities," and "monstrosities" of the freak show. As popular amusements, many *Völkerschauen* resembled these commercial, fairground freak shows. They were not only "cultural" displays—of dancing, dwellings, mock battles, and the rest—but commercial displays of strange bodies—bodies marked by ritual scarification, steatopygia, exotic ornament, black skin, nakedness—the bodies of pygmies and African albinos and the pop-Darwinian "missing link."[43] They presented a form of racial grotesque, producing the "shock of anatomy and lecherousness of appearance" that the philosopher Ernst Bloch ascribed to the fairs.[44]

Savages and freaks at the fair: postcard view of a giantess and a South Seas islander before a gawking crowd (1898). Markt- und Schaustellermuseum, Sammlung Erich Knocke, Essen. Courtesy Archiv Markt- und Schaustellermuseum Essen.

Ethnographic and freak shows shared common contents, style, and historical origins. Exhibitions of Africans or Asians earlier in the nineteenth
century had often taken the form of carnival freak shows. A review in the
Leipziger Illustrierte Zeitung of the 1904 "Somali-Negro" exhibition at the
Berlin zoological garden traces the now respectable *Völkerschauen* back to
their coarse, often fraudulent, freak show origins:

> Just fifteen or twenty years ago, for us Europeans on the Continent, it was
> still a curiosity when representatives of exotic peoples were seen among us. At
> best, one could sometimes catch sight of a true Negro in the large cities, on the
> coach box of a prince or else a well-to-do member of the "upper ten thousand."
> The public was always very distrustful of the so-called savages—in the form of
> pitch-black Moors or Indians or cannibals in show booths at the fairs—when
> they appeared ever so savage and consumed living rabbits and chickens for the
> spectators. One would only put one's faith in them when convinced that the
> Moor was the real thing [*waschecht*—literally "color-fast"]. In modern times,
> with perfected communications and active trade relations with the most distant
> lands, the Dark Continent in particular, this has changed. One reads daily now
> of visits from every possible savage or half-civilized people, who can offer the
> public any sort of scientific interest.[45]

The popular display of "exotic peoples" was rooted historically in the tradition of traveling mountebanks touting fake savages and the vulgar spectacle of the sideshow "geek," the carnival "wild man" who devoured live
animals. Only when Europe's imperial and scientific infrastructure had developed sufficiently to permit the regular traffic in native performers could
audiences count on seeing "legitimate primitives."

Although it changed over time, the relationship between ethnographic
and freak shows persisted into the twentieth century. Archives preserve the
proximity of freak shows to the *Völkerschauen*, whose traces lie scattered
among the historical ephemera of these popular amusements. The files of
the Augsburg police, for example, provide a clue as to how local authorities, charged with the surveillance of commercial entertainment, perceived
ethnographic shows at the end of the nineteenth century. These catalogues
of the fin de siècle popular imagination, which randomly juxtapose African
performers with microcephalics and midgets, supply the original context for
the popular reception of ethnographic shows. An exhibition like the Togo
Troupe appears in this context as another fair booth amusement, one in a
succession of curiosities including a 226-pound giant child; a "mouth-artist"
born without arms; the giant Spanish sisters Isabella and Flora; Apollonia,
Queen of the Giantesses; albinos; dwarves; a Siberian "torso-artist"—born
without arms, hands, legs, or feet; Siamese twins—"This monstrosity to be
seen for only a short time," warns the flyer; a Lilliputian; and a "human fish,
the man from the sea—strange phenomenon of nature."[46]

"Ethnographic Troupes, Abnormalities, and Every Sort of Natural Wonder":
advertisement for the Passage-Panopticon, Berlin (circa 1900). Page from an illustrated
catalogue for the Passage-Panopticon, Berlin, reproduced in Stephan Oettermann,
"Alles-Schau: Wachsfigurenkabinette und Panoptiken," in *Viel Vergnügen: Öffentliche
Lustbarkeiten im Ruhrgebiet der Jahrhundertwende*, ed. Lisa Kosok and Mathilde
Jamin (Essen: Ruhrland Museum, 1992), 45. Courtesy Ruhrland Museum Essen.

There was nothing inevitably extraordinary in the commingling of ethnographic shows and the traditional stuff of the fair. There was a flash of
greasepaint, an air of cheap illusionism, about both. The "cannibal" and the
"savage," like snake charmers and fakirs, had long been staples of carnival
sideshows. In the ethnographic shows, the Africans and Pacific Islanders
quite literally performed their own primitivism according to the specifica-
tions of the European impresarios.[47] Indeed, the indexical "ethnographic
typology" of performers in Hagenbeck's shows was layered over more pressing attributes of performance, or entertainment value, which took prece-
dence in recruitment of troupes.[48] Yet viewing the ethnographic exhibitions
as sites of commercial entertainment and transitory pleasure hardly exhausts
the question of their content. German science, too—early anthropology in

particular—laid claim to the ethnographic shows and collaborated with their commercial producers.[49] Hagenbeck, for example, emphasized ethnographic type over corporeal oddity in his respectable shows.[50] The leading anthropologists of the day—men like Rudolf Virchow and Felix von Luschan—and their museums, research institutions, and scientific associations, looked to the exhibitions as both opportunities for collecting data about primitive peoples and as tools for the broad dissemination of science.[51] The association with science helped over time to transform the meaning of the shows. It conferred respectability on them.[52] But the record of sober, scientific engagement nevertheless confirms persistent links between freaks, "vulgar" popular culture, and the *Völkerschauen*.

In 1895, the impresario Ludwig Neumüller, speaking on behalf of the Association of Traveling Showmen in Hamburg, addressed the Munich Society for Anthropology, Ethnology, and Prehistory at a celebration of its twenty-fifth anniversary. He expressed boundless gratitude to the anthropologists for, as he put it,

> the diverse expertise, etc., with which they have lent support to the various proprietors of racial exhibitions [*Volksracen-Ausstellungen*] and individual abnormality [exhibitions]. Because the distinguished Anthropological Society, or its members, used exhibitions of this sort for the purpose of anthropological study, such undertakings became educational for the masses, and many prejudices of the authorities, the press, and the broader public were eliminated. The Munich Anthropological Society and its president, the esteemed Professor Dr. Johannes Ranke, have supported such undertakings in the most outstanding way. I remember only the relevant anthropological performances of the 'Fuegians,' 'Kalmucks,' 'Sinhalese,' 'Somalis,' 'Buffalo Bill's Wild West,' 'Bedouins,' 'Dahomean Amazons,' 'Laplanders,' 'Hula Hula Dancers,' 'Dinka-Negroes,' [and] 'Matabeles,' not to speak of the abnormalities coming in between them. Through this generosity of the honored Geographical Societies of the different [German] states, large-scale exhibitions have become all the more viable.[53]

Once more, we see the connections—both scientific and commercial—between ethnographic and freak shows, between race and anatomical deformity, between instruction and entertainment. Neumüller twice mentions the display of "abnormalities"—or freaks—among the "racial exhibitions" made respectable by the anthropologists.[54] In a period when critics routinely condemned the trash, filth, and vulgarity of popular amusements, and tended to pathologize their effects on the masses, the participation of scientists conferred an indispensable respectability.[55] (Of course, the Munich anthropologists took in these numerous ethnographic shows—Bedouins, Ashanti, Tunisians, Samoans—always in private or special viewings in which science supplanted crass commercialism and the crowd.)[56] Carl Hagenbeck, for example, won formal declarations of support from the Berlin and Munich anthropological societies and the Leipzig Museum of Ethnology.[57] Under the sign of science, the so-called "anthropological performances"—both racial and medical—became legitimate, authentic, and "educational for the masses" as the "prejudices of the authorities, the press, and the broader public" dissipated.

The association of popular science, race, and entertainment reached far beyond the ethnographic shows, ultimately forming a dense web of connections between colonialism and German culture. The particular resonance of the *Völkerschauen*—and this is also true of colonialism—can be understood only in the context of a pervasive, burgeoning popular science that appealed to all classes and subcultures in Wilhelmine Germany.[58] Popular anthropology in particular attracted a wide audience: both middle- and working-class Germans, both educated bourgeois and Social Democrats. The "races of the world"—the colonized world in particular—appeared in ethnographic dioramas, illustrated encyclopedias, wax museums, travelogues, magazines, adult education lectures, and lantern-slide shows.[59] Indeed, the growing popular audience ultimately helped transform the very logic and style of exhibition in Germany's leading ethnographic museums.[60] The popular "Geography and Ethnography" sections of not only public but also SPD lending libraries in this period contained mostly books about the German and European colonies.[61] A revealing series of advertisements in the SPD's *Augsburger Volkszeitung* recommended to its socialist readers a "richly illustrated," "easy-to-understand," and "popular" "General Geography and Ethnography" *(Allgemeine Länder- und Völkerkunde)* as an "outstanding Christmas present for everyone." For just three marks, anyone "striving for education [could] . . . enrich his knowledge from the entertaining readings in this work" ("Wissen ist Macht!" trumpeted the ad. "Populärwissenschaftlich!" "Knowledge is power! Popular-Scientific!").[62] Popular "anthropological" works, usually in the form of travelogues, often presented primitive Africans in popular-Darwinist terms as the "missing link"—as examples of evolutionary atavism—reproducing a theme common to the freak show.[63]

Not just the *Völkerschauen*, but all sorts of traveling shows participated in the "scientific exhibition" of exotic peoples. The grandly named Kullmann's Museum for Art and Science advertised a respectable-sounding "Ethnology Section" and an "Anthropological Collection" and, among its "mechanically moving automatons," a series of races and peoples, or "Menschen- und Völkerrassen."[64] The famous panopticon *(Panoptikum)* was one of the most popular attractions of the period.[65] The original versions—Castan's Panoptikum and the Passage-Panoptikum in Berlin—began as wax museums and housed extraordinary collections of human oddities, historical curiosities, rare wonders of nature, and medical and criminological artifacts. Panopticons were also prominent venues for freak shows, *Völkerschauen*, and the anthropological *Wachsfigurenkabinette*, wax figure collections. As the big-city panopticons grew in popularity, they spawned both branches and imitators, bringing this particular constellation to towns across the country. A traveling panopticon "à la Castan," for example, exhibited—presumably in wax—a "Congo Negro" and "Hottentots, or Bushmen."[66]

Spectators at the Panopticon (1892). *ÜLuM* (1892). Courtesy Butler Library, Columbia University.

The panoptical survey of the "races of the world" was the pop-cultural simulacrum of the global-as-human-diversity. Commercial entertainments brought living specimens from the farthest reaches of the colonized world, or fabricated them in wax, for inspection, classification, edification, and pleasure. The racial differences and hierarchies rehearsed in travelogues and fifty-pfennig shows—and the dissemination of a racist grotesque through the ethnographic freak show—confirmed and amplified the racist politics of the colonial movement. The many forms of ethnographic entertainment conveyed images of the aboriginal, often carefully constructed, that gratified colonialists' sense of "racial" and cultural superiority and legitimized their endeavors. And yet, the experience of the *Völkerschauen*, following Carl Hagenbeck's leading example, was anything but uniform or stable. Once again, the inculcation of correct, controlled knowledge—anthropological, colonial, racial—proved elusive in the sphere of popular reception. Innumerable moments of exchange and interaction between spectators and performers—not least reciprocal currents of eroticism—threatened to undermine hierarchical barriers of race and authority, a cause of protracted concern to members of the Colonial Society and others. And bourgeois colonialists complained of increasingly vulgar lower-class audiences who, with their ill-disciplined voyeurism, transformed respectable ethnographic shows into sensationalized spectacles. The crowd proved itself, once again, stubbornly uncontainable.[67]

If bourgeois colonialists and scientists mingled with the masses under the sign of science, they also of course, found irresistible the propaganda potential in mass-cultural forms. This was something of a devil's bargain, promising great powers but also eliciting a certain uneasiness about the superficial and vulgar world of popular culture. Propagandists frequently borrowed from the techniques and style of showmen, particularly in the construction of colonial exhibitions around the turn of the century. Throughout metropolitan Europe, such exhibitions represented efforts to realize the overseas empires visually, and to simulate a thrilling experience of visiting them. They normally took the form of fabricated city streets or villages, their imitation souks and forts peopled with authentic "natives."[68] The German colonial exhibitions—in Berlin in 1896 and 1907, in Leipzig in 1897, and elsewhere—followed this pattern of reconstructing the colonies in miniature. To attract a mass audience, their creators embraced—with some hesitation—popular ethnographic amusements, blurring the distinction between propaganda and entertainment. The first German Colonial Exhibition opened on 1 May 1896 in Berlin's Treptow Park.[69] It formed part of the much larger Berlin Trade Exhibition, together with a North Pole exhibit, an Alpine Panorama, a Cairo exhibit surrounding a "monumental Cheops pyramid," and—somehow distinguished from all this by contemporaries—an amusement park. The organizers intended that the exhibition "give a true picture of our colonies and their inhabitants."[70] This would not entail so much analytical description, as at the sober Colonial Congresses of 1902, 1905, and 1910, with their learned lectures on botany, mineral extraction, tropical medicine, and economics. Rather, as Georg Simmel wrote of the adjacent Trade Exhibition, "here the abundance and diversity of the offerings" would "ultimately permit as the sole focus and distinguishing characteristic only amusement."[71] But that, of course, was not how the colonialists wanted to see it.

The colonial painter Rudolf Hellgrewe, "artistic director" of the exhibition, spared no artifice in designing an "authentic" experience of the exotic: Moorish architecture, trompe l'oeil landscapes, primitive ornament and ethnographica, palm trees, and fake villages. "A whole new world takes us captive when we set foot into the exhibition through an entrance—already recognizable from a distance by its flag poles—preserving the style . . . of New Guinea, and fantastically decorated with distorted masks and palm fronds."[72] The exhibition covered 60,000 square meters along the southeastern shore of the Carp Pond, just below "Old-Berlin" and across the street from the "North Pole." Once inside, visitors encountered a Machine House, an Africa House, a Tropical House, an Arab Temple, a Scientific Hall, a reading pavilion, an East African fort (the Quikuru), villages from Togo, Cameroon, and New Guinea, and other colonial scenes. The official report on the exhibition captures the kitsch-eclecticism of a colonial "Potemkin village":

> Stepping further along the main path through the beautiful Treptow Park, whose greenery provided a charming setting for the West African native villages, the visitor reached a lovely open area. Emerging from the depths of the African bush he will have experienced—so important in this sort of exhibition— a new sense of, so to speak, revelation. An enchanting view across the pond, whose waters reflected—menacingly, defiantly—the red walls and towers of Old Berlin! Fantastic structures—their domes glimmering in the sunlight—rose up, standing out against deep green stands of trees and dense foliage on the opposite shore. On the lake, black Venetian gondolas intersected with electric motorboats, disturbing the motionless swans, as boats of Negroes passed by with singing and the beat of drums, while from the center the spray of the fountain glittered in all the colors of the rainbow. It was a picture as full of the greatest activity and modern life as of singular poetic charm, so that this corner of the pond truly deserved to be called, on purely aesthetic grounds, the pearl of the Colonial Exhibition.[73]

"Savages" were obligatory in the miniaturized empire. The exhibition had, after all, to break even. Critics, including the German Colonial Society, resisted the idea of bringing colonial subjects to Berlin, in view of the ill effects on the Africans themselves.[74] The organizers, however, considered native performers essential for reasons of both finance and propaganda. This was not the first time the colonial movement had used the *Völkerschauen*, nor would it be the last.[75] In particular, the desire to attract the masses, rather than just the colonialist bourgeoisie, made theatrical spectacle necessary: "The board was of the opinion that to have a truly great, comprehensive exhibition that would be visited not only by those well-disposed to the colonies but above all by the broad masses of the people . . . could scarcely be accomplished without natives. Dead collections alone are never able to draw the great mass of the people."[76]

Observers also emphasized the performers' origins exclusively in the German colonies, which was unusual for *Völkerschauen*, as justification for including them in the exhibition. Among the performers were eight Papuans, fifteen Duala, twenty-six Togolese, seventeen Masai, five Herero, and four Nama ("Hottentots"). All together, they represented nearly every geographical region of the empire. "The wildest, most robust tribe in the medley of peoples . . . were the Masai, whose dances depicted the rapacity and lust for killing of these warriors, so feared by all neighboring tribes in their homeland."[77] The Hottentots and Herero, on the other hand, "showed true-to-life scenes of domestic life and activity," and "in rainy weather . . . applied themselves to making hippopotamus-hide whips [sjamboks]."[78] Because, according to the *Deutsche Kolonialzeitung*, "it is a matter here of tribes who live in our colonies, rather than whatever other black tribes with whom we have not come into contact, one will encounter them with more interest."[79]

Berlin Colonial Exhibition: "Dance of the Swahili" (1896). Arbeitsausschuß der Deutschen Kolonial-Ausstellung, *Deutschland und seine Kolonien im Jahre 1896: Amtlicher Bericht über die erste deutsche Kolonial-Ausstellung* (Berlin: Dietrich Reimer, 1897). Courtesy Deutsche Bücherei, Leipzig.

Colonial postcard: "Heathen Herero" in Southwest Africa.

This would confer on the ersatz villages a greater air of authenticity, and on the whole exhibition, by extension, a certain educative legitimacy. Furthermore, the "natives" were not only German colonial subjects, but were supposed to be uncontaminated by previous contact with commercial ethnographic shows. "What lends greater interest to the 'savages' displayed at the Colonial Exhibition is the fact that they are specially selected by the colonial administrations of the various German protectorates and consist without exception of representatives of tribes that do not lend themselves professionally to shows."[80] This was thought to eliminate the taint of vulgar entertainment—perhaps a flaw of the neighboring Cairo show—by making the exhibition more scientific and instructive.

And, indeed, the great spectacle drew Germans of all classes, from the Kaiser to servants and factory workers. Weekdays might bring only the relatively well-to-do, those with sufficient free time. "More colorful was the mixture of the crowd that spent Sundays at the exhibition," the only free day for most workers.[81] Over six months some one million visitors toured the pavilions and artificial villages.[82] Group visits to the Trade Exhibition—and so, we presume, to the Colonial Exhibition—included the workers of a Hamburg-Berlin venetian blind factory and a Brandenburg tinning factory; the Association of German Barbers, Hairdressers, and Wigmakers; twenty pages to the King of Bavaria; the workers of the Haucke & Kuntze perfume and toilet soap factory; the workers of the Kraft & Jacobi linen factory; 350 workers from a hat factory; and 900 metalworkers from F. Butzke & Co.[83] The price of admission, though probably too high for many working-class Germans, did not entirely exclude them.

This kind of popular success brought with it a certain anxiety. The bourgeois colonial movement existed to win popular support for the empire, but, as we have seen, disdained the very masses whose support it sought—and particularly the sort of spectacle calculated to appeal to them. "There are many thousands," complained the *Kolonialzeitung*, "who made the pilgrimage to Treptow only for the satisfaction of mere curiosity, in order to see the blacks for once, and who profited little." Organizers lamented free interaction between spectators and performers that yielded intimations of erotic desire and the blurring of colonial hierarchy.[84] The colonialists, of course, thought of themselves as educators, as transmitters of colonial knowledge. In 1900, the Colonial Society debated the question of importing "natives" from the German colonies, airing doubts about the scientific purpose of the shows. Here, again, the tensions within the public sphere of colonialism showed themselves as the ethnographic shows, ostensibly furthering colonialist aims, disclosed unintended effects in the field of reception.[85] The colonialist appropriation of commercial mass amusements—including the ethnographic shows—was often reluctant, but it was unavoidable. Many ordinary visitors came to gawk, conceded the colonialists, "but the thought certainly impressed itself on the great majority . . . that we stand here at the beginning of a highly significant development, and many were forever won for the colonial interests."[86] Not for the last time, colonial propaganda fused, uneasily, with forms of popular entertainment: counterfeit villages, magic lantern shows, and displays of exotic abundance. The climate of amusement and distraction—part of what Simmel called the "passive and receptive" varieties of experience in the metropolis—furthered a specific, overriding propaganda objective.

But colonialists took from the relative success of the 1896 exhibition the wrong lesson, retreating into the respectable precincts of the museum, the objectification of colonial knowledge as material culture: as "dead collections." For it was the exhibition that gave rise to the Berlin Colonial Museum, to which the exhibitors bequeathed the larger part of their collection of colonial commodities and other materials.[87] The museum was conceived to further its purpose, but failed to quite preserve the popular style in its exhibitionary logic. Founded by "friends of the colonial empire" in 1896, it opened in the imperial capital in 1899.[88] Like the exhibition, it was formally independent of—though supported by—the German Colonial Society, which saw in it a potentially powerful instrument of propaganda. Yet, although the Colonial Museum became a center for the transmission of colonial knowledge in Berlin, it was never very successful in attracting the urban masses.[89] By the summer of 1911, after twelve years, it counted a total of fewer than 500,000 paying visitors.[90]

Created to popularize colonialism, the museum subordinated its scientific and pedagogical mission to the larger purpose of propaganda, but certainly retained that mission.[91] One of many national museums and cultural institutions

Oriental East Africa: Indian street at the Leipzig Exhibition (1897). *DKZ* 10 (1897). Courtesy New York Public Library.

in the capital, it aimed its educational program—the dissemination of geographical, ethnographic, and economic knowledge about the colonies—at Germans of all classes, but particularly at the less educated. The executive board of the Colonial Society, discussing the uncertain future of the museum, emphasized its "valuable collections . . . that were perfectly suitable as illustrative materials for teaching." Lantern-slide lectures—and eventually cinema—supplemented the dioramas, ethnographica, and commodity collections on permanent display. The Colonial Society noted in particular that the "visitors consist predominantly of circles that did not belong to the Colonial Society, for whom colonial matters remain otherwise distant concerns."[92] And while the museum never reached the popularity of the 1896 exhibition, it did draw a steady, if modest stream of patrons from different social backgrounds. In April 1904, it determined that nearly 40,000 tickets had been sold over the preceding year.[93] In 1908 it sponsored 357 lectures and counted 60,000 visitors (including school children). The following winter, the Berlin-Charlottenburg chapter of the Colonial Society used museum materials for seven "public, popular" lantern-slide lectures given to associations of factory workers and artisans in the "largest halls in Berlin."[94] With limited success, the museum disseminated knowledge to a constituency beyond the educated, propertied enthusiasts of organized colonialism.

The museum occupied a vacant panorama building—the former Marine-Panorama, opposite the Lehrter Bahnhof—and traces of this original purpose survived, not only in the architecture but also in the insistent reality effect.[95] The prospective task of the museum was "representation of life in the colonies . . . according to nature, as in panoramas."[96] Rudolf Hellgrewe, scene painter of the colonial movement, had himself worked as a panorama painter, and he brought the techniques of monumental illusionism to his design for the museum.[97] An enormous glass-roofed court—the site of the old panorama painting—cut through the center of the building, providing the massive scale and viewer perspective that had underpinned the panoramic effect.[98] This was to be "the highlight of the museum," its dimensions "so enormous that an absolutely imposing exhibition—as much in its originality as its design—can be created."[99]

But at the same time the museum was supposed to transcend the panorama, then sinking into obsolescence, by amplifying the massive, overpowering effect of three-dimensional, "panoramic" reality surrounding the viewer, and infusing this effect with a contemporary political and national significance: "On the whole, the panorama exhibition no longer has the appeal it had upon first appearance. The reasons lie substantially in the nature of panoramas, which have little or no prospect of development, while a museum such as is proposed here, through the use of the advantages of the panorama, accompanies a political and economic current—the colonial movement—and with it produces growing inner strength."[100] The panorama had grown out of the tradition of trompe l'oeil painting, magnifying and inflating it until it literally enveloped the viewer within a total illusion of reality.[101] The ambitions of the Colonial Museum both incorporated and surpassed the panorama form. In the smaller, surrounding rooms the colonies would be represented through a series of "landscape paintings (panoramas)" integrated with colonial artifacts and artificial human figures in dioramic configuration.[102] The rotunda itself would be transformed into an artificial tropical river valley. The technique of total simulation, the experience of a synthetic, fully self-enclosed, miniaturized colonial world, was calculated to exert an irresistible fascination.[103]

An early prospectus for the museum, a pamphlet with floor plans and reproductions of paintings by Hellgrewe, asks the reader to imagine himself on a "Visit to the Colonial Museum." It leads the imaginary visitor on a walk through the great rotunda and smaller adjoining rooms:

> The visitor, standing at the great globe in a richly decorated entrance hall magically illuminated by skylights, walks first to the right, into the grandly designed room dedicated to the colonial past and the spread of colonial knowledge. The picture presented by the rotunda is quite overpowering. One is conscious of being in the middle of a room spacious enough for some six hundred people, the walls covered up to half their height in rock, upon which tropical vegetation

flourishes in gay profusion along a miniature waterfall. Through openings in the rock, he glimpses the exhibitions of Cameroon, Togo, and Southwest Africa, illuminated from above and from the sides. Each colony is, of course, treated individually; not only the activities and way of life of Europeans and natives, but also the character of the landscape is represented in dioramas.[104]

The prospectus suggests how colonialists imagined the overseas empire from an expansive, global perspective collapsing distance and difference, and how they envisioned a powerful, simulated experience of it. The overall scheme combined disparate, even contradictory tendencies: a fetishized kitsch-realism in the representation of the different colonies, and the weird unreality of their artificial proximity as "empire." Each colony was to be represented by individual dioramas made to look as real as possible, with "lifelike groups" of figures and dwellings "built of real material," and all of these displays were somehow to be "harmoniously united with one another."[105]

The museum in its final form fully realized—perhaps even surpassed—the intentions of its designers. Entering the building, visitors encountered the edifying—or, rather, misleading—symmetry of a "Hall of Imports" and "Hall of Exports" constructing the global through flows of commodities, as well as a small naval exhibition. But it was the central rotunda that would transport them to an exotic, unspecified "colonial" terrain: "Before us opens a densely jungled tropical river valley, over whose boulders a small stream gaily splashes, and beyond which, framed by an arrangement of large palms and flanked by Chinese guns taken at Kiaochow, rises the statue of the Kaiser. High above the rock, an unusual scene presents itself in the shimmering colors—red, gold, and green—of a replica Chinese temple from Kiaochow."[106] The vines, palms, and ferns—lush vegetation spilling over the rocks of the enormous "grotto"—provided a setting for the emblems of imperial conquest: the Chinese temple and artillery and the Kaiser himself. The hand-painted dioramic scenes in the surrounding rooms depicted an Arabian house, Togolese huts, and part of a New Guinea village.[107] Behind a replica of a noncommissioned officers' mess there opened up a dioramic vista on a miniaturized Mount Cameroon.

The kaleidoscopic arrangement produced a simulacrum of the global as "empire," a painstaking orchestration of artifice and illusion that ultimately represented no real place. The museum was simultaneously panoramic—in scale and technique—and panoptical: visitors could see the whole of the empire—Africa, China, the South Pacific—in a sweeping glance around the rotunda. The sight was, as the museum guide pointed out, a "surprising one" indeed: "On one side the New Guinea Village is next to a European residence, while the great Chinese temple with the view of a Kiaochow street occupies the middle, and the panorama is limited by the Arabian Café, with a large Arabian building and a lighthouse. Especially in the evenings, in the glow of the Arabian lighthouse, the picture revealed before our eyes is downright magical."[108] The uncanny ("magical," "enchanting") effect of this patchwork was perhaps more disorienting than scientific or educational. Indeed, with its waxworks mannequins and ethnographic clutter, the museum elicited dismissive comparisons with popular commercial amusements. Berlin anthropologists sneered at the museum, Felix von Luschan predicting that it would amount to "nothing better than a second-rate '*Tingl-Tangl* or at best, a panopticon.'"[109] (Even as critics derided Luschan's own overstuffed Berlin Museum of Ethnography as a mere curiosity cabinet, suggesting the double-edged ubiquity of the discourse opposing respectable science and cheap wonder.)[110] And perhaps, not unlike a fifty-pfennig fair booth "Savage Africa," the fabricated environments of the museum became for visitors a brand of simulated, commodified adventure: the prospect of imagining themselves in the faraway colonies. But the ideological framework of colonialism stamped the experience with a certain unity and purpose as a simulation site for instructing on the urgency of colonial empire for resource extraction and German labor. And, for a moment, at least, the combined panoramic realism and panoptical vantage point might permit the viewer—the factory worker, the schoolteacher, the office clerk—to be lord of all he surveyed.

The Colonial Museum, like the Colonial Society itself, was no hit with the masses, perhaps precisely to the extent that it musealized the empire, transmuting adventure into an object lesson in commerce, production, and geography—into respectable colonial knowledge—the trappings of the panorama notwithstanding. The museum boasted no cannibals, no Amazons, no African princes. It furnishes another example of the gulf between organized colonialism and ordinary Germans, or between colonial knowledge and the sensation of the fair. Yet, certainly, if colonial enthusiasts never overcame their broad—though not total—disinclination to open their organizations to members from the lower classes, they did increasingly seek to incorporate the masses into their program through the means available to them. These came increasingly to include the technologies, styles, and arenas of the new mass culture, opportunities which the Colonial Society had begun to discuss explicitly at least by 1898. This was a halting and awkward process, in which ambition was always intermingled with anxiety. In 1911, debating the relative costs and advantages of lantern slides and the cinematograph, one member insisted, with more than a trace of condescension, that "the great mass of the population wants some kind of razzle-dazzle [*etwas Klim-bim*]."

The elections of 1907—fought over the intractable war in Southwest Africa—clarified the growing interpenetration of mass culture and politics. In the struggles over colonial policy, we see the crystallization of a new political style: the style of colportage, of the fair. Colonialism was perhaps uniquely suited to this development precisely because it united politics and the exotic. The "picturesque" empire of mass culture spanned the globe, from China to the paradise of the South Pacific to East, Southwest, and West Africa. The aesthetic pretensions of Colonial Secretary Dernburg, speaking during the campaign, belied the actual infusion of politics with the idiom of mass culture. Lamenting the lack of German colonial art, Dernburg insisted on its momentous future. Because, he said, it is the task of art "to arouse in every man the best and noblest that lies within him and to infuse sensation with consciousness, then it also has a great task in our colonies. . . . Art has a mission there to heighten the sense for the noble and the beautiful in a free and untouched world; writers, musicians and artists of the German nation will perform a great service by fostering their ethical and aesthetic sensibility."[111] But—the contradiction between the war of extermination in Southwest Africa and Dernburg's "sense for the noble and the beautiful in a free and untouched world" notwithstanding—German writers and artists were already producing great quantities of pictures and books about the empire, popular ones. What these lacked in "nobility," they made up for in mass appeal, which lent them a particular political significance.

Constrained by a certain aloofness, by a sense of the vulgarity of the masses and their amusements, colonialists nevertheless drew on the tremendous propaganda potential in mass culture. If the economics and ideology of colonialism frequently met with hostility, incomprehension, or indifference, there was a thriving market for exoticism and adventure. As one colonial propagandist put it in the *Kolonialzeitung*, "Interest in our colonies among the lower middle class [*Mittelstand*], and among politically uncommitted workers, is easy to increase. Our people's attraction to the foreign, their interest in novelty, their pleasure in the wider world, their joy in adventure, and wanderlust are useful here. Certainly it's a gain when, after the kind of colonial evenings I hold, factory workers say to their employers 'That was good, that sort of thing should be done more often.' "[112]

Nationalist propaganda increasingly imitated and appropriated the representational forms and novel devices of mass culture. The national spectacle of 1907 called for visual and narrative entertainment at least as much as rational discourse. According to members of the government, what was wanted for the campaign was not facts and figures, "but rather real, vivid stories, the bloodier the better, since the masses with their need for melodrama always seek colportage literature. [And] if a few good pictures from the life of the soldier in Africa are to be got hold of, so much the better. People out in the small towns cut them out, stick them on the wall, and the [element of] suggestion begins to have an effect."[113] By 1906, dramatic depictions of colonial warfare were already long familiar to working- and middle-class readers and panorama spectators. Now, mass-produced images in election propaganda demonized the Herero and bathed colonial soldiers and settlers in the penumbral haze of national honor and heroism.[114]

A satirical attack in the socialist *Leipziger Volkszeitung*—"The Colonial Circus in the Election Campaign"—evokes the new carnival style of politics:

In order to show the productivity of our colonies, the [colonial] association will doubtless bring in a great menagerie of animals bred there. Several giraffes will dance the national anthem and parrots will recite speeches by Bülow and others. Children of loyal [*reichstreu*] voters may ride zebras spotted in black, white, and red. . . . At the end of each performance, Dr. Peters and Puttkammer, in original Herero costume, will eat fire and mimic the "savage man," and much better, much truer to life, than real Negroes from the waxworks or the master's coach-box can do it. . . . The national Colonial Circus could even charge a reasonable entry fee and thereby help fill the consumptive cash-box of the bourgeois parties. [Circus impresarios] Busch and Schumann, however, might want to look for new sensations.[115]

The separate spheres of propaganda and mass-cultural entertainment overlap, and perhaps even merge, reflecting both the transformation of political style and the commercial popularity of overseas adventure and patriotic fervor. In the "colonial circus," electoral politics converge with the Völkerschauen, waxworks, and menageries, the sites of commercial exoticism. Political speech becomes a rousing chorus. Voters are transformed into spectators as audience begins to supplant constituencies conventionally divided by interest and social class.

Through channels both direct and indirect, then, colonialism was becoming ubiquitous by 1907. The Colonial Society and similar institutions had gradually developed their ideological arsenal and techniques of propaganda since the early 1880s. These more conventional forms of political propaganda seem to have had a somewhat limited effect, due both to the power of SPD counter-propaganda and the sluggishness and social exclusivity of the Colonial Society. Mass amusements with colonial content, on the other hand, were pervasive, reaching large audiences in all parts of the country from all classes. The new mass media combined the exotic, the scientific, and patriotic into lucrative entertainments with broad appeal, making them ultimately more powerful than traditional propaganda. Indeed, in terms of the popularity of ethnographic exhibitions, early cinema, and the like, Germany came increasingly to resemble other European countries in the "age of imperialism."

CHAPTER FIVE

Ethnographic-Fantastic

Working-Class Readers at the Colonial Library

> The present has, rightly, been referred to as an age of travels and of
> geographical surveys.... The number of our geographical periodicals,
> ... as of our geographical societies is steadily growing; interest in
> geographical, ethnographic, and anthropological studies has been
> powerfully stimulated by scientific research and popular illustrated
> accounts.... But are we to be and remain only theoreticians in this
> field too...? Are we to continue sitting in our studies and making
> ourselves familiar with all the quarters of the globe, without finding a
> second national home anywhere overseas?
> —Friedrich Fabri, *Bedarf Deutschland der Colonien?* 1879

The colonial library crystallized the formation and dissemination of colonial knowledge in an expanding field of travelogue, novel, memoir,
ethnography, natural history, lexicon, and report. Institutionalized, or materialized, in a series of public, factory, associational, and socialist collections and reading rooms, it projected the ideal of an informed public. It
was hierarchical, distinguishing "good" literature from "bad," science from
fable, intellection from distraction and escape. Its object was the German
masses, and above all the working classes, whom it sought to enlighten and
instruct. In this it was hopeful, but frustrated: bedeviled by the stubbornness
of the workers, their obstinate reading against the grain of knowledge, but
also beset by the ambiguities and instabilities of its own system of hierarchy
and distinction. The colonial library retraced the deep ambiguity of colonial
discourse, and its defining class antagonism.

For Habermas, the public originated in the "reading public," the "public
sphere" in "the world of letters."[1] If the public sphere was ultimately an
abstraction, subsuming gender and class into a universalized subject that
concealed the hierarchical exclusion of women and the plebeian, its origins
in the reading public signified irreducible difference. "The circles of per-
sons who made up the two forms of public"—literary and political—"were
not even completely congruent," he says. "Women and dependents were
factually and legally excluded from the political public sphere, whereas female readers as well as apprentices and servants often took a more active
part in the literary public sphere than the owners of private property and

family heads themselves."[2] The world of reading, the very foundation of the public sphere, reveals its internal tensions. In the case of colonialism as knowledge, irrepressible subaltern reading practices in the new mass culture disrupted rationalizing "colonial enlightenment." They forced colonialists to confront a perplexing, infuriating world of mass pulp literature, from which they shrank; a socialist reading subculture, which they abhorred; and the imbrications of popular amusement and popular science, which confounded them for lack of any stable distinction. But these same reading practices also reinforced the claims of colonial knowledge to truth, through precisely opposition to the enchantment of mass culture. And the reiterated experience of division, subjectively powerful, obscured deeper continuities binding knowledge and enchantment together. Here again, distance conceals proximity—of the colonialist bourgeois and the proletarian reader—and indeed defines it.

If by the end of the nineteenth century some 90 percent of Germans could read, literacy by itself was no guarantee that German workers, with little free time or money for books, would become readers.[3] Widespread literacy, cheap colportage literature, and networks of public and workers' libraries did form the basis for a broad working-class reading culture, but only a minority of workers patronized libraries, and traces of the ephemeral, novelty-driven world of colportage literature have largely faded. Not surprisingly, workers left virtually no record of how they actually read particular books. Only scattered evidence survives, usually lists of most-read books in libraries, but also some contemporary speculation on how or why workers read certain kinds of books, among them books on colonialism.

Commercial mass culture, with all its enticing novelty and ideological ambiguity, was perhaps the most important arena for working- and lower-class readers of colonial literature. The enthusiasm for colonies in Germany coincided with a series of advances in print-capitalism that had far-reaching effects on mass culture. The colporteur novel, sold door-to-door in ten-pfennig installments, helped create a mass market for books already by the 1870s.[4] In the late 1880s, cheap pamphlet fiction—American detective stories and frontier tales, pirate stories and exotic adventures, with covers illustrated in vivid color—surpassed the colporteur novel in popularity. By 1910, Germans were buying tens of millions of dime novels every year, along with illustrated newspapers and mass-circulation magazines, from peddlers, kiosks, and tobacco shops.[5] A new working-class reading culture emerged with the formation of the mass market, just as the age of high imperialism was unfolding. Colonial exploration and the "scramble for Africa" generated a stream of travelogues, war stories, and ethnographic exotica that became the stuff of working-class readers' encounter with faraway worlds.

Workers got their hands on books in the new public and Social Democratic libraries, in railroad stations, and from peddlers. In a publishing center, like Leipzig—where typesetters, printers, and binders produced

Black Ivory from Cameroon: colonial dime novel.

books by many popular colonialist writers—they doubtless got their hands on them in other ways besides, whether from binderies and warehouses or from secondhand bookshops.[6] In a small village in Württemberg, in 1912, rural readers chose their wintertime reading from among war stories and travelogues at the modest local library.[7] Still, colportage was probably the most common and effective means of distribution. In an industrial city like Leipzig, for example, there were in 1896 more than 150 such dealers selling cheap prints, postcards, and dime novels with "enticing titles" in pubs, beer gardens, and door to door. According to one critical observer, the "better novels" appealed to shop girls and milliners, while most readers of sensationalist pulp novels in Leipzig were factory workers and servants.[8] Moritz Bromme, a socialist worker and bibliophile in a machine-building factory in the Thuringian town of Gera, described turn-of-the-century colportage and proletarian literary taste:

> At first, the workers read mostly the *Berliner Illustrierte* and the *Reporter*. . . . [Some] read the newly established *Gerichtszeitung*, which contained mainly sensational illustrations of murder. The younger fellows were of course consumers of *Hintertreppenromane*, with a murder on every page. Only those with whom we enlightened ones came into direct contact followed our advice and subscribed to *Freie Stunden*, or . . . Langkavel's *Der Mensch und seine Rassen*, [or] Bommeli's *Geschichte der Erde*. . . . The nineteen-to-twenty-two-year-old skilled people loved war stories or something racy, showing as many naked women as possible, like *Album, Frauenschönheiten, Das kleine Witzblatt, Flirt, Satyr*, and *Sekt*. Then there were the compulsive readers with *Buch für Alle* and *Gartenlaube*.[9]

Tales of faraway battles and adventures set in colonial Africa, Asia, or the South Seas easily fit the paradigm of the colporteur novel. Dashed off by hack writers and cheaply produced for the mass market, they have left relatively few traces. Surviving titles like *In Kamerun! Erlebnisse eines jungen Deutschen an der Westküste von Afrika* or *Unter den Battacks, den Menschenfressern auf Sumatra* suggest the commercial appeal of colonial stories.[10] Cannibalism, especially, was an enduring theme. At the turn of the century, following the German seizure of Kiaochow and coinciding with the Boxer Rebellion, readers could purchase in fifty installments the 1,202 pages of the breathlessly titled *Prinz Tuan, der geheimnißvolle Kaiser von China. Oder: Die Giftmischerin von Peking. Schicksale eines deutschen Mädchens im Wunderlande China. Chinesisch-deutscher Sensationsroman*. The "Unter deutscher Flagge" series—"Koloniale Unterhaltungsliteratur für Jugend und Volk"—included ten-pfennig titles like *Patrouillenritte in Deutsch-Südwest, Auf Grenzwacht in Südwest-Afrika* and *Die Eroberung von Kamerun*: "lively, thrillingly told tales based for the most part on true experiences," their covers illustrated in vibrant color. Inevitably, though, colonial themes represented only a small part of dime-novel plots encompassing everything from enslavement and murder to fortune-telling and royal scandals to emigrant misadventures and every sort of "schreckliches Schicksal." Around 1900, with the appearance in Germany of the cheap American serial novel, it was the Wild West tales of Buffalo Bill and the Nick Carter detective stories, rather than the trash novels of empire, which became enormous bestsellers.[11] A cheap, popular colonial literature flourished, but on a smaller scale.

Popular illustrated magazines supply another example of the multiple, indirect channels through which colonialism circulated as entertainment and education. These are to be distinguished from the more specialized geographical magazines, which projected a forthright, thoroughly colonialist position in the heyday of exploration and imperialism. General-interest magazines, intended for the edification and diversion of middle-class families—*Die Gartenlaube, Daheim*, and *Westermanns Monatshefte*—were popular among both workers and the "Geography, Tourism, and Colonial Affairs" reader generally.[12] Peddlers sold the magazines, like dime novels, door to door and in factories, and the panoply of family, fashion, and other titles consistently made up the largest share of colportage sales.[13] Bound annual volumes of these middle-class magazines were frequently among the most-read works at both public and workers' libraries. As a Nuremberg metalworkers' association library reported, there was "not much interest among our members for the rubric 'Geography and Travelogue,'" because magazines were sufficient to satisfy the workers' appetites in this area.[14]

There was no mass-circulation magazine in Germany that did not give the colonial empire a prominent place in its pages. They ordinarily displayed a broad, inclusive patriotism that remained as removed from divisive party politics as from the cheap thrills and violence of colonial colportage. The texts and pictures in *Westermanns Monatshefte, Über Land und Meer*, and *Die Gartenlaube* all served to popularize a brand of German colonialism that was not stridently political but rather forward-looking, scientific, and exciting.[15] Which is not to say that they were free of the exoticism, racism, and celebrations of war typical of colonial literature. The standard fare of racist cartoons, colonial battles, and exploration accounts filled the pages of *Über Land und Meer* throughout the 1880s and 90s. Pygmies and other human "curiosities" excited interest, but in a different key: more restrained and respectable than in dime novels (or, for that matter, at the fair). Maps, ethnographic reports, and descriptions of flora and fauna in the colonies were calculated to transmit colonial knowledge and cultivate an informed public. *Westermanns* contained the same sort of stuff but was much more explicitly political and procolonialist. It published articles on the slave trade, on settler life in Southwest Africa, on Stanley and the Emin Pasha story, as well as reviews of colonial literature and long pieces on the "colonial women question" and on German colonial cities. Among contributors were Carl Peters and Karl Dove, two of the best-known exponents of colonial expansion.

The new mass-reading culture challenged colonialists to identify books suitable for the ordinary reader and to distinguish good from bad. The *Kolonialfreund*, a guide to colonial literature for booksellers, librarians, and teachers, attempted to "separate the wheat from the chaff," reminding readers that "in the field of German colonial literature, alongside much chaff, there are also hundreds of good books that have remained completely unknown in broad circles." A number of the titles belonged to the world of cheap colportage literature and seemed to merit only grudging recognition. Twenty-pfennig booklets from the "Hurra! Durch alle Welt!" series, for example, were often filled with "too much blood and impossible, exaggerated adventures." That they were "nevertheless more worthwhile than the awful Indian-literature" was "beyond question." The editor recommended Langheld's *Im schwarzen Erdteil* and Liebert's *Im Kampf gegen die Wahehe* from another series, but warned that "not all authors in [the series] are 'outstanding,' and many remind one of colportage literature." And among twenty-pfennig books brought out by Globus, he points out *Afrikanische Sklavenräuber*, its illustrations "as horrible as the text."[16] But it was better to have workers reading books on colonialism, even the bad ones, if it might spark their interest and cultivate an inclination toward the better colonial literature: "The colorful covers of the booklets are very enticing to the youth, but remind one in many cases of the notorious Indian dime novels. In terms of content, they for the most part cannot be characterized as unobjectionable. . . . Still, it is commendable that these series provide quite enthusiastic colonial descriptions and can serve partially to encourage the reading of more substantial colonial works."[17]

Of course, colportage brought not only the penny dreadful, but also other kinds of books, including religious works and popular science, into the working-class household.[18] Missionary tracts, travelogues, and popular ethnographic lexicons all treated colonial themes in more explicit, more serious ways. A peddler might offer, for example, Gaetano Casati's *Zehn Jahre in Aequatoria und die Rückkehr mit Emin Pascha*, an "impartial account" of the sensational Emin Pasha story, "awaited with feverish impatience and suspense by the whole world." (In 1897 Casati was one of the most popular authors in the library of the educational association of Leipzig engravers.) A book "of the highest geographical, colonial, and topical interest," promising answers to "many burning questions about the Dark Continent," it could be had in forty installments—rather expensive ones at fifty pfennigs each.[19] More affordable were the sentimental and exotic stories sold in pamphlet series by religious colporteurs. Peddlers of bibles, prayer books, portraits of the emperor, and the like, the religious colporteurs worked with the churches, religious associations, and missionary societies.[20] They sold titles like the ten-pfennig *Wie der Herero lebt und stirbt, oder, Die Gottlosen haben keinen Frieden*: the work of missionary societies eager to popularize their role in spreading German Christianity and culture overseas.[21] The "heathen world" of the colonies was an inexhaustible source of variously exciting, inspirational, and affecting tales of missionary life, costing from five to fifty pfennigs each. Pamphlets like *Erlebnisse im Hinterlande von Angra-Pequena* and *Unter den Zwartboois auf Franzfontein: Ein Beitrag zur*

Missions- und Kolonialgeschichte Südafrikas, copiously illustrated with missionary genre scenes and portraits of local converts and chieftains, were calculated to appeal to a popular audience, although for many readers the aspect of exotic adventure perhaps eclipsed the intended Christian message.[22]

In any case, it was not religious and scientific works but the sensationalist, scandal-ridden *Hintertreppenromane*—the "backstairs novels"—that critics associated with the colportage trade. This was worthless "trash literature," morally corrupting, a "school for crime." "In the hovels of the poor, in workers' apartments, among families of artisans—everywhere we find the colorful booklets whose outward appearances are just as odious to educated taste as are their contents."[23] "Is it not a disgrace," wrote Ernst Schultze, leader of the movement for public libraries, "that in Germany and Austria some twenty million among the 'people of thinkers and poets' obtain their intellectual nourishment from 45,000 dime-novel colporteurs?" The notion that the "educational elevation of the people also entails an increase in love of fatherland" served to underscore the appeal of libraries to bourgeois social reformers.[24] Interpreting the new mass-reading culture as a serious moral and social problem, they vied for influence over workers' taste and reading habits by building libraries and conducting studies of their working-class patrons. Reformers hoped to ensure the transmission of national culture—the culture of the cultivated bourgeoisie—represented by the canon of classical German literature developed during the nineteenth century.

Around 1910, the public librarian Walter Hofmann undertook an analysis of Dresden workers' reading patterns in order to penetrate the murky "psychology of the proletariat." "We are better informed about the living conditions of half-savage African peoples," he observed, "than about the lower classes among our own people." As it turned out, workers, too, shared the interest in colonial topics. Of the fifty proletarian readers analyzed most carefully, over a fifth read books about African exploration and colonization. Both a typesetter and a turner, for example, read Margarethe von Eckenbrecher's *Was Afrika mir gab und nahm*. An unskilled worker borrowed Hedwig Irle's *Wie ich die Herero lieben lernte*, as did a construction worker, who also read Max Schmidt's *Aus unserem Kriegsleben in Südwestafrika* on the Herero and Nama wars, both volumes of Rochus Schmidt's *Deutschlands Kolonien*, and other books on the Boer War and Sumatra.[25] One thirty-year-old worker, apparently consumed by interest in the colonies, read almost exclusively books about German Africa, colonial wars, and cannibals.[26]

Such works were common in public lending libraries and reading rooms. In Hofmann's Dresden library, the "Länder- und Völkerkunde," or geography and ethnography section, included "among other things, numerous exciting true accounts, travel adventures, and descriptions of exotic cultures," many of which treated colonial themes.[27] Some 6 percent of the 1895 catalog of the Schmidt Lending Library in Dresden appeared under

"Reisebeschreibungen, Land- und Völkerkunde."[28] In the public library in Leipzig-Gautsch, the same section contained Frieda von Bülow's *Reiseskizzen und Tagebuchblätter aus Deutsch-Ostafrika*, a five-volume *Europas Kolonien*, and Schmidt's popular two-volume *Deutschlands Kolonien*.[29] Authors in this category generally recommended for the new public libraries included the widely read Henry Morton Stanley and Hermann Wissmann, former governor of German East Africa and something of a bestseller among German colonial explorers.[30]

Patronized by over a quarter of Hofmann's adult male working-class readers, and over a fifth of adult male bourgeois readers, the geography and ethnography section was "typically the most requested among the educational categories in the whole library." And among the subcategories of the belletristic section, it was what Hofmann called the "ethnographic-fantastic" to which specifically working-class men resorted, where "a tangible need for excitement and experience finds gratification." According to Hofmann,

> the by and large quite unsophisticated category of ethnographic, fantastic, and adventure novels . . . is overall (within the belletristic category) the most commonly used by workers. The 2,376 volumes borrowed by adult male workers once more give expression to the need to expand the narrow, everyday reality of existence through imagined excursions into the faraway and exotic, the same need that drove lending figures for the geographical and ethnographical section of the educational category so extraordinarily high.

Over the course of 1907 and 1908, 1,372 male workers borrowed 11,638 volumes of German belletristic literature, of which 2,376 belonged to the ethnographic-fantastic category. (The figures exclude the belletristic subcategory of new fiction where we find the colonial novels of Frieda von Bülow, who was, in any case, most popular among bourgeois women.) Not all of these readers, however, were inclined towards the specifically colonial titles among the ethnographic-fantastic. While "Länder- und Völkerkunde" in this period signified colonialist literature, the ethnographic-fantastic included not only Rudyard Kipling or Gustav Frenssen's *Peter Moors Fahrt nach Südwest*, but also and more importantly the works of wildly popular authors like Friedrich Gerstäcker, whose tales of emigrant adventures in the New World are more indirectly related to German colonial literature.[31] Only nine workers borrowed *Peter Moor*, while the library lent various volumes by Gerstäcker 489 times.[32] Still, together with the 3,232 volumes of geography and ethnography, this indicates a substantial, and perhaps surprising, interest in books—other than dime novels—about German and European colonies.

By 1906, the *Volksbibliotheken* in the forty largest German cities counted between them some 1.4 million readers borrowing 5.4 million books. Around 400,000 of these readers were workers, borrowing some 1.6 million books.[33] But it was ultimately the libraries of the Social Democratic Party that most working-class readers patronized. In 1890, just over 4 percent of readers in the twenty-five Berlin *Volksbibliotheken* were workers, although many more than that were small merchants, craftsmen, and journeymen.[34] At the turn of the century, about 33 percent of readers in the Danzig public libraries were workers, and working-class youth and artisans comprised about 25 percent each. In Breslau nearly 40 percent were craftsmen, apprentices, and workers, while in Düsseldorf only about 12 percent were workers and another 40 percent were artisans and small merchants. In Leipzig, only about 6 percent of readers in the public libraries were workers and another 31 percent artisans.[35] In 1906, the municipal and Saxon state governments, together with the Association for Public Welfare, supported seven public libraries for which, according to the police, "there was much demand among workers."[36] But apart from the thriving colportage trade, it was the SPD, not the *Volksbibliotheken*, which supplied working-class Leipzig with books. According to the *Bibliothekar*, the journal for the socialist library movement, the "bourgeois" public libraries in 1912 lent 87,844 volumes to 4,547 readers, while over 16,000 readers borrowed nearly 200,000 books from the 59 SPD and trade union libraries in Leipzig.[37] A fairly small, but significant and constant number of working-class readers sought out colonial literature—mainly in the form of "geography and ethnography"—in the public libraries. But many more workers in Leipzig—the heart of the "Red Kingdom of Saxony"—patronized the SPD libraries. And, surprisingly, these socialist workers reproduced this reading pattern in their own libraries.

Like the *Volksbibliotheken*, workers' libraries and reading rooms emerged in response to the flood of colportage literature. As Wilhelm Liebknecht put it in a speech to the Leipzig Workers Educational Association in 1872, the colporteur novel was "in its form, miserable trash, and in its content, opium for the mind and poison for morality."[38] The socialist libraries, too, sought to divert workers from mass-produced dime novels and offer them the chance of self-improvement through reading: "Our youth and our adult comrades have other, better things to read than Karl May's fantastic 'travel accounts' of the Orient—Persia, Turkistan and so on—or of America, of the Indian territories."[39] They also, of course, hoped to inculcate workers with socialist ideas, and in this sense competed with public, company, and school libraries. The Leipzig librarian Gustav Hennig, editor of the *Bibliothekar*, observed that the latter "contain an enormous amount of worthless stuff, and moreover, all the jingoist [*hurrapatriotisch*], bigoted rubbish and fabrications of history that wreak devastation among our youth. There are even notable educators," he went on, "who do not hesitate in the least to allow the books of Mr. Karl May into school libraries."[40] Theoretically, then, the SPD libraries would have served to filter out literature exhibiting vulgar or reactionary tendencies. We might therefore expect that colonial literature would find no place in workers' libraries. Yet it did, and largely because SPD librarians recognized important "scientific" discoveries in a lot of contemporary colonial literature. The reach, the credibility, of colonial knowledge was extensive.

Classified variously as geography, ethnography, or travelogue, German and foreign—particularly English—colonial literature consistently appealed to a small segment of the readership in workers' libraries. For example, of 1,432 responses to a survey of Berliners enrolled in workers' education courses (1906–8), 168, or 11.7 percent, named "Erd- und Völkerkunde" the subject most interesting to them.[41] In the library of the Berlin Woodworkers Association, an average of about 20 percent of the books borrowed each year (from 1891 to 1911) came from the "Reisebeschreibung und Völkerkunde" section.[42] A workers' library in Bremen reported in 1913 that the "travel narratives were almost always out, so that this area . . . had to be substantially expanded through new acquisitions." The SPD *Norddeutsches Volksblatt* printed in over one hundred installments Friedrich Gerstäcker's novel *Die Missionare: Ein Roman aus der Südsee*.[43] To help socialist librarians satisfy "the well known appetite for travelogues, which one can observe in every library," the *Bibliothekar* provided a list of books. It includes accounts by the heroes of African exploration—Gerhard Rohlfs, Wilhelm Junker, Gustav Nachtigal—and of course the celebrated work of Henry Morton Stanley. It also includes titles by three former colonial governors, several volumes on the Herero uprising and other episodes of colonial violence, and even a book by the notorious Carl Peters.[44]

In Hennig's own library—that of the Social Democratic Association of Leipzig-Plagwitz-Lindenau-Schleussig—the situation was much the same. In a brief history of his library over a ten-year period (1898–1907), Hennig includes a list of most-read works from the "Reisebeschreibungen und Naturwissenschaften" section. During this period, workers borrowed altogether over 80,000 books. More than half were novels, and only about a quarter belonged to "educational" categories, including the colonial literature grouped under "Travel Accounts and Natural Sciences." The most popular among these titles was *Unter Menschenfressern*, borrowed 199 times, followed by *Fünf Jahre unter den Stämmen des Kongostaates*, borrowed 122 times. Workers borrowed Stanley's *Im dunkelsten Afrika* and Wissman's ubiquitous *Unter deutscher Flagge* 81 times each, and *Unter den Kannibalen Borneos* 68 times. By way of comparison, the library lent adventure novels by Friedrich Gerstäcker—the most popular author—over 2,800 times, and 32 titles by Emile Zola over 2,000 times.[45] The pattern in the library of the Leipzig Association of Printers' and Typesetters' Assistants was similar. In the late 1890s, about 500 workers per year used the library. During the three years from 1896 to 1898, readers took home, respectively, 274, 332, and 328 volumes from the "Geographie, Länder- und Völkerkunde" section. Among them was *Im dunkelsten Afrika*, borrowed 19, 10, and 29 times over the three years, as well as eighteen volumes by Gerstäcker borrowed 177, 106, and 200 times.[46]

Wherever they were, workers consistently sought out and found books about the German and European colonial empires, or about the American frontier, whether in public or workers' libraries or through colportage. Not much, it seems, distinguished SPD from public, or even factory, libraries. At the small library in the Heye works in Gerresheim, for example, Gerstäcker and Cooper were among the most popular authors. The factory owner, Heye—not unlike his counterparts in the socialist library movement— "found among his workers a particular love of travelogue." When it came to enlarging the library, "this need was therefore taken into account and a number of works on Africa were acquired." And this turned out to be "a step in the right direction, since in just two months *Tigerfürst von Abessinien* was read twelve times, *In Kamerun* nine times, and *Sklavenjagd im Sudan* nine times."[47]

Social reformers and colporteurs, capitalist factory owners and socialist librarians made for odd bedfellows in all this, but there is no denying the curious similarities between them, the common appeal of colonial literature under the sign of science. And yet, what does this tell us? That workers were aware of and interested—sometimes passionately—in the distant, exotic world of the colonies; that, through reading, colonialism in some sense penetrated the interior world of the worker's imagination. But *how* did workers read these books? Did reading about the colonies make one a colonialist, as many hopeful propagandists seemed to think? Did it imply the transmission of a stable, transparent colonial knowledge, the enlargement of the rational-critical reading culture of the bourgeois colonial movement? Or, rather, knowledge contaminated by sensationalism, by colportage monsters and magic? Certainly contemporaries attributed talismanic powers to the book, often tracing the impulse to overseas exploration and colonial exploits back to reading. The travel writer Eugen Wolf described how "accounts of the epoch-making travels of Schweinfurth, Stanley, Livingstone and others made a deep impression" on the young Hermann Wissmann, who grew up to enjoy fame as an explorer, hunter, and governor of East Africa.[48] Frieda von Bülow, the colonial novelist, reported how on her first visit to Zanzibar *Arabian Nights* "came to life."[49] But it is not altogether clear that reading narratives of exploration and colonization actually inculcated colonial knowledge, or really inspired colonialism in the masses. Friedrich Fabri, Germany's leading colonial publicist in the heyday of African exploration, celebrated the widespread interest in geography and anthropology expressed by the new illustrated magazines, but wondered whether so much reading would ever translate into action. In "an age of travels and geographical surveys," he asks, when "interest in geographical, ethnographic, and anthropological studies has been powerfully stimulated by scientific research and popular illustrated accounts," would Germans "remain only theoreticians . . . sitting in our studies?[50] Examining the period after 1884, we observe no transparent link between colonialist literature—exploration accounts or geographical magazines like *Globus*—and colonialism itself, and no guarantee that working-class readers "profited" from their readings, gleaning colonial enlightenment and resolve. The evidence suggests that different readings were likely, and various effects—effects not excluding the dissemination of colonial enthusiasm.

To be sure, most of these travel and scientific books popular among workers were explicitly, even stridently, colonialist. Their authors—men like Karl Dove, Hermann Wissmann, and Carl Peters—were among the leading propagandists of empire and their works were emphatic exhortations to patriotic colonialism.[51] Colonialists identified this kind of reading, along with the ubiquitous magic lantern, as the principal means of instructing the masses in colonialism and inculcating in them the ardent feelings of the colonial movement. "The elementary schoolteacher may seek out predominantly youth literature, which he is accustomed to recommend," argued one colonialist, "but I believe our youth can be edified just as much by Wissmann and Emin Pasha, by Stanley and Livingstone. Teachers in the higher schools, on the other hand, will direct their students more to scientific travel readings, which always awaken interest in overseas subjects even when they do not directly concern the colonies."[52] Few seemed to doubt the power of reading to fire the colonialist imagination—but only by reading the *right* books.

The real problem, indeed, was to counteract the influence of colportage—of enchantment—and of the socialist press. "We start from below, among the working classes, where two paths to enlightenment present themselves: the printed and the spoken word." The "literary propaganda" of the printed word most often took the form of political flyers and pamphlets, but also books of various genres.[53] *Die deutschen Kolonien*, for example, based on a lecture series at the Colonial Museum in Berlin, making its way into the hands of workers in Dresden.[54] The propagandist's ideal was a "true *Volksbuch*"--a book for the people—defined as both "thrilling and easily understood." Frenssen's infamous novel *Peter Moors Fahrt nach Südwest*, about the war in Southwest Africa, evidently fit the colonialists' purpose. The story of Peter Moor, a North German blacksmith's son who goes to fight the Herero, it describes the harsh, alien colonial landscape, the agony and sacrifice of German soldiers, and the immense, destructive violence of the war. In Germany itself, "Frenssen's book was an event. It contributed like no other to the German people's laying aside its indifference to colonialism, learning to value the heroism of its sons, and taking increased interest in 'New Germany.'" The book's descriptions—"full of vigor, gripping simplicity, . . . and artistic perfection"—were said to "stir youth to pure, unadorned heroism and plant loyalty to the fatherland deep in their hearts."[55]

Colonialists frequently resorted to books and libraries to generate enthusiasm for the empire. The German Colonial Society erected at the 1896 Colonial Exhibition in Berlin a reading room that was emblematic of the broad effort to get colonialist books into the hands of German readers of all classes. Here, among potted palms, elephant tusks, and busts of famous explorers, visitors could examine maps of the colonies, enjoy picture books and albums, or read magazines and books on colonial topics. When they left, they could take a free colonial atlas home with them. Many local branches opened small libraries, sometimes to the public.[56] In Munich, the scholar Friedrich Ratzel and other members maintained a library "open to everyone free of charge."[57] In 1905, the Bochum section of the Colonial Society introduced a "proposal from industrial circles" at the national board meeting in Berlin. Turning the discussion "from the Masai in distant Africa to a people somewhat closer to home," the speaker envisioned "approaching the working class" and inspiring "whole masses with enthusiasm for colonial policy." (The comparison of German workers to African "savages" was becoming by this time something of a rhetorical convention.) Anecdotes about workers reading colonial literature formed the better part of his "particular observations made in Bochum." He reported with enthusiasm that

> in a large school for continuing education attended almost exclusively by workers, a library of two hundred books—a large part of them colonial books—is nearly always entirely out. It's a thought-provoking observation. It shows that students, who . . . after their day's work attend the continuing education school at night, still find time to read books of this sort at home. And when the school's director calls in the books, they repeatedly explain that 'my parents are still reading the book,' and that sort of thing. That shows that there are people among the working class who display understanding for and interest in our colonial goals.

Similarly, having "arranged for a number of copies of the *Deutsche Kolonialzeitung* to be left in a restaurant"—one, he suggested, "that was not of the very first rank"—he affirmed with satisfaction that "after some time he could either no longer find the papers or noticed that they showed signs of heavy use."[58] The Augsburg section likewise enjoyed some small success with the reading public after depositing its book collection in the Augsburg Municipal Library. Its local chairman expressed his particular pleasure at news that the book collection had been "extraordinarily heavily used by the reading public."[59] And again, months later, it seemed that the "hope that this might also be a way to make propaganda for the colonies has not been in vain since, according to the municipal librarian, the colonial library has been frequently in demand."[60] While such "thought-provoking" examples may reveal more about the wishful naïveté or profound aloofness of bourgeois colonial propagandists than about the tendency of working-class readers to develop colonial knowledge and enthusiasm, they nevertheless demonstrate how colonial literature became part of direct, unmediated attempts to win workers over to imperialism.

Reading room of the German Colonial Society, German Colonial Exhibition (1896).
Arbeitsausschuß der Deutschen Kolonial-Ausstellung, *Deutschland und seine Kolonien im Jahre 1896: Amtlicher Bericht über die erste deutsche Kolonial-Ausstellung* (Berlin: Dietrich Reimer, 1897). Courtesy Deutsche Bücherei, Leipzig.

And they illuminate the paradox of socialist libraries stocking colonial literature. What explains this curious overlap? Friedrich Fabri's linkage of reading, science, and colonialism points, it seems, to an important configuration in working-class reading culture: the equation of colonial literature with popular science. For the status of science, of "scientific knowledge" among all social classes in the nineteenth century, helps explain the appeal of colonial literature. We have seen how both public and workers' libraries catalogued various genres of colonial literature under educational and scientific headings—"Länder- und Völkerkunde" or "Reisebeschreibungen und Naturwissenschaften," for example. Publishers developed inexpensive popular science series like the "Geographische Bibliothek," consisting of slender, well-illustrated volumes costing eighty pfennigs apiece.[61] The many volumes on scientific research expeditions and anthropological encounters with strange peoples were one facet of the burgeoning popular-science world of lantern-slide lectures, evening enrichment courses, illustrated magazines, and popular ethnographic lexicons.[62] The traveling wax museums, with their "ethnographic collections," and the mise-en-scènes of "primitive" everyday life in the *Völkerschauen*, extended the scientific "sensibility" into the sphere of popular culture and commercial mass amusements and amplified it. The accumulating colonial library was the materialization of colonial knowledge in its most respectable, traditional form.

Their reverence for science certainly explains to a considerable extent SPD librarians' willingness to buy and recommend colonialist books. It is no doubt true that many socialist librarians offered travel literature and ethnography in spite of strong political and pedagogical convictions, and that they did so out of the need to compete with *Volksbibliotheken* and colportage.[63] They were certainly aware at some level of the contradictions inherent in lending colonialist texts in socialist libraries. Social Democratic newspapers poured forth scorn, sarcasm, and ridicule on the colonial enterprise. Of course, frequent, biting criticism of colonial scandals and violence concealed growing fissures within the party leadership on the question of colonialism, and indeed the acceptance of colonial travelogues as science reflected broad ambivalence about the utility and ethics of the empire—and a growing acceptance of its scientific, economic, technological modernity, its progressive inevitability. Still, the socialist daily press was unremitting—and could be scathing—in its criticism of colonialist literature. In response, for example, to the enthusiastic reception of Frenssen's *Peter Moor*, the *Schwäbische Volkszeitung* accused reviewers of either not having read the book at all or having "become so hardened that the most terrible accusations of human barbarism and blind madness no longer arouse in them any feeling." The novel—as a representation of reality, of colonial violence—was "more reliable than any government report or colonial travelogue, a ringing accusation against the decay of German culture apparent in our colonial policy."[64]

Colonial literature could nevertheless find redemption in science. The *Bibliothekar*, for example, recommended *Im Goldlande des Altertums*, by the

"African Peoples": the work of Leipzig lithographers and bookbinders (1906). "Afrika," *Meyers Großes Konversations-Lexikon,* 6th ed. (Leipzig: Bibliographisches Institut, 1906).

loathed Carl Peters, with the parenthetical assurance that the "results of the investigations described in it are recognized by science." A review of Duke Adolf Friedrich of Mecklenburg's account of his travels in Central Africa negotiates the problem in similar fashion. The reviewer advises SPD librarians that

> the contents are to be read critically, not only because various passages work as a peculiar sort of propaganda for German colonial policy but also on account of contradictions in judging the savages, their morality, etc. . . . These are neither the only—nor the most glaring—contradictions. One has only to read how . . . the duke praises the embarrassing justice that the German colonial authorities exercise over the natives. . . . That the work contains other jingoist [*hurrapatriotisch*] passages need astonish no further. Alongside these, to be sure, one finds abundant material on land and people, and reading the work pays handsomely.[65]

The geographical and ethnographic information—the innocuous sounding "abundant material on land and people"—somehow counterbalances the jingoist-colonialist content, as if these aspects of the work contradicted one another. Socialists thus seemed to count on a discerning reading public to grasp and preserve this distinction when reading colonialist texts. That the distinction, validated by "science," was dubious in the first place does not appear to have come up.

The development of geography and ethnography as popular science was, of course, an important point in the dense discursive formation of colonialism in the Kaiserreich. To emphasize workers' readings of colonialist literature as science—even within the context of the SPD library—implies no simple suppression or displacement of the ideological function of these texts. Rather, popular geography and anthropology in this period constituted a particular form of colonial knowledge that operated within the broader discursive field. As Leipzig professor and publisher Hans Meyer insisted, science was itself political: beginning with the acquisition of the African protectorates in 1884, "scientific research assumed a *national character.*" Both chair of the Leipzig Geographical Society and member of the board of the Colonial Society, Meyer exemplified the connections between science, commerce, and colonialism. "Just as the English, French, and Belgians have for a long time pursued political and mercantile aims on their research expeditions," Meyer continued, "so now the Germans follow this example in their own colonies."[66] Popular "scientific" literature—exploration accounts above all—reflected this constellation. Science did not redeem a popular book from its jingoist-colonialist contents; it could sanction and legitimize them, just as colonial adventure could add luster to science. But it is at the deeper level of "colonial enlightenment," the development of an unanswerable colonial rationality—against a field of colportage enchantment, through fierce social antagonism—that colonial discourse discloses its political implications.

The intertextual play of popular Darwinism and Stanley's bestsellers suggests one way that respective working-class readings of scientific and travel literature may have produced discursive effects. Popularizers of Darwin—including prominent colonialists like Friedrich Ratzel—attracted widespread interest among both workers and SPD party functionaries.[67] A 1914 brochure entitled "Hausbüchereien für Arbeiter," published in Leipzig as a guide for workers interested in acquiring personal libraries, included popular Darwinist books like Wilhelm Bölsche's *Abstammung des Menschen*, Rudolf Bommeli's *Die Weltalter*, and *Moses oder Darwin?* by Arnold Dodel.[68] Edward Aveling's *Die Darwin'sche Theorie* was the first volume in the SPD's low-priced Internationale Bibliothek, and Bommeli, Dodel, and Aveling all published with the SPD's Dietz Verlag, their works advertised in SPD newspapers.[69]

And of course the celebrated Stanley had many working-class fans. For example, among the most-read titles under "Naturwissenschaft und Reisebeschreibungen" in an SPD library in Leipzig in 1911 were four titles by Darwin, borrowed altogether twenty-seven times, and three copies of Richard Roth's *Stanleys Reise durch den dunklen Weltteil*, borrowed twenty-one times. A dozen years earlier, Stanley's *Im dunkelsten Afrika* and various volumes on Darwin were consistently prominent among "works with educational content" borrowed by Leipzig printers' and typesetters' assistants.[70] Aside from their popularity, there was no obvious connection between Stanley and the Darwinists, and it is not necessarily the case that the same workers read both. Still, given the broad popularity of Darwinist theory and the tendency to think of colonial literature as science, it is not unreasonable to infer a kind of cross-fertilization linking the discourses represented in the different texts. This is especially true of their respective representations of racial difference.

The circulation of Darwinist theory—itself often associated with progressive socialist politics—shaped conditions for the working-class reception of colonialist texts just as colonial travelogues—associated variously with both science and reactionary politics, shaped readings of popular Darwinism. Darwinists turned to colonial Africa to illustrate evolutionary theories of race just as explorers invoked Darwin when describing Africans. Both genres used the common racial idiom of the colonial era; they were among its most important sources. In his *In Darkest Africa*, Stanley indulges in displays of pseudoscientific erudition that lent the work an aura of scholarly respectability in the minds of many readers. Inclined toward physiognomic readings of race, Stanley perceives in one African the "true negroidal cast of features," distinguishes in others between the semi-Ethiopic and the full. Though his typologies appear vaguely scientific—they were borrowed from popular Darwinism—he wears his science lightly as, shifting his gaze from one specimen to the next, he tosses off spontaneous racial classifications: "The monkey-eyed woman had a remarkable pair of mischievous orbs, protruding lips overhanging her chin, a prominent abdomen, narrow, flat chest, sloping shoulders, long arms, feet turned greatly inwards and very short lower legs, as being fitly characteristic of the link long sought between the average modern humanity and its Darwinian progenitors, and certainly deserving of being classed as an extremely low, degraded, almost a bestial type of a human being."[71] Images of the primitive, the apelike, the bestial, degenerate, and prehistoric African filled the pages of colonial literature in its variously respectable and trashy forms. In "scientific" travel accounts like Stanley's, they counted as anthropological observations.

The images bear unmistakable resemblance to what working-class readers encountered in the pages of Darwin's German interpreters. There was a simple, powerful reciprocity between colonial-scientific and popular-Darwinist discourses about race. The various African peoples were "incapable of a true inner culture and of a higher mental development," according to Ernst Haeckel. The geographical distribution of the four lowest species of mankind—the wooly-haired Papuan, Hottentot, Kaffir, and Negro—happened to correspond precisely (if not exclusively) to native peoples in German colonies in Africa and the Pacific. This was natural and inevitable, for among men the "more highly developed, the more favored . . . possess the positive inclination and the certain tendency to spread more and more at the expense of the lower, more backward, and smaller groups." Europeans, "by means of the higher development of their brain . . . have already spread the net of their dominion over the whole globe."[72]

These symmetrical, linked representations of race reinforced a discourse whose origins are scarcely evident in Darwin's work. Of course, nineteenth-century racism had an intellectual history of its own, preceding Darwinism. In the case of Darwin's advocates in Germany, whose variations on evolutionary theory relied upon the example of the primitive black African or Pacific Islander, the origins of racism lay in colonial literature itself—in travelogue. This aspect of popular Darwinism was, as Alfred Kelly suggests, "little more than an updated version of the old travel literature on exotic peoples."[73] Indeed, the popularizer Ludwig Büchner, in a "hasty sketch of the natural and moral history of savage peoples" emphasizing their "brutal degradation and irrationality," identified the travelogues as the single most valuable source of scientific information: "Whoever then wishes to form a judgment as to the true nature of man . . . must . . . grasp at nature itself with both hands and draw his knowledge from the innumerable springs which flow there in the richest abundance. Nowhere do we find these springs richer and more copious than in the reports of travelers in distant lands as to the savage men and tribes which they have met with."[74]

The racial aspect of popular Darwinism in Germany was inseparable from colonial travel literature, and the travelogue was indebted to the Darwinists.

Popular science, as distinct from pure colonial politics, formed an important framework of reception among working-class readers, for whom both genres were popular. Both, however, also supplied explicit cultural and scientific justifications for colonialism, "naturalizing" it as ineluctable modern reality. The political and scientific strands are so closely interwoven that it is difficult to attribute to either a dominant influence over working-class reading. For some readers—the SPD librarians, for example—the spell of science was sufficient to justify recommending colonialist books. For others, science—as exploration, civilization, progress—no doubt explained colonialism itself. Whether or not this ultimately translated into enthusiasm for the colonial empire, the popularity of both genres suggests a broad familiarity with the brand of racist and "rationalizing" worldview that sanctioned and sustained colonialism.

But if the boundary between science and political colonialism proved porous and unstable, this was no less true of the division between respectable scientific literature and the sensationalized adventure that haunted it—between colonial knowledge and enchantment. If, by the end of the nineteenth century, the scientific monograph and the travelogue had evolved into distinct genres, municipal and workers' libraries, for all the anxiety about trash literature or colonial chauvinism, did not yet reflect this.[75] As we have seen, ambivalence about the nature of colonial literature was deep and commonplace. Already in the 1870s, the controversy surrounding the objectivity and credibility of Stanley's *Through the Dark Continent* had marked a high point in discussions about the scientific validity of travel accounts.[76] In the contradictions between, on the one hand, their broad popularity and bestseller, adventure-story style and, on the other, their scientific pretensions, Stanley's books embodied the genre confusion that remained typical of colonial travel literature up to 1914. By 1896, in the preface to his *Südwestafrika*, Karl Dove is still making careful claims for "the scientific rigor of [the book's] geographical content as much as for the truth of the actual accounts of travel and war," promising that the book will "serve as a means of instruction" even as it offers "something to those who pick it up only for entertainment."[77] Working-class readers frequently encountered this generic ambiguity in the interplay of science, politics, and entertainment. Books that counted as science for some readers appealed to others as tales of exotic, dangerous, and thrilling adventure.

"Of all the sciences," observed Joseph Conrad, it is geography that "finds its origin in action, and what is more, in adventurous action of the kind that appeals to sedentary people who like to dream of arduous adventure in the manner of prisoners dreaming behind bars of all the hardships and hazards of . . . liberty."[78] We might well extend the analogy to explain the appeal of colonial travelogues to modern industrial workers in Germany's big cities. Among working-class patrons of a Berlin library in the 1890s, for example, one group of readers "regularly studies scientific works," while "another, larger part of the membership are only casual readers, plagued by boredom, who wish to while away the time with easily understood readings (novels, travelogues)."[79] Indeed, travel and adventure literature in general appealed to working-class men more than it did to bourgeois readers, or to women readers in general.[80] For these seekers of amusement and distraction from everyday life, accounts of colonial adventures promised, perhaps, an occasional escape for a few hours from an oppressive existence.

The many "true accounts" of scientific exploration and military action teemed with gripping stories of brave soldiers at war, heroic explorers deep in the jungle, and encounters with pygmies, cannibals, and snake worshipers. Wissmann's famous account of his journey in the 1880s from the Angolan coast to Lake Tanganyika and on to Zanzibar is representative of the more respectable layers of the genre. Sponsored by the Africa Society in Berlin, Wissmann could write as a kind of heroic geographer-explorer whose entertaining tale of guns, crocodiles, Arab slave traders, and jungle primitives served both science and fatherland. The botanist-explorer Georg Schweinfurth became famous for travels among pygmies and cannibals.[81] Herbert Ward, an Englishman living along the Congo in the days of Stanley's Emin Pasha expedition, revealed the "secrets of tropical Africa," among them amulets, charm-doctors, fetish-men, and human sacrifice. Anthropophagi abound in all accounts, "indulging in a light repast off the limbs of some unfortunate slave" or, gathered in "orgies," "banqueting upon the bodies of the enemies slaughtered in some recent conflict." They live in houses "decorated with human skulls" and wear necklaces of human teeth.[82] Elements of the fantastic and the exotic, the dark secrets of the fabulist's Africa or South Seas, likely excited many—perhaps most—proletarian readers of colonial literature, and at the expense of proper "colonial enlightenment." Certainly this was the fear of cultural crusaders, colonialists, and socialists alike.

Walter Hofmann, the Dresden librarian, emphasized the enchanted mode of reading colonial literature in his curious "psychological" typology of the working-class reader. Most books identified by colonialists or socialists for their propagandistic or scientific value appeared to Hofmann as unredeemed fantasy. Hofmann did recognize that workers might read the same book in different ways, as science or adventure, and tried to resolve the ambiguity by considering individual books within the context of a worker's broader reading pattern. When requesting books, workers rarely made a distinction between "war literature, travelogue, and descriptions of exotic cultures" on the one hand and scientific works on the other (a distinction, for that matter, that most librarians did not seem to make, even as, paradoxically, they insisted on hierarchies of science and entertainment). "Whenever a travelogue was clearly read in the context of other educational or scientific works . . . and to the exclusion of all other travel literature, it was listed in the corresponding scientific section" of his typology, Hofmann explains. Having recognized this problem, he goes on to show that workers were much likelier to

Illustrating the ethnographic-fantastic: "A Visit to the Snake Temple of Waida" (1878). Richard Oberländer, ed., *Westafrika vom Senegal bis Benguela: Reisen und Schilderungen aus Senegambien, Ober- und Niederguinea* (Leipzig: Otto Spamer, 1878). Courtesy New York Public Library.

read for amusement than enlightenment. There were occasional exceptions, like the young mechanic who was "driven by a strong interest in geography and ethnography, which thrilling travel accounts by no means satisfy." Instead of the usual fare, he consumed "volume for volume Alexander von Humboldt's classic travels in the equinoctial regions of the new continent."[83] But most working-class readers—like the twenty-year-old millworker who read Thonner's *Im afrikanischen Urwald* or the forty-three-year-old instrument maker who borrowed Buchholz's *Reisen in Westafrika*—were drawn to the merely exciting—the ethnographic-fantastic—whether in the form of colonial war and travel accounts or adventure novels.[84]

Hofmann interpreted the similar division among readers of belletristic works in terms of, once again, a proletarian need "to expand the narrow everyday reality of existence through imagined excursions into the faraway and exotic." And he observed that this "need in a given reader is seldom paired with an interest in modern realist and naturalist descriptions of the present, making it clear that what we have here before us is something like two types." These were the "Zola reader" and the "Gerstäcker reader," the latter especially drawn to the pleasures of the ethnographic-fantastic. In Hofmann's hierarchy of proletarian readers, the Zola reader, with his naturalist appetite, is the more sophisticated, while readers almost exclusively of travel and war accounts "represent a whole other type"—indeed, a pathologically escapist one—though they are "somewhat more developed, rather more distinctive" than "the simpler minds" attracted to Jules Verne and *Die Gartenlaube*.[85] Reading Zola implied a sober grappling with social reality, while reading colonial travelogues amounted to a flight into the realm of enchantment.

The story of colonial literature and its proletarian readership does not quite fit into conventional accounts of either colonialism or working-class culture in Wilhelmine Germany. Historians most often depict colonialism as the emblem and vocation of the nationalist bourgeois, who fought the hostility of anticolonial workers and lamented the *Kolonialmüdigkeit* of most other Germans. The fundamental ambiguity of colonial literature, however, mirrors the equally fundamental heterogeneity of its audience. As it turns out, Social Democratic industrial workers and Colonial Society notables read many of the same books. Aspects of colonialism appealed to a broader, more diverse public than just the propertied and educated enthusiasts organized in nationalist pressure groups. Similarly, colonial literature tended to spill over boundaries within working-class society. The Social Democratic subculture of structured leisure developed in this period into an extensive network of associations, libraries, and educational institutions. This was in important ways a world apart from respectable, middle-class Germany, just as it distinguished itself from the burgeoning new commercialized mass culture.[86] Yet colonial literature appears to have found readers in each of these spheres, in SPD libraries no less than in public libraries or the colportage trade, irrespective of class or political factors.

The interplay of ideology, science, and fantasy in German colonial literature, and the multiple, overlapping frameworks of reception, complicate the attribution of particular social and political functions to such literature among workers. It might be that an imagined terra incognita provided a kind of idealized space for the projection of workers' utopian longings, an effect entirely unrecognized by contemporary observers and critics.[87] More certain was the propaganda function in the dissemination of colonial literature, an attempted manipulation of the masses to secure broad support for empire, naval expansion, and their corollaries. And there was the sheer entertainment, the pleasure of exoticism and adventure, which may have had the additional political function of diverting workers' attention away from the everyday dissatisfactions of political and social inequality endured in crowded industrial cities.

This double mechanism of manipulation and distraction leads us back, perhaps inevitably, to the concept of "social imperialism," obviously applicable in the case of workers reading about the empire.[88] It has become clear that some workers were quite receptive to the colonialist dimension of bourgeois culture, to colonial knowledge, even in SPD reading rooms. More often, though, the diffusion of colonialist writing among working-class readers was less direct than this. The organized colonial movement played a relatively small role in getting colonial literature into workers' hands. And in any case, the concept by itself does not suffice to explain the transmission and function of colonial knowledge and sentiment among and across different social classes. As we have seen in the case of literature, the mediation of colonialism was indirect and uncertain, following intricate channels and conducted by an unlikely combination of bourgeois pressure groups, SPD librarians, and colporteur peddlers. Understanding the effects of this dissemination depends upon knowledge of much more than libraries and reading patterns: the many dimensions of popular culture and associational life, local politics and social structure, economy and labor relations. Still, it is clear that colonialism did not finally succeed in peeling workers away from the SPD, even as it divided the ranks of party leaders and intellectuals. The working class did not, for the most part, abandon the SPD in the "Hottentot elections" of 1907. Nor did workers defect to colonialist associations or parties—who, as we have seen, scarcely knew what to do with them. It appears that a broad consensus gradually emerged in Germany on the advantages, necessity, and even the inevitability of colonialism, a consensus founded in part on the unremitting barrage of patriotic, racist, and violent language and imagery in popular colonial literature—but perhaps more importantly on the codes of science and colonial knowledge, constituted through the anxious conflict around reading. It is remarkable that, under such circumstances, so many workers persisted up to the outbreak of war in 1914 in their indifference or outright hostility to the blandishments of the colonialists.

CHAPTER SIX

The Hottentot Elections

Colonial Politics, Socialist Politics

> *The type of industrial worker created by capitalism is always
> vigorously anti-imperialist. In the individual case, skillful agitation
> may persuade the working masses to approve or remain neutral . . . but
> no initiative for a forcible policy of expansion ever emanates from this
> quarter. On this point official socialism unquestionably formulates not
> merely the interests but also the unconscious will of the workers. Even
> less than peasant imperialism is there any such thing as socialist or
> other working-class imperialism.*
> —Joseph Schumpeter, "The Sociology of Imperialisms," 1919

> *The signs of the times are a "general" enthusiasm regarding
> [imperialist] prospects, a passionate defense of imperialism, and every
> possible embellishment of its real nature. The imperialist ideology also
> penetrates the working class. There is no Chinese Wall between it and
> other classes. The leaders of the so-called "Social-Democratic" Party of
> Germany are today justly called "social-imperialists," that is, socialists
> in words and imperialists in deeds.*
> —V. I. Lenin, *Imperialism, The Highest Stage of Capitalism*, 1916

We imagine the scene: a cold, damp December night in Hamburg, ten
or twelve people in a small pub in the Nagelsweg, the dim room thick
with tobacco smoke and the smell of beer. A man named Hinz, a spy for
the Hamburg police, arrives about twenty minutes before ten o'clock, to
listen. It is mid-December 1904, several months after the Herero revolt in
German Southwest Africa, and a conversation among four of the patrons—
they appear to be workers—turns to the unfolding German war there. One
worker, pessimistic about German prospects, predicts that the "uprising in
Southwest Africa will not be put down for a long time yet and that probably at least as many soldiers as are already there now must be sent over."
His companion, bitterly resentful, condemns as "a scandal" that "so many
people have been sacrificed" for "a worthless desert that will yield nothing
in the foreseeable future." It's regrettable, he thinks, that so many people
are drawn into such "nonsense," to which another retorts, "If people are so
stupid and care so little for their own lives then it's their fault, and one has
to just let them go." More important, he wants to know, "who is supposed

to pay the huge costs" of the war? Still another is thinking about how to educate and mobilize Germans, complaining that there had been insufficient protest, that the "protest rallies must be repeated at brief intervals and extended all across Germany."[1]

When, with our police spy Hinz, we overhear such rancorous working-class talk of worthless sacrifice, of blood and money squandered in the desert, and of hatching plans to mobilize the indifferent or misguided masses, we hear a kind of collective ventriloquism: the embodied rhetoric of countless Social Democratic headlines and slogans, articles and leaflets, lectures and speeches. Ordinarily, of course, beer and brutishness—pubs and empire—are thought to go hand in hand. As J. A. Hobson put it in *Imperialism* just two years before, " 'Panem et circenses' interpreted into English means cheap booze."[2] Cheap booze and, moreover, cheap talk. "The saloon, the club, the train, and other common avenues of conversation helped in the work of propaganda," he argued, feeding a political discourse of "short stories and bar tittle-tattle."[3] But in Germany, with its strong Social Democratic Party, circumstances were quite different. The machinery of imperial propaganda, and of commercial mass amusement, was powerful, but, as we shall see, the force and momentum of the SPD critique and mobilization nevertheless enabled a stubborn working-class resistance. Such bar-room chatter, right in the bustling imperial entrepôt of Hamburg, is but one vivid reflection of a discourse widely diffused among workers and local organizers of the SPD.

By February 1907, two years on, such working-class anticolonialism would be severely tested—although events in Southwest Africa had vindicated the pessimism and anger voiced in the Hamburg pub. By all accounts, even among many Social Democrats, that winter marked the apotheosis of colonial enthusiasm in Germany: the dramatic dissolution of parliament and fierce elections following it—national elections fought for the first time over the "colonial question." These were the so-called "Hottentot elections," occasioned by the protracted, brutal, very costly war in German Southwest Africa, first against the Herero, and then against the Nama, the eponymous "Hottentots." Nationalist fervor and the passions stirred by war combined, crystallizing in a new mass enthusiasm that, for the first time, substantially transcended class divisions that had bedeviled and defined German colonialism from its origins.

By 1907, of course, the German Colonial Society was powerfully shaped by these divisions: by a membership carefully limited to the propertied and the educated, by a pessimistic, sharply attenuated apprehension of "the masses," and by a fundamental antagonism with the vigorously anticolonial SPD. After some twenty years of perplexed, halting efforts to make the overseas empire popular, colonialists in 1907 believed they had finally achieved some success among the "broad masses" of factory workers, peasants, shopkeepers, and artisans. It was the heyday of a robust and vicious propagandism against the "enemies" of the Reich: the bloodthirsty savages of Southwest Africa and their sympathizers, Social Democracy and the Catholic Center Party. As one colonialist put it, with characteristic derision, there was "gradual clarification, too, of the colonial policy of the bar-room [*Stammtisch*]. One no longer looks for Southwest Africa in the South Seas, and even knows better now than to mistake Togo for Tokyo."[4] The ordinary German seemed, at last, within reach.

Even Lenin, driven by no less antipathy toward German Social Democracy than were the bourgeois colonialists themselves, argued in his 1916 work *Imperialism* that "The signs of the times are a . . . passionate defense of imperialism, and every possible embellishment of its real nature. The imperialist ideology also penetrates the working class. There is no Chinese Wall between it and other classes."[5] This in response to the enthusiasm for war in 1914, but also to the quickening revisionism among German Social Democrats, the growing acceptance of a "reformed," "humane," and "scientific" idea of imperialism that had taken root already before 1907, part loss of political nerve, part surrender to the economic axioms of colonial discourse. The electoral defeat of 1907 energized this tendency. Leading Social Democrats like Eduard Bernstein, Gustav Noske, and Richard Calwer produced controversial analyses portending a socialist embrace of some version of empire.

But what of the workers themselves? What do we find if we look beyond the world of party intellectuals and leaders, into the proletarian public sphere, into actual *political* life at the grassroots? If ever there was a moment in the Kaiserreich when the machinery of imperial manipulation might implant among the German working class its particular racist and economic worldview, it had come. Certainly this is how Hobson understood the Boer War, which had, he wrote, opened up a "panorama of vulgar pride and crude sensationalism to a great inert mass."[6] But there was no real jingoist mob, no working-class *Hurrahkanaille* in Germany, nor even anything to match, for example, the more extreme passions of the middle-class Pan-German League. The popular reception of empire was often less vivid, and altogether more elusive. The revisionist drift in the national SPD at precisely this moment belies the local reality of a persistent, unmistakable anticolonialism among workers. There is a history of powerful anticolonial conviction in the Kaiserreich; it flourished among politicized working people even as the leaders who had given it direction and momentum began themselves to succumb to the promise of empire. The "colonial policy of the bar-room" turns out to be sober socialist critique.

In the effort to say something about the mass politics of colonialism, historians tend to scrutinize the response to empire by the leadership of the Social Democratic Party, ostensibly the party of the German working class.[7] Conclusions about working-class attitudes scarcely gesture toward the everyday action and opinion of rank-and-file Social Democrats, much less the ill-defined proletarian world beyond the party.[8] Yet if, in 1907, Social

Democracy seemed to waver before the powerful strategy of the Right, and indeed to grow ever more receptive to colonialism, the experience of workers themselves tells a different story. With the elections, German colonial policy became an important political issue for workers. Colonialism made headlines, filled newspaper columns and public meetings, and pulled thousands of new working-class voters into the electoral process. But it was really only the scale of the working-class response that was new. The SPD had worked since before the turn of the century to shape a discourse among working people that would enable a broadly based critique of empire. Working-class responses to the war in Southwest Africa evolved out of this older, broader discourse on colonial violence and exploitation, provoked especially at the turn of the century by the Boer War and the Boxer Rebellion.[9] In the multiple forms of working-class engagement in early 1907—through local party institutions and in the language of local party organs—we observe the fruition of this strong countervailing force. If revisionism had begun to erode the powerful, united front of SPD anticolonialism at the top, among the leadership, the very success of anticolonial policy, its rhetoric and activism, suggest that any neutralization or retreat among the more radical rank and file was anything but a foregone conclusion, in the immediate aftermath of 1907 or in 1914.

The elections followed immediately upon Chancellor von Bülow's dramatic dissolution of the Reichstag on 13 December 1906, prompted by the Center Party's rejection of a request for 29 million marks in supplementary funding for the expedition in Southwest Africa.[10] The previous two years had been a trying time for supporters of German *Weltpolitik*—and an extended field day for their critics. In 1905, the Maji Maji Rebellion had broken out in East Africa, and the Kaiser's trip to Tangier had precipitated the First Morocco Crisis.[11] Colonial scandals continued to generate sensational press reports of greed, corruption, brutality, and sex. Most troubling of all, however, was the army's inability to crush the uprising in Southwest Africa. Despite the expenditure of nearly 600 million marks and General Lothar von Trotha's notorious extermination policy, the Herero, and later the Nama, had been able to tie down some 14,000 troops in the colony. Disease and the implacable, waterless terrain prolonged the bitter campaign.[12]

With the rejection of the colonial spending measure, however, the nationalist Right had its own scandal to conjure with: the betrayal by Center and SPD politicians of German youths struggling against cruel savages under a pitiless sun. The elections would not be about suffrage, tariff, or tax reform or any of the myriad matters of conflicting material interest that commonly defined politics. They were to be about national honor and loyalty to the nation on the field of empire. Bülow's government, together with the Colonial Office, the parties of the nationalist Right, and the powerful *nationale Verbände*, orchestrated the elections as an appeal to patriotic sentiment, colonial race hatred, and fear of socialism.[13]

Postcard view: the war in Southwest Africa (ca. 1906).

Already, with the lapse of the antisocialist laws and the rise of the SPD in the 1890s, colonial discourse had changed. Whereas previously the lower classes represented an object of collective anxiety, as pauperized, deracinated "dangerous classes" in need of homes overseas (colonialism as what "we" need to do about "them"), by the later 1890s they were increasingly the targets of colonial propaganda. Colonialists began to address the working classes directly and tried to persuade them that the overseas empire offered solutions to the ills of industrial society. They emphasized the place of workers in a broad scheme of colonial production and consumption, in which jobs depended on rubber, tobacco, cotton, and other imports, and rising income in turn bought *Kolonialwaren* for working-class households. A reinvigorated, if naïve and often maladroit colonial movement had begun in the late 1890s to reach out to broader masses of people through veterans' associations, the "yellow" trade unions, Evangelical Workers Associations, lending libraries, lantern-slide lectures, the 1896 Colonial Exhibition, and the Colonial Museum.

At the same time, colonial political discourse became more shrill and divisive, reflecting the fragmentation and polarization of German society. Far from uniting Germans around a great national task, or distracting them from problems at home, the *Kolonialfrage* magnified conflict. The SPD took every opportunity to expose the contradictions at the base of colonial ideology: the impossibility of proletarian emigration, the high price of colonial goods, and the marginal value of colonial imports. Colonialists, infuriated by the jeering obstructionism, became increasingly explicit in framing their politics in terms of nationalism and strident antisocialism. The elections of 1907 crystallized these differences, amplified them, and transformed the nature of colonialist politics. Whereas the colonial debate had in previous years provided both socialists and the Center Party with a string of scandals and failures, the drama of the war in Southwest Africa enabled the nationalist Right to recast the issue as one of patriotism and loyalty. The elections proved a watershed moment, marking the transition of colonialism from an emblem of class division to a potential force for national integration.

Working-class voters were important targets for the barrage of colonialist and nationalist propaganda. "Up to now," complained Colonial Secretary Bernhard Dernburg in an election speech, "only the industrial workers have had true benefits from the colonies—they who now want to condemn wholesale the entire colonial policy."[14] The president of the Colonial Society urged its members to take advantage of the "exceptional and auspicious opportunity" to "strengthen the colonial conscience of the voting masses."[15] The society collaborated with the Pan-Germans, the Navy League, nationalist publishers, and others to distribute flyers, brochures, postcards, and newspaper articles, often through factory owners.[16] They distributed some 150,000 copies of "Soldiers' Letters from German Southwest Africa" and over one million of "Germany, Hold on to Your Colonies."[17] A propaganda leaflet headlined "That Is the Truth!" depicted the horrors of war in Southwest Africa,

"Advancing against the Enemy": postcard view from Southwest Africa (ca. 1906).

the terrifying black enemy, German heroism, and the criminal responsibility of the SPD and Center. The dramatic picture on the cover shows a family of German settlers under attack by demonic blacks, the sky aflame in the lurid red and yellow of their burning farm.[18] At a lecture to some 1,000 people in Solingen over 350 brochures on the war were sold to workers for 10 to 60 pfennigs.[19] The Colonial Society also coordinated the performance of short dramatic pieces and patriotic tableaux vivants in "theaters, circuses, and similar institutions," where patriots acted out scenes from military life in uniforms furnished by the army.[20] The Social Democrat Carl Severing later remembered how, since the main elections had been scheduled for the Kaiser's birthday, by electing "deputies loyal to the government the voters were supposed to offer the monarch a kind of birthday present."[21] Propagandists railed against the "Hottentottenblock" of SPD and Center, the "black-red League for the Defense of Kaffirdom against Germans."[22] In Nuremberg, the local paper complained of "a leaflet from the Social Democrats," seeking "to entirely cover up the fundamental issue of this election. It deals quite thoroughly with the colonial scandals objected to by all parties, and with the costs of German colonial policy, but entirely conceals that the Center and Social Democracy refuse the means necessary to maintain the military readiness of the German troops standing against the savage and cruel enemy."[23]

The Colonial Economic Committee issued streams of commodity propaganda pamphlets, some one million of them distributed through some 5,000 manufacturers directly to their workers: "Copper and the German Colonies," "Cotton and the German Colonies," "Rubber and the German Colonies," and so on.[24] The Berlin-based Colonial Political Action Committee provided pamphlets nationally to firms for distribution among workers, for example to some 1,300 workers in the factories of Elberfeld, in the Rhineland, or another 600 in Ruhrort.[25] Colonialists tried to lure workers away from the SPD both by appealing to feelings of national identity and solidarity and by reiterating the material benefits—markets and tropical commodities—of colonialism to workers.[26] Colonial Secretary Dernburg insisted in a Berlin speech that popular discontent with colonial sacrifice was a problem most often of knowledge, knowledge that had "not yet penetrated to broad segments of the people." Colonization, properly understood, would speak for itself: "the exploitation of the soil, its natural resources, the flora and fauna, and above all the people, for the economy of the colonizing nation."[27]

Still, it does not automatically follow that local contests revolved around colonial policy in the way suggested by the national political discourse. Leading Social Democrats later disagreed about whether the elections had really been about colonialism in the first place. There were many other social, political, and economic matters of particular municipal or regional significance for working-class voters.[28] In Leipzig, for example, the unequal franchise for both the city government and the Saxon Landtag excited strong feelings and had already alienated many working-class voters from the parties of the Bülow bloc. In Düsseldorf, the particular local configuration of politics, together with SPD ambivalence toward the whole issue of empire, similarly marked the contest.[29] Whatever the appeal of jingoism to local workers, nationalists had to contend with longstanding class antagonisms over food prices, housing, labor issues, and glaring inequalities in the political and judicial systems. The nationalist parties exerted every effort to transform the elections into a rush of patriotic feeling, a mass rite of devotion to the fatherland. If their victory suggests that they were successful, neither their intentions nor the overall results are by themselves sufficient evidence that, for workers, the elections turned mainly on the matter of empire or fatherland among so many longstanding issues.[30]

Very often, though, they did. Whatever fissures divided party leadership, local branches of the SPD frequently took up the challenge of the nationalist parties and fought the elections squarely on the national-colonial ground chosen by the Bülow government and its allies.[31] As Eduard Bernstein observed following the elections, if "the parties, and not least Social Democracy, also raised an abundance of other questions in election speeches and literature," it was "still the colonial question that set the tone of the campaign."[32] Colonialist discourse that had already penetrated the experience of working-class voters or readers or spectators at the panoramas or cinematographs now became prominent in the arena of SPD electoral politics. Colonialism by no means eclipsed other contentious issues. It did, however, supply the main topic of SPD headlines, meetings, posters, speeches, and pamphlets as organizers and journalists wove anti-imperialism into their propaganda: "Down with all brutal men who by their cruelty have shamed Germany's reputation! Down with reaction and the prison bill! Down with the three-class voting law in Saxony!"[33] The drama of the election, the vivid rhetoric of both socialists and nationalists, and the ultimate loss of parliamentary seats by the SPD transformed colonialism for the first time into a general theme of working-class politics. Even if many working-class voters remained politically indifferent to German colonialism, after the winter of 1907 they could no longer ignore it.

The party sharply attacked the large, unevenly shared costs of empire-building, the brutal violence of colonialism, and laid the blame for the Herero revolt at the feet of settlers and colonial officials.[34] But it is at the local, grassroots level that we see the real vigor and reach of working-class anti-colonialism. Eduard Bernstein, looking back on working-class mobilization that year, observed that the rank and file collectively amounted to a "proletarian army," many of them "vigorous enthusiasts in the prime of life, and ready to take upon themselves any work necessary for the distribution of the electoral literature of the party and the working up of the electors." And not only in cities. "Clubs of Socialist Cyclists exist in large numbers and train their members for efforts in rural districts."[35] Across Germany, the forms of local engagement had been prepared over the previous eight or ten years. In Leipzig, SPD newspapers and public meetings had long before introduced many workers to a clamorous anti-imperialism.[36] As early as 1900, an urgent address "To Our Readers!" in the *Leipziger Volkszeitung* had begun to interpret the seizure of Kiaochow, the Boxer Rebellion, and the Boer War as related parts of a single capitalist-imperialist system that threatened to bring about world war. In October 1906, a series of articles on "Colonial Policy" criticized and condemned both the economic and the emigrationist strands of German colonialism. The paper explained imperialism in the conventional economic terms of capitalist overproduction, the acquisition of markets, and the export of capital. It went on to ridicule the German colonies as a costly failure by comparison with other European colonial empires: "The difference consists only in that, in other countries, where a continual stream of gold flows in from the colonies, these riches are realized from the plundered natives, while in Germany, where the colonial policy is only a failed caricature—not producing gold but consuming it—gold for Tippelskirch and Woermann must be raised from German taxpayers, and 'colonial policy' is only a pretext to exploit their own people for the benefit of a few capitalists."[37] The failed colonial policy was not even successful in the brutal exploitation of native peoples, scoffed the *Volkszeitung*, relying instead on the exploitation of overtaxed German workers to provide "colonial profits" for a few firms and individuals.

In parts of Bavaria, local SPD branches had successfully mobilized workers to protest colonial violence in Africa and Asia. In 1900, for example, workers rallied in Lechhausen, Augsburg, and across southern Bavaria against *Weltpolitik* and the China expedition.[38] The socialist *Augsburger Volkszeitung* continually attacked colonial policy, even comparing the condition of German workers to that of colonized Africans. "The very ruling classes who brutalize and enslave the workers here in Germany carry on the same fine business with the blacks there," in the colonies.[39] And it was the workers who were the "worst affected" by the "monstrous, heavy consequences" of the China expedition, which "cut so deeply into the life of the German people."[40] The 1905 Berlin Colonial Congress was painted as a "colorful society of dukes and counts, generals and Christian servants of God, of privy councilors, professors, and bankers, ever ready to grant, in uncounted millions, the money of the German worker" for a "desert sand policy" (*Wüstensandpolitik*) that served only the lust for adventure of the few.[41] After the turn of the century, readers encountered ever more sensational headlines: "COLONIAL SWAMP," "HORRIBLE REVELATIONS FROM SOUTHWEST AFRICA," "COLONIAL FIASCO," "THE ADVENTURE IN SOUTHWEST AFRICA," "COLONIZATION WITH THE WHIP," "COLONIAL ABOMINATION," and "A BLOODY DEFEAT IN SOUTHWEST AFRICA."

When in 1900 a Hamburg worker accuses the European powers of "snipping off" Chinese lands and introducing "European culture by force," or in

1905 a Saxon factory worker sarcastically mocks the "stroll to China" by "defenders of the fatherland," they reproduce the language and tone then being popularized by the SPD.[42] The same rhetoric colored the *Leipziger Volkszeitung* during the elections, when it attacked the "colonial swindle" perpetrated by the National Liberals and the Conservatives—the "*Schutztruppe* of corruption"—who concealed a "barbaric war of extermination" caused by the dispossession and mistreatment of the Herero by German settlers. "Robbed of their property, often ill-treated, almost without rights, abandoned to . . . foreign intruders," the Herero "finally grasped at the most extreme means, rebellion against the oppressor."[43] Reasoning of this sort represented bold dissent from the jingoism and racist demonization of the Herero common in the German press. Indeed, the Leipzig police observed a stubborn radicalism in the *Volkszeitung*, even as other elements in the SPD were beginning to articulate a more moderate position on colonialism. Police reports warned that in 1907, as in the previous year, the paper "represented the radical faction in the Social Democratic Party," by continuing to condemn men like Eduard Bernstein, Richard Calwer, Max Schippel, and other "opportunists and revisionists on the military question and colonial policy."[44]

The scandal mongering and hyperbole in the *Leipziger Volkszeitung*, then edited by Franz Mehring, were but one aspect of a local politics in Leipzig that became, as police observers put it, "extraordinarily lively" in January 1907. Immediately following the dissolution of the Reichstag, the national parties united into a local cartel against the SPD. According to Leipzig police reports, they were "extremely active," holding "numerous large election meetings, at which Social Democrats were usually present in large numbers, so that some of these meetings took on a truly tumultuous character."[45] The full panoply of nationalist associations worked to excite patriotic fervor. The Colonial Society itself sponsored three meetings in Leipzig.[46] Also very active were the "many national 'Patriotic Associations' [*Vaterländische Vereine*], the *Vereine reichstreuer Männer*, etc., district associations and groups, which through their painstaking work contributed substantially to the election of the national candidates. They held numerous district meetings, nearly always well attended, distributed appealing leaflets, and in particular helped the nationalist press win voters."[47] Even the local Evangelical Workers Associations entered the fray, going so far as to recommend outright that their members vote for the bloc candidates.[48]

The SPD Leipzig responded with energy and venom. The *Volkszeitung* attacked Colonial Director Dernburg's campaign as a "rivulet of the shallowest phrases [that] burbles, burbles, burbles along. The imagination of an Arabian storyteller"—Dernburg himself—"unfolds enchanting pictures for the listeners." The task of disenchantment fell to the propagandists of the SPD, for whom Dernburg was like "a drunken petit bourgeois making bar-room propaganda for a veterans' association; the more pitying smiles he gets, the wilder and more enthusiastic he acts."[49] The SPD agitation committee coordinated the campaign in Leipzig, flooding the city with propaganda, leaflets, and posters publicizing colonial corruption and brutality, the Carl Peters affair, and the worthlessness of Southwest Africa.[50] SPD campaign workers plastered the four central and outer districts with nearly 12,000 posters and distributed over 100,000 handbills. A half-million leaflets blanketed outlying districts, and as many more the center of the city, although "snow, cold, and bad road conditions hindered the agitation profoundly."[51]

The intense excitement of the contest was keenest in the many political meetings held throughout December and January. There were great election rallies at which, for example, Bebel or Heinrich Lange, the SPD candidate for central Leipzig, addressed crowds of Social Democrats on the theme of colonialism. There were also numerous smaller meetings in different working-class neighborhoods across the city. Many of these occurred under the surveillance of the municipal authorities, whose handwritten reports describe something of their atmosphere. On 12 January, for example, the SPD sponsored a meeting at the Gasthof zu den drei Linden in Liebertwolkwitz, in the mostly working-class thirteenth district. Some 250 to 300 people came to hear the speaker Ludwig Bartels, who, according to the official report, at first "spoke very slowly, agreeably, [then] maliciously and sneeringly and then became in his lecture extraordinarily abusive. He began with the "murderer Peters" and repeated, 'He is a murderer! . . . [T]he government is pursuing a criminal, a bestial and murderous colonial policy.' . . . At the end of his performance, Bartels's speech received lively applause."[52] Bartels addressed another crowd the following day on the Peters and Puttkamer scandals, the extermination order of General von Trotha in Southwest Africa, and the "bestial atrocities" committed there.[53]

The Social Democrats held nearly three hundred such meetings in Leipzig, and particularly in the new industrial suburbs.[54] Speakers did not always emphasize colonialism as the principal theme; tariffs, food costs, and the Saxon franchise were among other topics addressed. German colonial policy was, however, either the most or among the most important matters discussed at virtually every one of the meetings subject to surveillance. Around 400 men and 5 women attended a meeting on colonialism in Möckern. Some 150 to 180 people attended a meeting in Eythra, where the SPD representative spoke on the "dissolution of the Reichstag, on domestic, foreign, and colonial policy, navalism and militarism, on indirect taxes, . . . and on the current condition of the German worker." The meeting was broken up by the police.[55] At a small meeting of about 50 in Schönau, the speaker attacked Trotha's extermination order, Dernburg as a "failed banker," and colonialism as the "cheap finery" and "plaything of the ruling classes." A few days later in Markkleeberg an SPD speaker addressed about 120 people on the Peters case and the economic injustice of colonialism, a policy "in the interest of a small group of capitalists like Krupp and Tippelskirch."[56] SPD members also displayed their fiery rhetoric in meetings held by opposition parties. Using tactics long employed to disrupt meetings like those of the Evangelical Workers Associations, hecklers attended 13 meetings in Leipzig and 71 more in outlying areas.[57]

In Augsburg during the elections, the party mobilized trade unions, the Women's Educational Association, and singing, gymnastics, and other clubs to distribute handbills both in town and in surrounding areas. A corps of "Rote Radler" — members of the Workers Cycling Association — carried leaflets to outlying villages.[58] On Sundays, organized leafleting in the mornings preceded large afternoon *Volksversammlungen* in local beer halls, not only in Augsburg but beyond, in comparative hamlets like Inningen, Bobingen, Schwabmünchen, Pfersee, and Steppach. In Kriegshaben, a woman speaker railed against the "colonial swindle." The meeting in Stadtbergen drew both workers and peasant smallholders, and in Langweid "a magnificent attendance from all circles of the population."[59] The *Schwäbische Volkszeitung* provided substantial coverage of the war — under headlines like "MOLOCH AFRICA" or "THE WHIP AS INSTRUMENT OF GERMAN CULTURE" — as it had of the stormy 1906 Reichstag debates on Germany's "desert policy" (*Wüstenpolitik*). Under the headline "THE BLEEDING DESERT," the paper attacked Gustav Frenssen's novel, *Peter Moors Fahrt nach Südwest*, "a ringing accusation against the decay of German culture apparent in our colonial policy," and its warm reception by critics whom it charged with shocking callousness.[60]

When the hard-fought elections were over, the intellectuals and ideologues of the SPD disagreed about the implications of colonialism for the party. Revisionists argued in favor of empire on both political and economic grounds.[61] Radicals insisted that, however potent the spell of colonialism over elements of the bourgeoisie, the working class remained largely unaffected. For Karl Kautsky, the SPD had "underestimated the power of the colonial idea in bourgeois circles."[62] Rosa Luxemburg argued in a Berlin speech that, among the mass of new voters whose participation proved decisive, the greater share "belongs to the *Mittelstand*, [though] a smaller part may belong to the working class." She interpreted the elections as a battle between Social Democracy and the *Kleinbürgertum*, "a struggle of a dying class against a rising one, a class struggle par excellence."[63] And indeed, in Protestant Germany as a whole, the parties of the bloc did benefit from the increased participation of farmers and the urban middle classes, whose votes went largely to the liberals. And many middle-class voters who had chosen the SPD in 1903 voted for the "National Cartel." Of course, in a certain light, the SPD defeat does not appear as dire as its loss of Reichstag seats suggests. Altogether, it received some quarter of a million more votes in 1907 than in 1903, but since it was unable to increase its percentage of the total vote, and overall participation was substantially greater (rising from 76 to 84 percent of those eligible), the parties of the Bülow bloc were able to claim victory.[64]

Still, even in the most unassailable concentrations of working-class Social Democracy there is evidence of imperialist gains among workers. In the longtime SPD stronghold of Nuremberg, the share of the vote fell from 60 to 56 percent.[65] In Leipzig, in the "Red Kingdom of Saxony," although the results were mixed, the SPD experienced them as a serious defeat at the hands of the local Cartel. After having "exerted all of their energies to keep the central Leipzig [Leipzig-Stadt] electoral district," which they had won from the Pan-German leader Ernst Hasse in 1903, they lost it to the National Liberal candidate.[66] There were 42,938 eligible voters in the twelfth district in 1907, of whom 38,637 (90 percent) voted. Of votes cast, 24,044 (62 percent) were for the cartel and only 14,366 (37 percent) for City Councilor Lange, the SPD candidate.[67] The SPD received 1,774 (10.9 percent) fewer votes than in 1903.[68] The local agitation committee advanced a sociological analysis of voting patterns in central Leipzig to explain the loss. In areas with heavier concentrations of workers, they reported, voter participation was the least, falling as low as 82 percent, while in bourgeois areas participation rose as high as 95 percent. The lower numbers they attributed partially to the wintertime absence of seasonal workers in the building trades and to areas where "many unskilled and barely organized workers" did not bother to vote at all. Their report also suggests that working-class voters were not immune to the appeal of nationalism and colonialism: "The loss of seasonal workers' votes does not, in and of itself, account for the Social Democratic loss. Rather, the conclusion that a substantial part of the working-class electorate must have voted for the bourgeois candidate is justified and well-founded. The 'affectionate coaching' on the part of the opposition must have been effective here, according to the results from wards inhabited almost exclusively by workers."[69]

The 1903 SPD victory in central Leipzig turned out to be exceptional in a district that was otherwise solidly National Liberal from 1871 through the elections of 1912.[70] The results for the surrounding industrial and working-class suburbs (Leipzig-Land), on the other hand, held much greater significance for the party. Even though the Social Democratic candidate won, the results for the much larger district, "populated for the most part by the industrial working class," were nevertheless "fully unsatisfactory" to the SPD.[71] There were 112,537 eligible voters in the thirteenth district in 1907, of whom 97,592 (87 percent) cast votes. Of these, 39,689 (41 percent) were for the Cartel, as against 56,712 (58 percent) for the incumbent Social Democrat Friedrich Geyer.[72] This represented a clear SPD victory and a slight gain of 1,893 votes (3.4 percent) over 1903.[73] The SPD nevertheless interpreted the outcome as a disappointment and a warning for the future. In this heavily industrialized, heavily working-class, and heavily Social Democratic part of the "Red Kingdom," the Cartel won some 16,000 votes more than in 1903.[74] The feeling that the thirteenth district was "an impregnable socialist stronghold" had turned out to be a dangerous illusion. Party analysts argued that the nonparticipation of nearly 15,000 eligible voters reflected insufficient propaganda and agitation among workers. At 87 percent, voter participation was higher than in 1903 (82 percent), and surpassed the national average of 84 percent.[75] However, the influx of new voters failed to help the SPD. Its share of eligible voters declined from 57 percent in 1903 to about 50 percent.[76] The appeal of nationalism and colonialism was clearly a factor even among working-class voters in a bastion of SPD strength.

Immediately following the elections, the Leipzig SPD dropped colonialism and once more took up the matter of the unequal Saxon suffrage. Yet the colonial question did not really go away. The local police noted that it—and the rancorous division between stalwart anticolonialists and revisionists—was much discussed at the congress of the Socialist International held that August in Stuttgart, and then again three weeks later at the Essen party congress.[77] Leipzig itself remained the stronghold of the SPD left-center during the last years before war, and left-wing radicals gathered around their banner paper, the *Leipziger Volkszeitung*.[78] According to the police, the SPD had been badly burned by anticolonialism in 1907 and the party was hesitant to muster its usual outrage in the face of the Second Morocco Crisis in July 1911. Such "considerations were not, however, shared by the most extreme elements of Social Democracy and its press, the *Leipziger Volkszeitung* in particular. These factors worked incessantly and with success to induce the party leadership to action against war and especially against Germany's efforts" abroad. The month after the Agadir Crisis, the SPD agitation committee organized a mass demonstration at a brewery in Stötteritz attended by some ten thousand protesters (and of course police agents).[79] In the 1912 elections, which the SPD again lost in Leipzig-Stadt (with 46 percent of the vote) but won in Leipzig-Land (with nearly 70 percent), colonialism persisted as an issue of the second rank, overshadowed by food prices and tax policy, but still marked by the local authorities.[80] Only the war would finally end the local battle over colonialism. As the ever-perceptive police put it, "The year 1914 stood in its first half still entirely under the sign of class struggle, while it was dominated in the second half by the World War and the political truce between parties."[81]

All parties, Kautsky argued in 1907, need a "program for the future" to "unite the broader sections of society under their flags." Accordingly, many workers dreamed of a future Social Democratic state, just as the nationalist middle classes looked to the colonial empire as the solution to economic problems and the intractable social question. "The more unsatisfactory and confused the conditions at home, the more longingly the bourgeois elements in all large capitalist states gaze toward the colonies." Socialism and colonialism, Kautsky pointed out, were linked. Fear of an expanding SPD fed enthusiasm for the colonial future. "The fascination exerted by the colonial state of the future on the entire bourgeois world . . . is closely related to growing fear of the Social Democratic future state."[82] But Kautsky's pairing of rival "future states" also, if inadvertently, suggests the outlines of an unrecognized utopian sodality encompassing socialists and colonialists. Perhaps colonialism appealed to some workers—readers of colonial adventure, visitors to the colonial wax museum or panorama—in the same way that the socialist *Zukunftsstaat* transfixed others: as an escape, a dream, a promise of hope for the future. Or a "rational," "scientific" worldview adequate to the times.

Nevertheless, the prevailing interpretation of German Social Democracy as "revisionist," as increasingly "colonialist," implies a distortion of perspective. At the *local* level, in terms of everyday political discourse and practice, the SPD was forcefully anticolonialist—in 1907, as over the preceding ten years, and beyond. The successful mobilization of rank-and-file workers, the wide penetration of critical rhetoric, indicate a substantial political anticolonialism belied by accounts of an acquiescent SPD leadership. If the elections marked "the beginning of the domestication of Social Democracy," its neutralization in the face of nationalist *Weltpolitik*, the momentum of grassroots radicalism and the actual majority of votes won by the SPD suggest that this development was not inevitable.[83] Widespread anticolonial feeling is one of the outstanding facts of the German colonial period, distinguishing it in comparison with other European societies. But what is key here is the *productive* nature of the conflict itself: a bitter antagonism between bourgeois colonialism and its SPD opponents that was political, intellectual, and moral. Colonialism both reproduced and eroded class difference in Germany, and it was out of this tension that, ultimately, a more supple, sinuous colonial discourse developed, reflected in revisionism and the ineluctable appeal of colonial knowledge—a discourse that penetrated all classes.

And not least the SPD itself. The party lost nearly half its seats, but it polled more than 3.2 million votes, over a million more than the Center and 1.5 million more than the National Liberals, the most successful among the parties of the Bülow bloc. The SPD experienced this as a traumatic defeat and a sign of the power, even the inevitability, of colonialism. That it did so in the face of strong countervailing facts suggests the implicit, growing acceptance of colonial knowledge, of global market modernity. The elections catalyzed this reshuffling of worldview.

And, of course, the politics of SPD anticolonialism and its mutations does not, by itself, tell the complete story, because it omits the more indirect mediations of colonialism, its assimilation into a specifically working-class culture, often in the form of "colonial knowledge," even as a robustly, surprisingly critical attitude flourished among ordinary working men and women. To understand the broader significance of colonialism in Germany, and ultimately its role in the dissemination of racism, it is necessary to consider how class difference shaped the reception and formation of discourse, and how discourse transmuted class difference. But the transmission of colonial

knowledge among socialists and workers occurred not just in electoral contests or the political arena more broadly but also, as we have seen, in the
diffuse sphere of culture—the world, much-maligned by contemporaries, of
dime novels, the cinematograph, the *Panoptikum*, and also, paradoxically,
in SPD libraries and adult education, as popular science. Whether as mass
culture or mass politics, colonial discourse acted gradually, as a form of
working-class or mass initiation into capitalist market modernity: into international exchange relations, via the discourses of commodity consumption,
mass production, and global competition. It was also, inseparably, a form
of initiation into the nation-state; and here, perhaps, the diffusion of racist
cultural codes and iconographies framed the formation, much contested,
of national subjectivity among German workers.[84] The elections marked
the apotheosis of "race" in Wilhelmine Germany, its "breakthrough to national consensus into which oppositional groups also integrated over the
long term."[85] But for the SPD, its leadership in particular, race was framed
within a compelling discourse of the economic, the modern, progress. It
was above all most susceptible of assimilation to this most modern image
of the global, and Germany's place within it—and not only in its revisionist
impulse, but even in the orthodox critique of empire that itself took colonial political economy increasingly seriously.[86] Still, the vigorous popular
engagement in anticolonial critique and protest, the strong countervailing
currents that long thwarted colonialist aims, above all in a time of war from
1904 to 1907, suggest that this was hardly inevitable.

Magic Lantern Empire

Reflections on Colonialism and Society

> *The* real *course of development ... results in the necessary victory*
> *of ... the avowedly restless, adroit self-interest of* enlightenment
> *over the parochial, worldwise, naïve, idle and deluded* self-interest of
> superstition.
>
> —Karl Marx, *The Economic and Philosophic Manuscripts of 1844*

In late October 1891 a traveling magic lantern show, the Original-Wandel-Theater, opened in Regensburg, in the Bavarian Oberpfalz. As good as its name, it conjured *Wandelbilder*, "dissolving views": a precinematic illusion of motion produced by projecting two or three pictures simultaneously. The "famous, instructive" show promised "picturesque geographical excursions and scientific expeditions," including the "newest results of the colonial endeavors in Central Africa from authentic reports by the famous African explorer Emin Pasha and Dr. Carl Peters, as well as Imperial Commissioner Major von Wissmann."[1] These shimmering images of a "Map of Central Africa" or "The Capital of the Isle of Zanzibar," and a "moving" image of "The Journey to the Dark Continent" captivate and elude. The dissolving views glow magically, and recede. Metaphorically, they suggest the strangely spectral reality of the German colonial empire, the contradictions defining colonial discourse. The distant colonies are brought closer; they appear as chimerical markets, impossible settlements, unattainable.

The language of this ephemeral advertisement is: instruction, geography, scientific expedition, authentic report, map. We encounter in this small-time traveling show, as in countless other examples, the language of colonial discourse, of its construction as knowledge. More generally, colonial discourse evolved a trope of *knowledge as disenchantment* that preceded German colonization itself and that was pan-European. In the fractured class society of Germany, it would realize unforeseeable influence. But it emerged first with the spectacle of exploration, not least as a phenomenon of the mass media, and developed with the establishment of a German colonial empire in the mid-1880s. When Stanley arrived in Berlin he was celebrated, as everywhere, for his "powerful pioneering work" in revealing in Africa "the last and the greatest of its secrets," the Congo. (Who then could imagine the veil of secrecy that would descend over King Leopold's Central African empire?) "Africa's earth alone is still virgin; great stretches are still undisturbed by colonization," observed one commentator in the German press, but exploration had finally dispelled rumors of strange wonders there. "A decade ago those areas still formed absolutely white spaces on our maps, and we had no other knowledge of them than those fantastic reports that peopled these regions with misshapen figures, with dwarves, cannibals, magicians, men with tails, and others."[2] Similarly, "the land of black men, the Egyptian Sudan," had been a "land of riddle and fable in earlier times," before colonial penetration.[3]

But, in a sort of return of the repressed, tattooed cannibals, Amazons, and magicians continued to reappear. No matter the extent of exploration, discovery, or colonization, the trope of secrets unveiled persisted. "While the island population of the South Seas becomes, through contact with Europeans, ever more civilized, and barbaric customs like cannibalism are dying out, new reports speak of . . . cannibals among the aboriginal population of the East Indies, where it stands, of course, in relation to religious ceremonies or blind superstition."[4] The "tireless Hugo Zöller," for his part, continued to produce "his interesting and partly scientifically important accounts of the west coast of Africa," drawing "a very interesting picture of the Amazons of the King of Dahomey."[5] Amazons continued to tour the country in sensational ethnographic shows.[6] And they excited scientific interest: in November 1892 the Munich Anthropological Society arranged a private viewing of "Dahomey Amazons," and the following January sponsored a lecture on "The Sexual Organs of a Dahomey Amazon."[7] As late as May 1914 the Homburg section of the Colonial Society hosted a lecture on life "Between the Cannibals and Dwarves in German Congo and Southern Cameroon."[8]

Looking back, from the 1920s, on the heyday of German discovery in West Africa, Zöller remembered that "what mostly amazed" him about the people of West Africa, "at least among the rich," was "a distinctive code of politeness, and, if one can put it so, a barbaric high culture, which well understood how to flaunt itself with champagne, with . . . silk beds, chandeliers, and the like. In any case, Dahomey was not a land of such savages as one was no doubt accustomed to imagine in those days at home" in Germany.[9] Such were the disappointments of disenchantment. Nor, according to the obscure West African explorer Ernst Henrici, had the Amazons themselves met expectations, even in the 1880s. "The black female guard of famously warlike Dahomey belongs to the romance of the Dark Continent," he observed, "but the recent African expeditions destroy more and more the nimbus around this legendary state and its bloody terror. . . . They are female niggers [*Niggerweiber*], nothing more . . . as lazy as all niggers."[10]

And yet, inevitably, a troupe of "authentic" Amazons performed their warlike ways all across Germany. We can imagine the arrangements with Zöller's champagne-swilling notables in West Africa, who procured them for the European showmen. According to Zöller, the "so-called Amazons"

that performed in Germany "truly came from the west coast of Africa, perhaps even from Dahomey itself or its surrounding area, but were not real
Amazons."[11] If there were no "real Amazons" anywhere, it was in any case
a positive aspect of the fakery and fantasy that ultimately mattered. For the
persistence of flim-flam popular wonders underwrote the legitimacy and
authority of colonial discourse that denied them. The tensions of the (broken) spell and the (unveiled) secret—of Africa or the East Indies or the South
Seas—would never be permanently resolved; they were dialectically constitutive of disenchanted knowledge.

"Tattooed Cannibals": from a brochure accompanying an ethnographic show (ca.
1883–96). Courtesy Museum für Völkerkunde, Hamburg, Nachlass Adrian Jacobsen.

Precisely where the claims of science and respectability appeared to counteract the vulgar, sensational, or trivial, the story itself—of the "missing link," of cannibalism, or Amazons—persisted, irrepressibly. The exchange of knowledge and enchantment continued over the years up to 1914 in constant tension and mutation. Even Carl Hagenbeck's ostensibly positivistic ethnographic representations expressed, over time, a growing impulse toward the theatrical, culminating in his famous *Tierpark* outside of Hamburg (a commercial logic that was not, however, inevitably inimical to their respectability).[12] There was a growing sense among bourgeois critics that many of the ethnographic shows were becoming ever more sensationalist; but Rudolf Virchow and his associates in Berlin, more and more repelled by the fairground atmosphere, simply began to make their visits in private.[13] In their ethnographic museums, these professional anthropologists sought to orchestrate an ordered, transparent, rational encounter with other cultures, to redeem the jumble of ethnographica from the idle wonders of the curiosity cabinet. But the broad public frustrated their efforts with a recurrent, incorrigible exoticism, pointing again to the continuous tension between the authority of science in the public sphere and an insistent popular estrangement, or enchantment. And in the end, anthropological theory and practice were inadequate to the sheer profusion of objects fetishized for their power to represent a global totality of human culture.[14]

The Amazon Corps: ethnographic show (ca. 1890). Courtesy Museum für Völkerkunde, Hamburg, Nachlass Adrian Jacobsen.

The much amplified trope of disenchantment evolved with the bitter conflict around empire. The fascination with superstitions or cannibalism that flourished in popular and mass culture—and not only there—closely retraced the deep social fissures that underlay the conflict. The still-strong vestiges—or projections—of a rational bourgeois public sphere that decisively shaped colonial discourse and institutions disposed them in turn to the formation of an irrational object in need of enlightenment. In the deeply fractured class society of Wilhelmine Germany, the educated and propertied bourgeoisie of the colonial movement never doubted that they were the qualified, licensed purveyors of legitimate knowledge. Popular ignorance about the colonies both amused and troubled them, and they made fun of the error and fantasy they attributed to the "masses," whether peasants, factory workers, artisans, or shopkeepers. As one writer observed after the 1907 elections, it was "especially among the broad masses of the so-called *Mittelstand*, where property and education are, after all, not always happily united, and where one is able to exercise a not inconsiderable influence through his property, [that] an Egyptian obscurity reigns in colonial matters."

> For that I can cite the opinions of competent gentlemen who, in giving election speeches, had contact with all sections of the *Mittelstand*—from the so-called "better" to the déclassé, from whom the Social Democrats get their camp-followers—and who, through encountering "absolute ignorance" in colonial matters, became very depressed. The fundamental question that I heard just before the election from a man who took the field with pikes and clubs against the advocates of German colonial policy—"What are colonies actually?"—has now been generally answered. . . . People no longer look for Southwest Africa in the South Seas, . . . are no longer astonished that it rains sometimes in Cameroon, and that the craneflies in East Africa sting worse than in the Black Forest.[15]

The links between class position and knowledge constantly surface in colonial discourse—requiring a history of German colonialism that is at once social and cultural, material and discursive. The bourgeoisie had perpetually to struggle against elusive, recalcitrant lower classes otherwise abandoned to sensationalism, misinformation, and rumor. Only with an unprecedented blitz of electoral propaganda—and the "influence of property"—did the rays of bourgeois *Kolonialaufklärung* begin finally to penetrate the mysterious, "oriental" recesses of the "popular mind." And even then the popular fascination with cannibalism or fetish priests—the stuff of dime novels and magic lanterns—pointed to the stubborn persistence of other modes of knowledge. A "slight shudder still creeps over German skin when one is told that cannibals still live on New Pomerania," the writer continued.

It is neither insignificant nor merely coincidental that the great colonial crisis of 1904–6, the period of revolts in East and Southwest Africa, of mounting scandal and expense culminating in bitter political controversy and the dissolution of the Reichstag, saw a powerfully renewed emphasis on colonial science, expertise, and education. The more critics attacked the irrational violence and futility of the colonial project, the more knowledge was rushed into the breach. Emblematic of this was the selection in 1906 of Bernhard Dernburg to direct the colonial administration. Technocrat, businessman, banker, he was above all a proponent of "scientific colonialism," a renovated colonial policy.[16] His tough style, practical business sense, and elaboration of a modern approach seemed to promise a rationalization, a kind of "Americanization" of colonialism.[17] In a campaign speech before an audience of scholars and artists in Berlin in January 1907, Dernburg invoked science and technology as "the modern means of developing foreign parts of the world," of "raising up lower cultures, improving the living conditions of blacks and whites."[18] During the elections, leading German social scientists including Adolf Wagner, Max Sering, and Gustav Schmoller established the Colonial-Political Action Committee to advocate for a renovated, reformed colonialism, and they worked closely with Dernburg to integrate the most up-to-date thinking into colonial policy.[19] In Hamburg, the Senate agreed in 1907 to establish a Colonial Institute that, opened in 1908, exemplified the connections between Dernburg, the social scientists, and German colonial policy.[20] And this is only the most well-known of a whole series of colonial academies or programs in *Kolonialwissenschaft* that formed at various universities, technical schools, and commercial colleges by the end of 1907. As its colonial policy faltered, Germany developed the most elaborate system of colonial education in the world.[21]

SPD critics perceived the deployment of bourgeois colonial knowledge, above all in its more specifically political contexts, as manipulation: colonialism as an instrument of the ruling classes, a diversionary tactic. Especially the strongest critics of empire shared this understanding, which came ultimately to shape histories of the period in terms of "social imperialism." Different classes seemed variously susceptible to it. Salaried, white-collar workers, for example, "are more easily seized by the ideology of imperialism, and because of their interest in the expansion of capital, they become prisoners of its ideology." According to the anticolonial theorist Rudolf Hilferding, these comprised "subscribers to specifically imperialist publications, partisans of racialist theory (which they frequently interpret in terms of competition), readers of war novels, admirers of colonial heroes, agitators and electoral fodder for finance capital."[22] And nor were workers immune, it seemed, to the lure of empire. Lenin, intent observer of the German scene, argued that imperialism "creates the economic possibility of corrupting the upper strata of the proletariat."[23] Colonialism would, in the theory of contemporary socialism, ultimately intensify class contradictions as capitalism descended into inevitable crisis.[24] But it had a prior power to unite across the class divide. According to Rosa Luxemburg, the elections of 1907 "found the whole of Germany in a paroxysm of imperialistic enthusiasm, firmly united under one flag."[25] Similarly, Hilferding emphasized the general power of imperialism to achieve social cohesion and defuse conflict. "The imperialist," he argued,

> observes with a cold and steady eye the medley of peoples and sees his own nation standing over all of them. . . . The subordination of individual interests to a higher general interest, which is a prerequisite for every vital social ideology, is thus achieved; and the state alien to its people is bound together with the nation in unity, while the national idea becomes the driving force of politics. Class antagonisms have disappeared and been transcended in the service of the collectivity. The common action of the nation, united by a common goal of national greatness, has taken the place of class struggle, so dangerous and fruitless for the possessing classes.[26]

The approach elides precisely the kind of social division and conflict that colonialism in fact both reproduced within its own institutions and discourse and intensified in its political opposition to anticolonialists. Colonialism was not principally integrative, ideologically or politically, in the Kaiserreich, although it had those potentials over the longer term—paradoxically through polarities of knowledge that retraced distinctions of class. Given the protracted antagonism around empire, and the anxieties surrounding colonial knowledge, this is too simple an account. Caught up in the model of manipulation from above, socialists failed to grasp the ways that the very conflict itself, the contested authority of colonial knowledge—continuously challenged, but continuously reasserted, in mass culture as in mass politics—gradually produced a certain elasticity, strength, sinuousness in colonial discourse, precisely in its "rationality."

Nor could these socialist critiques, reproduced in the most important subsequent histories of the subject, account for the ways that discourse shaped the German bourgeoisie itself. Stanley wrote that Bismarck, in 1884, had perceived in the quickening German colonial movement the "strong throb of modern life." The progressivist trope of science, technology, economic expansion—of modernity—slowly enveloped the educated and propertied classes and made colonialists of them. They were not themselves simply *outside* of discourse, detached from it, somehow free to wield it as a tool of manipulation. Colonial discourse operated to frame and materialize their own worldview, and to universalize it vis-à-vis the objectification of both the colonized and the lower classes. The geographical, oriental, and colonial societies; the ethnographic museums; the chambers of commerce, merchant associations, and Colonial Economic Committee; the state; schools and universities; the School of Oriental Languages; the Colonial Institute and the Colonial Council—these institutions did not simply represent the objective interests of a particular class and conceal them in a universalizing propaganda.[27] Indeed, given the stark reality of a costly, unprofitable empire, they suggest the heterogeneity of class interest and its complex mediations.

And ultimately, colonial knowledge—the progressivist discourse of colonial inevitability and modernity—insinuated itself within Social Democracy. This was famously true of a right-wing socialist like Gustave Noske, who straightforwardly took up colonial discourse, if in a renovated "socialist sense": "Trade with the colonies," he conceded, "represents only a very small fraction of Germany's total world trade. But it is no longer of really minor significance for the German economy, since a hundred million marks more or less in commodity exports mean work or unemployment for thousands of German workers." And, moreover, he argued, imports of colonial raw materials met Germany's most urgent needs.[28] The unanswerable force of brute economic "fact" was likewise typical of arguments by Eduard Bernstein, the leading SPD revisionist: "Without the colonial expansion of our economy the misery that we can still observe in Europe today . . . would be infinitely more severe."[29]

More telling was the way that colonial discourse left traces even in the thinking of fierce critics of empire. Rudolf Hilferding, precisely in his attack on colonialism as opening territories to monstrous flows of capital, appears to assume an economic logic that was really more an axiom of colonial discourse than an empirical development. It is in "overseas colonial territories" that "have not yet been opened up," he observes, that "capital has the opportunity to invest on the grand scale." Hilferding's critical impulse belies the ways his line of thinking strangely reflects colonial discourse itself: "Capital becomes the conqueror of the world, and with every new country that it conquers there are new frontiers to be crossed."[30] Sounding uncannily, but for his withering critical tone, like a pamphlet from the Colonial Economic Committee, Hilferding describes colonies as "outlets for capital investment"—particularly when they provide goods that "can be produced by capitalist methods, have an assured sale on the world market, and are important to industry in the home country."[31] Rosa Luxemburg's powerful theory of imperialism similarly insisted on a certain logic to empire building as "the political expression of the accumulation of capital in its competitive struggle for what remains . . . of the non-capitalist environment."[32] Here, again, capital, "impelled to appropriate productive forces for purposes of exploitation, ransacks the whole world. . . . The process of accumulation, elastic and spasmodic as it is, requires inevitably free access to ever new areas of raw materials in case of need."[33]

And yet the workers themselves, as the mobilization of 1907 shows, represented a great reservoir of actual or potential anticolonialism, developed in intense antagonism between the SPD and the colonial movement over the previous years, which casts in stark relief the progress of colonialism among the political leadership of the SPD. Revisionists began to accept empire, and even radicals began to assimilate a vision of colonial dynamism to their theories of capitalism, but the grassroots continued to suggest the possibility of resistance. Frank Sobich disposes of the myth of socialist defeat in the 1907 elections, an experience of failure among the party leadership that obscured the quotidian reality of working-class mobilization and anticolonial conviction, as well as important aspects of the election results. The SPD, after all, polled some 250,000 more votes than in its great victory of 1903, and still took more votes than any other party.[34]

But of course, in the quiet of their reading rooms or before the peepholes of the Kaiser Panorama, the empire exerted real fascination on workers, too. The knowledge that many workers struggled to acquire—in libraries, lantern-slide lectures, and adult education courses—was often geography, ethnography, or popular Darwinism: knowledge so often shaped by the colonial context, if derided by bourgeois colonialists. In the library, as in the museum or cinematograph, workers—men and women—encountered the effects of both propaganda and cultural reformism. Surprisingly, in view of the sustained sense of distinction, of class difference, bourgeois colonialists and the cosmopolitan lower classes had much in common. If colonialists perceived themselves as bearers of reason and truth against the distortions of colportage, objectively they were reproducing the monstrous, the fantastic, and the sensational, albeit within a discourse of science, progress, and the civilizing mission.

Ethnographic shows and wax museums, united in the *Panoptikum*, were coded as popular science—as anthropology and geography—and thus presented as legitimate and respectable. Here the fair, with its oddities and freak shows, resurfaced in new, ostensibly modern, rationalized forms. But popular science, in its representations of the colonial exotic—whether in magic-lantern shows, traveling anthropological cabinets, or colonial travelogue—enacted its own kind of "reenchantment of the world," or counterenchantment—an irrationalism of the racial grotesque and a fetishized economics appearing as its opposite: rational, empirical, modern science. Bound up with the insistent facticity of commodity propaganda and a transnational "labor question"—the growing economic objectification of the world—this points to the "master fetish," so to speak, of colonialism, enmeshing bourgeois and socialist intellectuals and, increasingly, the lower classes in a new, hegemonic sense of the global.

The nineteenth-century elaboration of "commercial geography" and its correlated languages of *Weltpolitik*—"world policy"—and *Weltmarkt*—the world market—linked colonial knowledge and capital and substantially produced the terrains of politics, class, and national identity from the turn of the century. In its origins, this discourse denoted commercial navigation and overseas trade. Gradually, however, with the rise of formal colonization and growing mobility, it signified broad new areas of urgent interest: global labor, in terms of both tropical commodity and metropolitan factory production, and global capital flows. The most recent transnational history of the Kaiserreich foregrounds these themes of labor mobility, commodity circulation, and markets in a colonial world. Sebastian Conrad argues for examining "the metropole and the colony within a single analytic framework," clarifying linked constructions of labor and laborer inside and outside of Germany, and showing their shared origins in transnational material histories and discourses.[35] Andrew Zimmerman illuminates the role of political, economic, and intellectual networks, spanning Germany, the United States, and Africa, in transfers of technology and knowledge for the mobilization of colonial labor and metropolitan capital to produce raw materials for international markets.[36] He shows how Max Weber, Gustav Schmoller, and other German economists developed "a global sociology of race and labor," how the categories of social science were themselves constitutive of the capitalist formation of a global South.[37] The Tuskegee expedition's transposition of the American New South, its racial and economic structures, to German Togo became integral to reformist, progressive, "scientific" colonialism; Dernburg's modernizers advanced, in essence, a "New South colonialism" in German Africa.[38]

Colonial knowledge—social scientific, racial, economic—not only reproduced class distinction, in the form of cultural capital, but inscribed it in a political economy of empire predicated on the objectification and subordination of labor in both colony and metropole. As Zimmerman argues, it was around the constraint of autonomous labor that social science, racial theory, capital, and colonialism converged. Here, again, we observe the "education of the Negro to work" as the analogue of the "colonial education of the German people." The idea of settlement colonialism, of colonies where Germans without means could make a new start, rapidly became an anachronism in the colonial period, eclipsed by a policy of exploitation of indigenous labor for commodity production. The persistence of such fantasies among many thousands of lower-class Germans marked their exclusion, ironically, from the colonial movement itself. And at the same time, colonialists worked to instruct the untutored masses in the ways that colonial commodities assured their labor in German factories. Metropolitan and colonial labor dwelt, in this sense at least, in the same world, one in which tropical commodities set *them* in motion, rather than the other way around. Contemporary socialists, of course, pointed out the symmetrical oppression of both German and colonial labor.[39] But just as significant was the linked initiation into a modern logic of world-as-market—an amplified "commercial geography"—conceived in terms of hyperextended commodity chains and an immense global division of labor.

The pluralized perspective of transnational social history in the age of empire brings the politics of the Kaiserreich—and especially nationalism—into new focus. The development of colonialism, its fractured and shifting forms, point to the inadequacy of models of either "social imperialism" "from above" or populist mobilization "from below," and by the same token refuses the accounts of both SPD revisionism and the decomposition of *Honoratiorenpolitik*, the politics of notables, in the age of mass politics.[40]

In the topsy-turvy world of the colonial period, socialist leaders assimilating colonial knowledge retreated from the radicalism of their own rank and file, while colonialist notables in search of mass support shrank from varieties of popular enthusiasm. The "social imperialism" model of manipulation belies the complex mediations of colonialism. It elides antagonism and fluid ambiguities, displaces capitalist dynamism, and flattens a disparate public into an inert, passive object.[41] Moreover, it obscures the way that colonialism exemplified, indeed helped to construct, German modernity. Colonialism signified not the manipulation of the broad masses by an anti- or premodern Right, but rather the assimilation of a heterogeneous Right to the global modern. Still, however fractious the Right was, however heterogeneous or pluralized the broader public, and however transformative the challenges of mass politics, the formation of colonialism cannot be understood outside of a context of tensional interaction with powerful local and national networks of notables engaged in the associational and discursive forms of a vestigial bourgeois public sphere.

Somewhat paradoxically, the opening up of the history of German nationalism to a global perspective tends toward a reformulation, however refined, of the integrative history of the German Right. To be sure, a transnational historical framework takes imperialist ideology seriously, rather than treating it as epiphenomenal, as an effect of internal class tensions in Germany and a tool of manipulation. This tends to transform our understanding of German nationalism in particular, to reframe it in terms of global, above all colonial, relations. As Sebastian Conrad argues, German nationalism around 1900 must be understood in a global context precisely in the projection of race onto the idea of nation.[42] But in the foregrounding of race, crystallized for Germans in colonial relations, there is reinscribed the concept of rallying together, integration, the forging of national unity. According to David Ciarlo, for example, by 1914 a powerful image of racial identity-as-difference, tied to colonial commodity production and stabilized and disseminated through the advertising iconography of a nascent mass consumer culture, functions to resolve social antagonism. Commercial advertising shows a "development not toward division, but toward integration—integration around hardening visions of race."[43] The prioritization of race hardly amounts to a revised concept of social imperialism, a refounded model of "manipulation from above," but it does reestablish, in a sense, a unifying function of colonialism that effaces the centrality of class division and antagonism precisely around the "colonial question."

Frank Sobich rejects the idea that the 1907 elections exemplified a kind of fundamental manipulation from above, focusing instead on the independent, dynamic formation of a "nationalist, racist and anti-socialist consensus."[44] But the elections were nevertheless a key moment in the forging of national unity through the identification of racialized outsiders and enemies. "The treatment of the 'Hottentot elections,'" he argues, "should be concerned with how, in a colonial context, a reformulated racist ideology managed to break through to national consensus into which oppositional groups also integrated over the long term."[45] By taking race and empire seriously, in a way that Rosa Luxemburg could not—she saw the elections as "conducted under the slogan of colonial policy," as "a symbol *of* politics"—Sobich complicates her sense of the "spiritual pogrom atmosphere" of 1907, but seems also to conserve something of her idea of the unifying power of nationalist imperialism.[46] Where Luxemburg saw the defeated working class of 1907 as prefiguring the passivity of 1914, Sobich, emphasizing instead the radicalism of 1907, sees in the SPD a fundamental revisionist transformation by 1914, and thus rupture rather than continuity, but their conclusions are the same. For Luxemburg the "pogrom atmosphere" of radical nationalism, for Sobich the "alleged 'defeat,' " produced, as he puts it, the "traumatization of the working-class movement," the rallying together of the nation.[47]

And yet, as Geoff Eley demonstrated, nationalism around 1900 was itself plural and contested rather than simply "integrationist," a terrain of political conflict in which the state, parties, and the *nationale Verbände* participated. Indeed, the Bülow bloc, the very fruit of nationalist-imperialist "victory" in 1907, marked not the forging of unity, but a "moment of fission in German politics," ultimately "fragmenting the government's accustomed parliamentary support."[48] Colonialism similarly developed in a field of contestation and division. Clearly the sense of national identity with which the Right conjured its visions was by 1907 constituted substantially through a global prism of race. But that same prism tied race fundamentally to issues of labor, production, and exploitation in a hierarchized, colonized world. The public sphere, as indeed the sense of nation, was constituted through the effacement of labor, both metropolitan and colonial, which is another way of linking metropole and colony. Colonialism refracted, reproduced, and retraced fissures in German politics and society. It mirrored the anxieties, energies, and ambiguities of a dynamic mass culture. It may be said that it was not so much that colonialism produced the nation—unifying and integrating it against the specter of race—but rather that it divided the nation and produced the global.

Abbreviations

AAZ	*Augsburger Abendzeitung*
ADV	Alldeutscher Verband
AVZ	*Augsburger Volkszeitung*
AH	Amtshauptmannschaft
ANN	*Augsburger Neueste Nachrichten*
AVZ	*Augsburger Volkszeitung*
BA	Bundesarchiv Berlin-Lichterfelde
BHStA	Bayerisches Hauptstaatsarchiv
DFV	Deutscher Flottenverein
DKG	Deutsche Kolonialgesellschaft
DKV	Deutscher Kolonialverein
DKZ	*Deutsche Kolonialzeitung*
FK	*Fränkischer Kurier*
GfDK	Gesellschaft für Deutsche Kolonisation
JSH	*Journal of Social History*
KWK	Kolonialwirtschaftliches Komitee
LAZ	*Leipziger Abendzeitung*
LIZ	*Leipziger Illustrierte Zeitung*
LNN	*Leipziger Neueste Nachrichten*
LT	*Leipziger Tageblatt*
LVZ	*Leipziger Volkszeitung*
MAAZ	*München-Augsburger Abendzeitung*
MNN	*Münchner Neueste Nachrichten*
PB	Polizeiberichte
RKA	Reichskolonialamt
SAA	Stadtarchiv Augsburg
SAB	Stadtarchiv Bamberg
SAL	Stadtarchiv Leipzig
SAM	Stadtarchiv München
SAN	Stadtarchiv Nürnberg
SM	*Sozialistische Monatshefte*
StAL	Sächsisches Staatsarchiv Leipzig
SPD	Sozialdemokratische Partei Deutschlands
SVZ	*Schwäbische Volkszeitung*
ÜLuM	*Über Land und Meer*
VZ	*Vossische Zeitung*
WIDM	*Westermanns Illustrierte Deutsche Monatshefte*
ZAfA	Zentral-Auskunftstelle für Auswanderer

Notes

Empire as World and Idea

1. "Das Panorama deutscher Colonien," *VZ*, 16 December 1885.
2. The Colonial Panorama opened in Berlin on 16 December 1885 and closed at the end of 1887. Stephan Oettermann, *The Panorama: History of a Mass Medium*, trans. Deborah Lucas Schneider (New York: Zone, 1997), 267–70.
3. "Das Panorama deutscher Colonien."
4. On the history of the Kaiserreich in transnational context, with emphasis on globalizing labor, commodity flows, markets, and imperialism, see Sebastian Conrad, *Globalization and the Nation in Imperial Germany* (Cambridge: Cambridge University Press, 2010); Andrew Zimmerman, *Alabama in Africa: Booker T. Washington, the German Empire, and the Globalization of the New South* (Princeton, N.J.: Princeton University Press, 2010).
5. "Besitzergreifung der deutschen Kolonien an der Westküste Afrikas durch S.M. Schiffe 'Möve' und 'Leipzig,'" *ÜLuM* 53, no. 22 (October 1884–85): 483.
6. "Der Aufstand in Kamerun," ibid., no. 20 (October 1884–85): 439.
7. "Das Panorama deutscher Kolonien in Berlin," *LIZ* 68, no. 2218 (January–June 1886): 11.
8. Ibid.; Oettermann, *The Panorama*, 270.
9. Max Buchner, *Aurora colonialis: Bruchstücke eines Tagebuchs aus dem ersten Beginn unserer Kolonialpolitik 1884–85* (Munich: Piloty & Loehle, 1914), 192.
10. Hugo Zöller, *Als Jurnalist [sic] und Forscher in Deutschlands großer Kolonialzeit* (Leipzig: Koehler & Amelang, 1930), 176.
11. *Globus* 47, no. 20 (1885): 320.
12. Zöller, *Als Jurnalist [sic] und Forscher*, 222.
13. The volumes on Togo and Cameroon appeared in a combined edition already in 1885. Hugo Zöller, *Die deutschen Besitzungen an der westafrikanischen Küste* (Berlin: W. Spemann, 1885). For the next several years he continued to publish widely in his new field. For example, Hugo Zöller, "Die Bewohner unserer westafrikanischen Kolonien," *Die Gartenlaube*, no. 15 (1889): 255–58.
14. Buchner, *Aurora colonialis*, 190. Buchner served as commissioner from 14 July 1884 to 17 May 1885.
15. Max Buchner, *Kamerun: Skizzen und Betrachtungen* (Leipzig: Duncker & Humblot, 1887), x.
16. *MNN*, 4 January, 20 February 1886.
17. Max Buchner, "Unsere Kamerun-Häuptlinge," *MNN*, 10, 12 January 1886; "Kamerun-Geschichten," ibid., 4, 5 September 1886; "Unser Export nach Westafrika," ibid., 5 January 1887.
18. "Das Panorama deutscher Colonien," *VZ*; "Das Panorama deutscher Kolonien in Berlin," *LIZ*, 11.

19. Buchner, *Kamerun*.

20. "Zwei schwarze Könige in Kamerun in Kamerun," *Die Gartenlaube*, no. 20 (1887), 639; Buchner, *Kamerun*, 22.

21. Henry M. Stanley, *The Congo and the Founding of Its Free State*, 2 vols. (New York: Harper, 1885), 2:378–408. Appeared in German as *Der Kongo und die Gründung des Kongostaates*, 2 vols. (Leipzig: Brockhaus, 1887).

22. "Die Kongokonferenz zu Berlin," *ÜLuM* 53, no. 14 (October 1884–85): 307.

23. "Jubiläums-Kunst-Ausstellung in Berlin: Supplement zur *Illustrirten Zeitung*," *LIZ* 86, no. 2237 (January–June 1886), 491; Oettermann, *The Panorama*, 257–58; R. Rönnebeck, "Panoramen," in *Berlin und seine Bauten*, ed. Architektenverein zu Berlin and Vereinigung Berliner Architekten, 2 vols. (Berlin: Wilhelm Ernst, 1896), 2:537.

24. Königliche Museen zu Berlin, *Führer durch die Sammlungen des Museums für Völkerkunde* (Berlin: W. Spemann, 1888), 67–68.

25. C. Falkenhorst, "Aus dem Reiche Emin Paschas," *Die Gartenlaube*, no. 20 (1888): 636.

26. "Ein heimgekehrter Afrika-Reisender," ibid., no. 8 (1887), 255.

27. Stephan Oettermann, "Alles-Schau: Wachsfiguren-Kabinette und Panoptiken," in *Viel Vergnügen: Öffentliche Lustbarkeiten im Ruhrgebiet der Jahrhundertwende*, ed. Lisa Kosok and Mathilde Jamin (Essen: Ruhrlandmuseum, 1992), 45.

28. Andrew Zimmerman suggests quite powerfully, in his transnational history linking the Verein für Sozialpolitik, the Tuskegee Institute, the American New South, and German colonization in Togo, how the categories of social science were constitutive of the "global," or the emergent "global South." See *Alabama in Africa*, 237–39.

29. Jürgen Habermas, *The Structural Transformation of the Public Sphere: An Inquiry into a Category of Bourgeois Society* (Cambridge, Mass.: MIT Press, 1989), 102.

30. Stanley, *The Congo*, 2:387.

31. Jeff Bowersox, *Raising Germans in the Age of Empire: Youth and Colonial Culture, 1871–1914* (New York: Oxford University Press, 2012); Suzanne Marchand, *German Orientalism in the Age of Empire: Religion, Race, and Scholarship* (Cambridge: Cambridge University Press, 2009); H. Glenn Penny, *Objects of Culture: Ethnology and Ethnographic Museums in Imperial Germany* (Chapel Hill: University of North Carolina Press, 2002); Sara Pugach, *Africa in Translation: A History of Colonial Linguistics in Germany and Beyond, 1814–1945* (Ann Arbor: University of Michigan Press, 2011); Jens Ruppenthal, *Kolonialismus als "Wissenschaft und Technik": Das Hamburgische Kolonialinstitut, 1908 bis 1919* (Stuttgart: Franz Steiner, 2007); Woodruff D. Smith, *Politics and the Sciences of Culture in Germany, 1840–1920* (New York: Oxford University Press, 1991); Andrew Zimmerman, *Alabama in Africa*; and *Anthropology and Antihumanism in Imperial Germany* (Chicago: University of Chicago Press, 2001).

32. As Nancy Fraser puts it, "discursive interaction within the bourgeois public sphere was governed by protocols of style and decorum that were themselves correlates and markers of status inequality." See Fraser, "Rethinking the Public Sphere: A Contribution to the Critique of Actually Existing Democracy," in Calhoun, *Habermas and the Public Sphere* (Cambridge, Mass.: MIT Press, 1992), 119.

33. The fundamental role of associational life in the formation of bourgeois society is treated in David Blackbourn, "The Discreet Charm of the Bourgeoisie: Reappraising German History in the Nineteenth Century," in David Blackbourn and Geoff Eley, *The Peculiarities of German History: Bourgeois Society and Politics in Nineteenth-Century Germany* (New York: Oxford University Press, 1984); Geoff Eley, "Nations, Publics, and Political Cultures," 296–98; Thomas Nipperdey, "Verein als soziale Struktur in Deutschland im späten 18. und frühen 19. Jahrhundert," *Gesellschaft, Kultur, Theorie* (Göttingen: Vandenhoeck & Ruprecht, 1976).

34. SAN, C7/V 1090 and 2327, Vereinspolizeiakten (Acten des Stadtmagistrats Nürnberg); SAA, 5/579, Magistrat der Stadt Augsburg, Acten, Gesellschaft Kamerun II (1890).

35. BA, DKG, R8023/254, Bl. 23, Satzungen der Deutschen Kolonialgesellschaft.

36. Michael Warner, "The Mass Public and the Mass Subject," in Calhoun, *Habermas and the Public Sphere*, 383.

37. As Habermas put it, the "privatization of civil society" had been the "social precondition" for a bourgeois public sphere, which became the legitimate arena for debating "rules governing relations in the basically privatized but publicly relevant sphere of commodity exchange and social labor." Habermas, *The Structural Transformation*, 74, 27.

38. Rudolf Hilferding, *Das Finanzkapital: Eine Studie über die jüngste Entwicklung des Kapitalismus* (1910); Rosa Luxemburg, *Die Akkumulation des Kapitals* (1913).

39. Habermas, *The Structural Transformation*, 236.

40. For Habermas, the *"plebeian* public sphere" was "a variant" of the bourgeois public sphere that, if ultimately "suppressed in the historical process," had remained "oriented toward the intentions of the bourgeois public sphere." Habermas, *The Structural Transformation*, xviii.

41. Buchner, *Kamerun*, 200.

42. Max Haushofer, "Die Phantasie als soziale Macht," *WIDM* 58 (April–September 1885), 349.

43. Habermas, *The Structural Transformation*, 29–43.

44. Enchantment already long opposed to the Enlightenment rationalism of "discovery." On the eighteenth-century disavowal of earlier, superseded accounts of marvels and strange geographies in a German context—the travelogue of Georg Forster—see Russell Berman, "The Enlightenment Travelogue and the Colonial Text," in *Enlightenment or Empire: Colonial Discourse in German Culture* (Lincoln: University of Nebraska Press, 1998), 42, 44. On the deeper history of the German *intellectual* mastery of the overseas exotic, see Christine R. Johnson, *The German Discovery of the World: Renaissance Encounters with the Strange and Marvelous* (Charlottesville: University of Virginia Press, 2008).

45. Penny, *Objects of Culture*, 165, 167–68, 193–96, 201.

46. Ibid., esp. chap. 5, 102–6; Zimmerman, *Anthropology and Antihumanism*.

47. The point that the public sphere perhaps always contained both rational discourse and its (popular) other, in the form of satire or the carnivalesque, is made in Harold Mah, "Phantasies of the Public Sphere: Rethinking the Habermas of Historians," *Journal of Modern History* 72 (March 2000): 163–64.

48. Roger Chickering, " 'Casting Their Gaze More Broadly': Women's Patriotic Activism in Imperial Germany," *Past and Present*, no. 118 (1988): 156–85; Krista O'Donnell, "The Colonial Woman Question: Gender, National Identity, and Empire in the German Colonial Society Female Emigration Program, 1896–1914" (Ph.D. diss., State University of New York at Binghamton, 1996); Lora Wildenthal, *German Women for Empire, 1884–1945* (Durham, N.C.: Duke University Press, 2001).

49. Mah, "Phantasies of the Public Sphere," 163–64; Eley, "Nations, Publics and Political Cultures," 304–7, 326; Fraser, "Rethinking the Public Sphere," 116–24.

50. Fraser proposes a complex and conflicted public sphere embracing "alternative publics" and "subaltern counterpublics," generators of "counterdiscourse." See Fraser, "Rethinking the Public Sphere," 116–24.

51. The most powerful statement of the theory is Hans-Ulrich Wehler, *Bismarck und der Imperialismus* (Cologne: Kiepenheuer & Witsch, 1969; reprint, Frankfurt/M.: Suhrkamp, 1984), esp. 112–26, 454–502; idem, "Bismarck's Imperialism, 1862–1890," *Past and Present*, no. 48 (1970): 119–55; idem, *The German Empire, 1871–1918*, trans. Kim Traynor (Providence: Berg, 1985).

52. See Geoff Eley, "Defining Social Imperialism: Use and Abuse of an Idea," *Social History* 1 (1976): 265–90; idem, "Social Imperialism in Germany: Reformist Synthesis or Reactionary Sleight of Hand?" in *Imperialismus im 20. Jahrhundert*, ed. Joachim Radkau and Imanuel Geiss (Munich: C. H. Beck, 1976).

53. Eley points out that historians neglect the popular dimension of imperialism, "rarely venturing into the streets outside, into the uncharted reaches of the committee-room, the working-men's club, the recreational society, the public house, or the family. There is still little understanding of how social imperialist mechanisms might have acted on the consciousness of real people." Eley, "Social Imperialism in Germany," 72.

54. Knowledge also, of course, underpinned the colonial state. George Steinmetz powerfully demonstrates the relationship of ethnographic knowledge and colonial administration in *The Devil's Handwriting: Precoloniality and the German Colonial State in Qingdao, Samoa, and Southwest Africa* (Chicago: University of Chicago Press, 2007).

1. Estrangement

1. See Wulf Otte, *Weiß und Schwarz—Black and White: Photos aus Deutsch-Südwestafrika/from Namibia, 1896–1901* (Wendeburg: Verlag Uwe Krebs, 2007).

2. On the Deutsche Kolonialgesellschaft (DKG) and its predecessors, the Deutscher Kolonialverein (DKV) and the Gesellschaft für deutsche Kolonisation (GfDK), see Klaus J. Bade, *Friedrich Fabri und der Imperialismus in der Bismarckzeit: Revolution–Depression–Expansion* (Freiburg: Atlantis, 1975), 169–85, 287–309; Elfi Bendikat, *Organisierte Kolonialbewegung in der Bismarck-Ära* (Heidelberg: Kivouvou, 1984); Richard V. Pierard, "The German Colonial Society, 1882–1914" (Ph.D. diss., State University of Iowa, 1964).

3. BA, DKG, R8023/254, Bl. 23, Satzungen der Deutschen Kolonialgesellschaft. This was a simple restatement of the statutes of the earlier DKV. See BA, DKG, R8023/253, 70, Satzungen des Deutschen Colonialvereins.

4. Pierard, "German Colonial Society, 1882–1914," 19–20; Fritz Ferdinand Müller, *Deutschland–Zanzibar–Ostafrika: Geschichte einer deutschen Kolonialeroberung, 1884–1890* (Berlin [East]: Rütten & Loenig, 1959), 51–53; Wehler, *Bismarck*, 165–66; Bade, *Fabri*, 176. The Westdeutscher Verein für Colonisation und Export, which preceded the Kolonialverein, was similarly restricted to the elites of the Rhineland and Westphalia. See Bade, *Fabri*, 167–68.

5. Bendikat, *Organisierte Kolonialbewegung*, 134.

6. Pierard, "German Colonial Society, 1882–1914," 109–11; idem, "The German Colonial Society," in *Germans in the Tropics: Essays in German Colonial History*, ed. Arthur J. Knoll and Lewis H. Gann (New York: Greenwood, 1987), 24–27; Roger Chickering, *We Men Who Feel Most German: A Cultural Study of the Pan-German League, 1886–1914* (Boston: George Allen & Unwin, 1984), 315–16; Geoff Eley, *Reshaping the German Right: Radical Nationalism and Political Change after Bismarck* (New Haven, Conn.: Yale University Press, 1980; reprint, Ann Arbor: University of Michigan Press, 1991), 121–23.

7. Pierard, "German Colonial Society, 1882–1914," 106.

8. On Peters and the GfDK, see Bendikat, *Organisierte Kolonialbewegung*, 88–94; Müller, *Deutschland–Zanzibar–Ostafrika*, 97–114; Wehler, *Bismarck*, 336–41.

9. BA, DKG, R8023/254, Bl. 20, Satzungen der Gesellschaft für Deutsche Kolonisation.

10. Peters's widely publicized Emin Pasha expedition of 1888 was similarly frowned upon by Bismarck, but undertaken nevertheless. See J. C. G. Röhl, "The Disintegration of the *Kartell* and the Politics of Bismarck's Fall from Power, 1887–90," *Historical Journal* 9 (1966): 75; Hartmut Pogge von Strandmann, "Domestic Origins of Germany's Colonial Expansion under Bismarck," *Past and Present*, no. 42 (1969): 152–57.

11. On the concept of *Volkskolonialismus*, see Bendikat, *Organisierte Kolonialbewegung*, 92; Pogge von Strandmann, "Domestic Origins of Germany's Colonial Expansion," 151.

12. Müller, *Deutschland–Zanzibar–Ostafrika*, 101.

13. Bendikat, *Organisierte Kolonialbewegung*, 91; Müller, *Deutschland–Zanzibar–Ostafrika*, 104–5; Ulrich S. Soénius, *Koloniale Begeisterung im Rheinland während des Kaiserreichs* (Cologne: Rheinisch-Westfälisches Wirtschaftsarchiv, 1992), 30.

14. Bade, *Fabri*, 305–6.

15. Soénius, *Koloniale Begeisterung im Rheinland*.

16. SAL, PB 1910, 160. In 1910, there were three separate branches in Leipzig: the general association, and one each for women and academics.

17. DKG Abteilung Leipzig, *Verzeichnis der Mitglieder* (Leipzig: DKG, 1899, 1910); *DKZ*, 6 April 1907 and 7 May 1910.

18. DKG, *Verzeichnis der Mitglieder*, 1910; SAL, PB 1910, 96.

19. John P. Short, "Colonialism and Society: Class and Region in the Popularization of Overseas Empire in Germany, 1890–1914" (Ph.D. diss., Columbia University, 2004), 313.

20. ADV Leipzig, *Jahresbericht der Ortsgruppe Leipzig des Alldeutschen Verbandes über das Jahr 1900* (Leipzig: ADV, 1901).

21. It has not been possible to find further details on the membership and activities of the Leipzig colonial veterans' association.

22. BHStA, MA 95355, GfDK (1887–1918), DKG Abteilung Regensburg, *Verzeichnis der kolonialen Sonder-Ausstellung auf der Oberpfälzischen Kreisausstellung zu Regensburg 1910* (Regensburg: DKG, 1910), 14–17.

23. DKG, *Jahresbericht 1895* (Berlin: DKG, 1896); SAN, C7/V 4840, Jahresbericht des Gauverbandes 'Bayern-Nord' der DKG, 1913 (Nuremberg, 1914).

24. SAN, C7/V 1300, Vereinspolizeiakten, DKG Abteilung Nürnberg-Fürth, 1888–1928, Mitglieder-Verzeichnis der Abteilung Nürnberg der DKG (as of 15 April 1905) (Nuremberg, 1905); Mitglieder-Verzeichnis der Abteilung Nürnberg-Fürth der DKG (as of 1 January 1913) (Nuremberg, 1913); Jahresbericht 1914, Abteilung Nürnberg der DKG (Nuremberg, 1915).

25. SAN, E6 487, Vereinsarchive, Jahresbericht 1913, Abteilung Nürnberg-Fürth der DKG (Nuremberg, 1914); C7/V 1300, Vereinspolizeiakten, DKG Abteilung Nürnberg-Fürth (1888–1928), Jahresbericht, 1914, Abteilung Nürnberg-Fürth der DKG (as of 26 April 1915); Mitglieder-Verzeichnis der Abteilung Nürnberg der DKG (as of 15 April 1905) (Nuremberg, 1905).

26. *AAZ*, 25 February 1912. It was one of sixty chapters in Middle Franconia, which together counted 4,200 members in 1912.

27. In 1888, when most Munich papers opposed Bismarck's colonialism, the procolonial *Münchner Neueste Nachrichten* had a circulation of 60,000, twenty times that of the anticolonial *Bayerischer Kurier*. See Liselotte Saur, *Die Stellungnahme der Münchner Presse zur Bismarck'schen Kolonialpolitik* (Würzburg: Konrad Triltsch, 1940), 95. In 1886, the *Münchner Neueste Nachrichten* printed at least 134 articles and notices concerning colonialism, making it a not unimportant part of everyday life for thousands of readers. In 1912, the Colonial Society credited the *Allgemeine Zeitung*, the *München-Augsburger Abendzeitung*, the *Münchner Neueste Nachrichten*, the *Münchener Zeitung* and even the "ultramontane" *Bayerischer Kurier* with being helpful to the cause of colonialism. See Karl Francke, *Festschrift zum 25-jährigen Bestehen der Abteilung München der Deutschen Kolonialgesellschaft, 1887–1912* (Munich: Deutsche Kolonialgesellschaft Abteilung München, 1912), 72. The *Süddeutsche Monatshefte*, established in Munich in 1904, published a number of articles on technical and geographical aspects of *Kolonialpolitik* and *Flottenpolitik* by Bavarian and other colonialists.

28. *DKZ*, 18 January 1908.

29. SAN, C7/V 4355, Vereinspolizeiakten, Zweigverband Nürnberg-Fürth der DKG (1907–21).

30. *DKZ*, 8 February 1908.

31. In 1899, the Schuckert Elektrizitäts-Aktien-Gesellschaft was, in terms of capital investment, the largest company in Bavaria. It employed 1,082 white-collar workers and 7,413 wage
workers. In 1903, it merged with Berlin-based Siemens. See Dieter Rossmeissl, *Arbeiterschaft
und Sozialdemokratie in Nürnberg 1890–1914* (Nuremberg: Stadtarchiv Nürnberg, 1977), 41.

32. SAN, C7/V 4355, Vereinspolizeiakten, Zweigverband Nürnberg-Fürth der DKG
(1907–21), Jahresbericht für 1912 des Zweigverbandes der Abteilung Nürnberg der DKG.

33. The membership in 1912 was 285 (162 Schuckert employees), in 1913, 294 (174), in
1914, 250 (146). SAN, E6 487, Vereinsarchive, Jahresbericht für 1913 der Abteilung Nürnberg-
Fürth der DKG; C7/V 4355, Vereinspolizeiakten, Zweigverband Nürnberg-Fürth der DKG
(1907–21), Jahresbericht für 1914 des Zweigverbandes der Abteilung Nürnberg-Fürth der
DKG.

34. SAN, C7/V 4355, Vorstand der DKG Nürnberg to Stadtmagistrat Nürnberg, 12 August
1913.

35. SAN, C7/V 1300, Vereinspolizeiakten, DKG Abteilung Nürnberg-Fürth (1888–1928),
Mitglieder-Verzeichnis der Abteilung Nürnberg-Fürth der DKG (1905, 1913); E6 487, Vereinsarchive, Jahresbericht für 1913 des Zweigverbandes der Abteilung Nürnberg-Fürth der DKG.

36. SAN, E6 487, Vereinsarchive, Jahresbericht für 1913 des Zweigverbandes der Abteilung Nürnberg-Fürth der DKG.

37. Chickering, *We Men*, 103–8; Peters, *Der Alldeutsche Verband*, 24.

38. Eley, *Reshaping the German Right*, 128, 129–30. As Eley puts it, "In terms of the social
identity of its leadership, formal and actual, at the national, regional and local levels, the German Navy League was clearly a movement of the middle classes, if that rather diffuse term is
used to encompass the industrial, professional and petty-bourgeoisie" (133).

39. DKG Abteilung Leipzig, *Verzeichnis der Mitglieder*, 1910.

40. Soénius, *Koloniale Begeisterung im Rheinland*, 42, 85–86; on the Frauenverein, 86–87.

41. The Frauenbund der Deutschen Kolonialgesellschaft, originally founded as the
Deutschkolonialer Frauenbund in 1907, joined forces with the DKG in 1908. On the organiza-
tional history, as well as German women's colonialism more generally, see Wildenthal, *German
Women for Empire*.

42. Many of these women were perhaps also members of the German Women's Naval Association, Munich Branch (Flottenbund Deutscher Frauen, Ortsgruppe München) (established
December 1905), or the Association for Germandom Abroad, Munich Women's Branch (Fraue-
nortsgruppe München des Vereins für das Deutschtum im Auslande).

43. SAA, E IV 3/1492, Deutscher Frauenverein für Krankenpflege in den Kolonien/Ab-
teilung Augsburg, Satzungen der Ortsgruppe Augsburg des Deutschen Frauenvereins für Krankenpflege in den Kolonien.

44. *AAZ*, 9 January 1908; 16 March 1911.

45. Wildenthal, *German Women for Empire*, 41; eadem, "Colonizers and Citizens: Bourgeois Women and the Woman Question in the German Colonial Movement, 1886–1914" (Ph.D.
diss., University of Michigan, 1994), 118. The Deutscher Frauenverein für Krankenpflege in
den Kolonien, originally founded as the German National Women's Association (Deutschnatio-
naler Frauenbund) in 1886, became the German Women's Association for the Red Cross in the
Colonies (Deutscher Frauenverein vom Roten Kreuz für die Kolonien) in 1908.

46. Wildenthal, *German Women for Empire*, 146–51, 41.

47. *AAZ*, 9 January 1908.

48. SAA, E IV 3/1492, Deutscher Frauenverein für Krankenpflege; *AAZ*, 12, 16 March
1911.

49. Chickering, " 'Casting Their Gaze,' " 177. As Chickering puts it, "patriotic activism
among German women, no less than among German men, was a class-bound phenomenon . . .
the product of the . . . social experiences, traditions and prejudices . . . of an upper-middle-class
milieu distinguished by *Besitz und Bildung*, by wealth and education" (184).

50. Rudolf Wagner, "Die deutsche Frau in den Kolonien," *WIDM* 108 (1910): 202.

51. Wildenthal, *German Women for Empire*, 146–51, 156; eadem, "Colonizers and Citizens," 181, 185–87.

52. On the ADV, see Chickering, *We Men*; Michael Peters, *Der Alldeutsche Verband am Vorabend des Ersten Weltkrieges, 1908–1914: Ein Beitrag zur Geschichte des völkischen Nationalismus im spätwilhelminischen Deutschland* (Frankfurt/M.: Peter Lang, 1992).

53. Pierard, "German Colonial Society, 1882–1914," 140; Peters, *Der Alldeutsche Verband*, 22–23.

54. Soénius, *Koloniale Begeisterung im Rheinland*, 81–84.

55. SAN, C7/V 726, Vereinspolizeiakten, Afrikanische Gesellschaft in Deutschland, 1879.

56. SAN, C7/V 1300, Vereinspolizeiakten, DKG Abteilung Nürnberg-Fürth (1888–1928), Jahresberichte 1912, 1913 Abteilung Nürnberg der DKG (Nuremberg 1913).

57. The Verein zur Erhaltung des Deutschtums im Auslande, founded in 1882 as the Munich chapter of the General German School Association (Allgemeiner Deutscher Schulverein).

58. Short, "Colonialism and Society," 319–25.

59. ADV, *Jahresbericht 1900*; DKG Leipzig, *Verzeichnis der Mitglieder*, 1899.

60. Chickering, *We Men Who Feel Most German*, 44.

61. Friedrich Ratzel (1844–1904), professor at the universities of Munich (1875–86) and Leipzig (1886–1904), was a geographer, early ethnographer, and popularizer of Darwin. He was the author of, among other works, *Die Erde und das Leben*, *Völkerkunde*, and *Anthropogeographie*, and originator of the *Lebensraum* concept.

62. On the significance of the deeply hierarchical structure of the DKG, see Eley, *Reshaping the German Right*, 119–21.

63. Soénius, *Koloniale Begeisterung im Rheinland*, 46.

64. Bade, *Fabri*, 177–81, on the early struggle to broaden the movement socially.

65. Pierard, "German Colonial Society, 1882–1914," 112–13.

66. See Wildenthal, *German Women for Empire*, 146–51.

67. Pierard, "German Colonial Society, 1882–1914," 161, 285.

68. Ibid., 118, 161.

69. Kenneth Holston, "'A Measure of the Nation': Politics, Colonial Enthusiasm and Education in Germany, 1896–1933" (Ph.D. diss., University of Pennsylvania, 1996), 49.

70. Eley, *Reshaping the German Right*, 121.

71. *DKZ*, 27 April 1907.

72. Soénius, *Koloniale Begeisterung im Rheinland*, 46–47.

2. World of Work, World of Goods

1. "Kolonialerziehung des deutschen Volkes," the title of a book from the period, and "Erziehung des Negers zur Arbeit" were constructions typical of German colonial discourse.

2. *SVZ*, 17 January 1907. *Kolonialkoller* is a play on the colonialist term *Tropenkoller*, or "tropical fever," the mental derangement that allegedly afflicted Europeans in the colonies and the etiology of numerous particularly brutal acts.

3. Wehler, *Bismarck*, 114–15, 230–57, 445–49.

4. BA, DKG, R8023/509, Bl. 228, "Arbeiter, Kolonien und Flotte."

5. SAL, Kap. 35/469, Deutsche Kolonialgesellschaft und das Kolonialwirtschaftliches Komitee, Bd. I (1896), Paul Lensch, "Der Arbeiter und die deutschen Kolonien" (KWK [Kolonialwirtschaftliches Komitee], n.d.), 7, 10, 14.

6. Buchner, *Kamerun*, viii.

7. KWK, *Unsere Kolonialwirtschaft in ihrer Bedeutung für Industrie, Handel und Land-wirtschaft* (Berlin: KWK, 1910), 18.

8. Ibid., 20. East African production rose to 2,077 bales in 1909. On the concerted effort by the German state and industrial interests to transplant the racialized labor practices and capitalist cotton production of the American New South to Togo, see Zimmerman, *Alabama in Africa*, 20.

9. Francesca Schinzinger, *Die Kolonien und das Deutsche Reich: Die wirtschaftliche Bedeutung der deutschen Besitzungen in Übersee* (Stuttgart: Franz Steiner, 1984), 124–28. By 1913, less than 0.5 percent of imports into Germany came from the German colonies. In 1912, British West Africa supplied 89 percent of the palm nuts, and the United States 83 percent of the cotton. German colonies supplied 13 percent of palm nuts, 0.2 percent of cotton, and less than 2.5 percent of cocoa imports. See also W. O. Henderson, "Germany's Trade with Her Colonies, 1884–1914," *Economic History Review* 9 (1938–39): 1–16.

10. BA, DKG, R8023/509, Bl. 228, "Arbeiter, Kolonien und Flotte."

11. *Kölnische Zeitung*, 17 February 1908.

12. BA, DKG, R8023/509, Bl. 441, "Deutschland halte fest an deinen Kolonien!"

13. Hans-Jürgen Teuteberg, "Wie ernährten sich Arbeiter im Kaiserreich?" in *Arbeiterexistenz im 19. Jahrhundert: Lebensstandard und Lebensgestaltung deutscher Arbeiter und Handwerker*, ed. Werner Conze and Ulrich Engelhardt (Stuttgart: Klett-Cotta, 1981), 70.

14. Walther G. Hoffmann, *Das Wachstum der deutschen Wirtschaft seit der Mitte des 19. Jahrhunderts* (Berlin: Springer, 1965), 126. In the mid-nineteenth century, this loose group of intoxicants, stimulants, and tropical semiluxuries formed the second most important category in the average German household budget—about 17 percent of personal consumption. Of this, some 34 percent went for spirits, and another 26 percent for beer.

15. Teuteberg, "Wie ernährten sich Arbeiter im Kaiserreich?" 69; idem, "Die Nahrung der sozialen Unterschichten im späten 19. Jahrhundert," in *Ernährung und Ernährungslehre im 19. Jahrhundert*, ed. Edith Heischkel-Artelt (Göttingen: Vandenhoeck & Ruprecht, 1976), 274–77.

16. Karl Helfferich, *Deutschlands Volkswohlstand, 1888–1913* (Berlin: Georg Stilke, 1913), 90. Among "Kolonialwaren und Südfrüchte," Helfferich estimated that per capita consumption of cocoa beans grew four times, tea fifteen times, and rice fifty-four times.

17. Hoffmann, *Wachstum der deutschen Wirtschaft*, 127.

18. Teuteberg, "Nahrung der sozialen Unterschichten," 238–41, 269–73. Before the war, the lower classes often drank ersatz forms of coffee—made of rye, wheat, or corn malts, chicory, acorns, or peanuts—or mixed them into more expensive real coffee, 269–73.

19. Hoffmann, *Wachstum der deutschen Wirtschaft*, 127–28.

20. Teuteberg, "Nahrung der sozialen Unterschichten," 273.

21. David Ciarlo, *Advertising Empire: Race and Visual Culture in Imperial Germany* (Cambridge, Mass.: Harvard University Press, 2011), 45.

22. Hannah Arendt, *The Origins of Totalitarianism* (New York: Harcourt Brace, 1973), 151.

23. Ciarlo, *Advertising Empire*. On the relationships between imperialism, advertising, and "commodity culture" in Victorian England, see Anne McClintock, "Soft-Soaping Empire: Commodity Racism and Imperial Advertising," chap. 5 in *Imperial Leather: Race, Gender, and Sexuality in the Colonial Contest* (New York: Routledge, 1995); Thomas Richards, "Selling Darkest Africa," chap. 3 in *The Commodity Culture of Victorian England: Advertising and Spectacle, 1851–1914* (Stanford, Calif.: Stanford University Press, 1990).

24. Erich Prager, *Die Deutsche Kolonialgesellschaft, 1882–1907* (Berlin: Dietrich Reimer, 1908), 119.

25. SAA, Hassler-Archiv/19: DKG, DKG to Theodor von Hassler in Augsburg, 26 February 1896.

26. Pierard, "German Colonial Society, 1882–1914," 212.

27. *DKZ*, 30 November 1899. In 1899, Karl Eisengräber founded a rival Kolonialhaus in Halle, which by 1902 had forty-four branches in Leipzig, Dresden, Munich, Frankfurt, Bonn, Mannheim, and other cities. See ibid., 27 November 1902.

28. On the façade, designed by the painter Rudolph Hellgrewe, see ibid., 10 December 1903.

29. On the Deutsches Kolonialhaus in general, see ibid., 21 March 1901; 30 October 1902; 10 December 1903.

30. Pierard, "German Colonial Society, 1882–1914," 213.

31. Richard V. Pierard, "A Case Study in German Economic Imperialism: The Colonial Economic Committee, 1896–1914," *Scandinavian Economic History Review* 16 (1968): 156; idem, "German Colonial Society," 213–14; *Satzungen des Komitees zur Einführung der Erzeugnisse aus deutschen Kolonien* (Berlin, [1896]).

32. *Fränkischer Kurier*, 7, 8 October 1898.

33. Pierard, "A Case Study," 156–58.

34. KWK, *Koloniale Produkte: Erläuterungen zu der Schulsammlung* (Berlin: KWK, 1910.)

35. DKG, *Jahresbericht der DKG, 1895* (Berlin: DKG, 1896); BA, R8023/911, Bl. 35–36; Bericht über die Sitzung des Ausschußes, 24 March 1896; Prager, *Deutsche Kolonialgesellschaft*, 119.

36. Walter Benjamin, *Charles Baudelaire: A Lyric Poet in the Era of High Capitalism* (London: Verso, 1976), 165.

37. DKG, *Jahresbericht der DKG, 1895*, 47.

38. Georg Simmel, "Berliner Gewerbe-Ausstellung," *Die Zeit* (Vienna), 25 July 1896, 60.

39. Ciarlo, *Advertising Empire*, 56, 61.

40. *DKZ*, 26 September 1896. Following the exhibition, the extensive commodity collections were divided between the Oriental Seminar (Berlin), the Württemberg Verein für Handelsgeographie, and the German Colonial Museum, the idea for which emerged from the 1896 exhibition. See Prager, *Deutsche Kolonialgesellschaft*, 120.

41. *DKZ*, 26 September 1896.

42. Ibid., 10 December 1903.

43. For striking images of the Berlin Trade Exhibition, see Paul Lindenberg, *Pracht-Album Photographischer Aufnahmen der Berliner Gewerbe-Ausstellung 1896* (Berlin: Werner, 1896).

44. Fritz Kühnemann, B. Felisch, and L. M. Goldberger, eds., *Berlin und seine Arbeit: Amtlicher Bericht der Berliner Gewerbe-Ausstellung 1896* (Berlin: Dietrich Reimer, 1898), 4.

45. Ciarlo, *Advertising Empire*, 56, 61.

46. Simmel, "Berliner Gewerbe-Ausstellung," 59. See also David Frisby, *Fragments of Modernity: Theories of Modernity in the Work of Simmel, Kracauer, and Benjamin* (Cambridge, Mass.: MIT Press, 1986), 75, 94–95.

47. On the growing criticism, doubt, and disappointment, including Bismarck's own exasperated pessimism, see Wehler, *Bismarck*, 407–11. On the discord between Bismarck and the colonial movement, and its role in the break between the Kartell and the chancellor, see Röhl, "The Disintegration of the *Kartell*," 75.

48. Carl Peters, "Kolonialmüdigkeit in Deutschland," in *Gesammelte Schriften*, ed. Walter Frank, vol. 1 (Munich: C. H. Beck, 1943), 421–22. The term *Kolonialmüdigkeit* was the "current expression for the undeniable standstill in the participation of the German public" in colonialism (*DKZ*, 6 November 1902).

49. *Alldeutsche Blätter*, 13 February 1904.

50. Karl Dove, "Kolonialer Pessimismus," *DKZ*, 6 June 1901; idem, "Zwei Jahrzehnte deutscher Kolonialbestrebungen," *WIDM* 102 (1907): 123.

51. *DKZ*, 14 March 1908.

52. Ibid., 19 July 1913.

53. Ibid., 17 June 1905.

54. "Koloniale Agitation," ibid., 3 August 1889.

55. "Arbeiter und Kolonien," ibid., 23 February 1907; "Koloniale Erziehung des deutschen Volkes," ibid., 4 May 1907; BA, DKG, R8023/1089, Bl. 24–28, Bericht über die Sitzung der Werbekommission, 8 October 1913. In the last years before the war, a traveling lecturer visited branches in Bochum, Kiel, Warmbrunn, Nuremberg, Weilheim, and many other towns and cities across Germany to give a talk entitled "The Significance of our Colonies for Industry and the Working Class." *DKZ*, 25 November 1911, 30 November 1912, 26 April, 29 November 1913.

56. Pierard, "German Colonial Society, 1882–1914," 361–62. Although the effort to win the working classes had begun much earlier, Pierard locates it in the last years before the war: "In 1913 the Society even began trying to reach the working classes" (361). Without much discussion or concrete detail, he concludes that there was "no indication that the propaganda had made much of an impact upon the working classes" (362).

57. BA, DKG, R8023/646, Bl. 324, Bericht über die Sitzung des Ausschußes, 29 October 1903.

58. BA, DKG, R8023/915, Bl. 266–67, Bericht über die Sitzung des Ausschußes, 13 November 1903.

59. BA, DKG, R8023/646, Bl. 349, Bericht über die Sitzung des Ausschußes, 25 March 1904; R8023/916, Bl. 67, Bericht über die Sitzung des Ausschußes, 18 June 1904.

60. BA, DKG, R8023/108, Bl. 127, Bericht über die Sitzung des Vorstandes der DKG, 28 November 1905.

61. *DKZ*, 24 October 1896. The exhibition was not, strictly speaking, organized by the DKG, but by a separate committee composed of some of its leading members.

62. Ibid., 11 April 1908.

63. BA, DKG, R8023/914, Bl. 233, Bericht über die Sitzung des Ausschußes, 15 November 1901. See also Bl. 261, 20 December 1901.

64. Finding evidence of rural colonial propaganda therefore presents numerous difficulties. Looking, on the one hand, "from above," one discovers very few signs of efforts by the DKG or other groups to orchestrate propaganda campaigns in the countryside. The geographically diffuse nature of localized propaganda efforts, on the other hand, means that surviving traces are dispersed across a wide field and are therefore extremely difficult to recover. Evaluating the reception of such propaganda presents even greater problems.

65. *Kölnische Zeitung*, 17 February 1908.

66. *DKZ*, 17 June 1905.

67. Ibid., 19 July 1913.

68. *Kölnische Zeitung*, 17 February 1908.

69. BA, DKG, R8023/915, Bl. 266–67, Bericht über die Sitzung des Ausschußes, 13 November 1903.

70. *DKZ*, 22 June 1912.

71. BA, DKG, R8023/22, Bl. 1, Bericht über die Sitzung des Vorstandes der DKG, 4 June 1912.

72. BA, DKG, R8023/21, Bl. 35, Bericht über die Hauptversammlung der DKG, 9–10 June 1911. See also Bl. 87, "Die Kolonial-Wirtschaftliche Ausstellung der Deutschen Kolonialgesellschaft auf der Jubiläums-Wanderausstellung der Deutschen Landwirtschafts-Gesellschaft" (Kassel 1911).

73. *DKZ*, 16 March 1912, 28 March 1914.

74. Soénius, *Koloniale Begeisterung im Rheinland*, 89–90. On the "yellow" unions, see Klaus Mattheier, *Die Gelben: Nationale Arbeiter zwischen Wirtschaftsfrieden und Streik* (Düsseldorf: Schwann, 1973).

75. Zentralverband christlicher Textilarbeiter Deutschlands, *Geschäftsbericht für die Zeit vom 1. Juli 1912 bis 30. Juni 1914* (Düsseldorf: Zentralverband christlicher Textilarbeiter Deutschlands, 1914), 106.

76. Ibid., 86.

77. Ibid., 128.

78. Ibid., 55, 128.

79. Pierard, "German Colonial Society, 1882–1914," 274.

80. Wildenthal, "Colonizers and Citizens," 200–203. Wildenthal unfortunately gives no information on readership or circulation.

81. BA, DKG, R8023/509, Bl. 228, "Arbeiter, Kolonien und Flotte"; Bl. 247, "Kolonial-National"; Bl. 316–17, "Das ist Wahrheit!"; Bl. 440–41, "Deutschland halte fest an deinen Kolonien!"; R8023/510, Bl. 414–39, "Kolonialpolitischer Führer"; Bl. 412–13, "Die Koloniale Lügenfabrik."

82. Pierard, "German Colonial Society, 1882–1914," 308.

83. BA, DKG, R8023/510, Bl. 34. Inspired patriots penned brief scenes like "Unsere Braven, Fünf Bilder aus dem Leben unserer Truppen in Südwestafrika von A. von Liliencron" and "Eine Viertelstunde in Südwestafrika, Dramatische Szene von Alberta von Frendorf" (Bl. 263–70).

84. *DKZ*, 26 April 1913; SAN, E6 487, Vereinsarchive, Jahresbericht, 1913, Abteilung Nürnberg-Fürth der DKG.

85. BA, DKG, R8023/1092, Bl. 186–93, Hauptversammlung Breslau, 4–5 June 1913.

86. *DKZ*, 14 June 1913.

87. BA, DKG, R8023/1092, Bl. 188, Hauptversammlung Breslau, 4–5 June 1913.

88. A year later, members of the DKG were still referring to the Harburg proposal as a catalyst for propagandizing among the workers. BA, DKG, R8023/17, Bl. 34, Bericht über die Sitzung des Vorstandes der DKG, 28 November 1913; *DKZ*, 7, 28 March, 16 May 1914.

89. "Werbung in Arbeiterkreisen," *DKZ*, 21 June 1913.

90. "Koloniale Werbung und Aufklärung," ibid., 19 July 1913.

91. Ibid., 7 March 1914.

92. Ibid., 28 March 1914; BA, DKG, R8023/1092, Bl. 49, Bericht über die Sitzung des Vorstandes, 4 June 1914.

93. "Koloniale Werbung und Aufklärung," *DKZ*, 19 July 1913.

94. Eley, *Reshaping the German Right*, 221.

95. *DKZ*, 12 December 1901.

96. Ibid., 10 June 1911.

97. Soénius, *Koloniale Begeisterung im Rheinland*, 88.

98. "Koloniale Werbung und Aufklärung," *DKZ*, 19 July 1913.

99. BA, DKG, R8023/917, Bl. 179, Bericht über die Sitzung des Ausschußes, 15 February 1907.

100. BA, DKG, R8023/17, Bl. 34, Bericht über die Sitzung des Vorstandes der DKG, 28 November 1913; R8023/916, Bl. 59, Bericht über die Sitzung des Ausschußes, 20 May 1904; R8023/917, Bl. 174, Bericht über die Sitzung des Ausschußes, 1 February 1907; *DKZ*, 27 June 1914.

101. Dieter Fricke, "Gesamtverbande evangelischer Arbeitervereine Deutschlands, 1890–1933," in *Lexikon zur Parteiengeschichte: Die bürgerlichen und kleinbürgerlichen Parteien und Verbände in Deutschland, 1789–1945*, ed. Dieter Fricke, vol. 3 (Leipzig: VEB Bibliographisches Institut, 1985), 19, 21.

102. *DKZ*, 23 January, 3 April, 20 November 1909, 16 March 1912, 14 June, 22 November 1913, 16 May 1914; BA, R8023/917, DKG, Bericht über die Sitzung des Ausschußes, 10 May 1907, Bl. 270.

103. *LNN*, 25 January 1908.

104. Naumann (1860–1919) was both a pastor and a liberal politician, and in 1896 a founder of the National Social Association. As a Reichstag deputy and author of many books and articles, he was a tireless publicist for his concept of national unity based on social reform at home and imperialism abroad. On Naumann's synthesis of Christian socialism and imperialism, see Dieter Düding, *Der Nationalsoziale Verein, 1896–1903: Der gescheiterte Versuch einer parteipolitischen Synthese von Nationalismus, Sozialismus und Liberalismus* (Munich: Oldenbourg, 1972); Peter Theiner, *Sozialer Liberalismus und deutsche Weltpolitik: Friedrich Naumann im Wilhelminischen Deutschland, 1860–1919* (Baden-Baden: Nomos, 1983).

105. SAL, Kap. 35/275, Evangelischer Arbeiterverein; Kap. 35/802, Evangelischer Arbeiterverein Leipzig-Gohlis.

106. Soénius, *Koloniale Begeisterung im Rheinland*, 88.

107. BA, DKG, R8023/1092, Bl. 190, Hauptversammlung Breslau, 4–5 June 1913.

108. *DKZ*, 20 May 1911.

109. Eley, *Reshaping the German Right*, 220–22.

3. No Place in the Sun

1. Lucie Böttcher to DKG, BA, DKG, R8023/171, Bl. 51–52, 18 January 1898. My deepest gratitude to Molly O'Donnell for so generously making available to me her transcriptions of women's letters from the Bundesarchiv.

2. BA, RKA, R1001/6266, Bl. 23, 9 August 1907.

3. Magda Henck to Colonial Department, Foreign Office, BA, DKG, R8023/171, Bl. 114, 20 February 1898.

4. Apollonia May and Johanna Demmel to DKG, BA, DKG, R8023/171, Bl. 201–2, 2 May 1898.

5. Ida Hofter to Colonial Department, Foreign Office, BA, DKG, R8023/171, Bl. 204, 7 May 1898.

6. BA, RKA, R1001/6262, Bl. 34–35, 16 December 1907.

7. Max Buchner, "Faktorei-Leben in Kamerun," *MNN*, 3 April 1886.

8. Minne Gotzen to Kaiser Wilhelm II, BA, DKG, R8023/171, Bl. 283, 26 April 1898.

9. BA, RKA, R1001/6257, Bl. 148, 26 July 1913 (from Leipzig-Stötteritz).

10. Eugenie Beez to the DKG, BA, DKG, R8023/170, Bl. 150, 27 December 1897. The DKG replies that "of slavery in a German protectorate there is self-evidently no question," even if "circumstances in the protectorate are substantially other than they are in Germany." Von Bornhaupt (DKG) to Eugenie Beez, BA, DKG, R8023/170, Bl. 161–63, 28 December 1897.

11. BA, RKA, R1001/6244, Bl. 145.

12. On German colonial ideology, see Woodruff D. Smith, *The Ideological Origins of Nazi Imperialism* (New York: Oxford University Press, 1986); idem, "The Ideology of German Colonialism, 1840–1906," *Journal of Modern History* 46 (1974): 641–62.

13. Helmuth Stoecker, ed., *German Imperialism in Africa: From the Beginnings until the Second World War*, trans. Bernd Zöllner (London: C. Hurst, 1986), 13.

14. On Hamburg's colonial and overseas interests, see Klaus J. Bade, "Imperial Germany and West Africa: Colonial Movement, Business Interests, and Bismarck's 'Colonial Policies,'" in *Bismarck, Europe, and Africa: The Berlin Africa Conference 1884–1885 and the Onset of Partition*, ed. Stig Förster, Wolfgang J. Mommsen, and Ronald Robinson (New York: Oxford University Press, 1988); Ekkehard Böhm, *Überseehandel und Flottenbau: Hanseatische Kaufmannschaft und deutsche Seerüstung, 1879–1902* (Düsseldorf: Bertelsmann Universitäts-

verlag, 1972); Percy Schramm, *Hamburg, Deutschland und die Welt: Leistung und Grenzen hanseatischen Bürgertums in der Zeit zwischen Napoleon I. und Bismarck* (Munich: Georg D. W. Callwey, 1943); Stoecker, *German Imperialism in Africa*; Helmut Washausen, *Hamburg und die Kolonialpolitik des Deutschen Reiches, 1880–1890* (Hamburg: Hans Christian, 1968).

15. On the early indifference of local magnates and merchants to colonialism, see Bade, *Fabri*, 185–89; Washausen, *Hamburg und die Kolonialpolitik*, 39–42.

16. Adolf Coppius, *Hamburgs Bedeutung auf dem Gebiete der deutschen Kolonialpolitik* (Berlin: Carl Heymann, 1905), 56.

17. See Böhm, *Überseehandel und Flottenbau*; Washausen, *Hamburg und die Kolonialpolitik*.

18. Wilhelm Hübbe-Schleiden, *Deutsche Colonisation: Eine Replik auf das Referat des Herrn Dr. Friedrich Kapp über Colonisation und Auswanderung* (Hamburg: L. Friederichsen, 1881); idem, *Überseeische Politik: Eine culturwissenschaftliche Studie* (Hamburg: L. Friederichsen, 1881). See also Woodruff D. Smith, *The German Colonial Empire* (Chapel Hill: University of North Carolina Press, 1978), 24–25; Washausen, *Hamburg und die Kolonialpolitik*, 35–36, 40; Wehler, *Bismarck*, 144–47.

19. Hundreds of letters from working- and lower middle-class Germans to the Reichskolonialamt comprise a rare record of popular colonial aspirations. Although most are very brief requests, either for information or government aid for colonial settlement, many letters describe the circumstances and hopes of the prospective colonists. Because most do not reveal the writer's profession, educational background, or other personal circumstances, I have not thought it worthwhile to quantify the data. See BA, RKA, R1001/6240–66: Anfragen über Auswanderungsbedingungen und Erlangung von Privatstellungen in den Kolonien and R1001/1170–96: Anfragen über Ansiedlungsverhältnisse in Deutsch-Südwestafrika.

20. The Zentral-Auskunftstelle für Auswanderer (ZAfA) was funded by a subvention from the Reichstag, but administered by the DKG in Berlin, as well as locally by numerous DKG chapters throughout Germany.

21. BA, RKA, R1001/6275, Bl. 25, Geschäftsbericht der ZAfA, 1902–3. The records do not indicate which potential destinations (whether the colonies, America, or elsewhere) were of interest to members of the different occupational categories.

22. BA, RKA, R1001/6275, Bl. 40, Geschäftsbericht der ZAfA, 1903–4; Bl. 72, Geschäftsbericht, 1905–6.

23. Peter Marschalck, *Deutsche Überseewanderung im 19. Jahrhundert* (Stuttgart: Ernst Klett, 1973), 82.

24. BA, RKA, R1001/6275, Bl. 223, Geschäftsbericht der ZAfA, 1907–8.

25. BA, RKA, R1001/6275, Bl. 355, Geschäftsbericht der ZAfA, 1910–11.

26. *DKZ*, 31 August 1912. Of the total number of requests, 11,427 concerned the colonies.

27. Marschalck, *Deutsche Überseeauswanderung*, 82. The *Siedlungswanderung* lasted from about 1815 to 1895 and the *Arbeitswanderung* from 1895 to 1914.

28. BA, RKA, R1001/6241, Bl. 145, 30 September 1909.

29. BA, RKA, R1001/6241, Bl. 9–10.

30. There is scattered evidence of colonization as an effort at upward social mobility. According to Christraud Geary, most missionaries of the Basel Mission in Cameroon came from the peasantry or old *Mittelstand*, had little formal education, and were "upwardly mobile and education-minded." See Geary, "Impressions of the African Past: Interpreting Ethnographic Photographs from Cameroon," *Visual Anthropology* 3 (1990): 296. Similarly, most applicants to the female emigration program for Southwest Africa were young servants or working-class women seeking a better future. See O'Donnell, "The Colonial Woman Question," 81–92.

31. BA, RKA, R1001/6265, Bl. 43, 16 September 1913.

32. BA, RKA, R1001/6262, Bl. 34–35, 16 December 1907.

33. BA, DKG, R8023/171, Bl. 145, n.d.

34. Bade, *Fabri*, 54–67, 80–85, 191–200, 354–62.

35. See figures in Marschalck, *Deutsche Überseewanderung*, 35–37.

36. Ibid., 10–12. On aspects of the emigration in its late phase, see also Klaus J. Bade, "German Emigration to the United States and Continental Immigration to Germany in the Late Nineteenth and Early Twentieth Centuries," *Central European History* 13 (1980): 348–77; idem, "Massenauswanderung und Arbeitsmarkt im deutschen Nordosten von 1880 bis zum Ersten Weltkrieg: Überseeische Auswanderung, interne Abwanderung und kontinentale Zuwanderung," *Archiv für Sozialgeschichte* 20 (1980): 265–323; Wolfgang Köllmann and Peter Marschalck, "German Emigration to the United States," *Perspectives in American History* 7 (1973): 499–554; Mack Walker, *Germany and the Emigration, 1816–1885* (Cambridge, Mass.: Harvard University Press, 1964).

37. Marschalck, *Deutsche Überseeauswanderung*, 36.

38. BA, DKG, R8023/255, Bl. 32, program of the General German Congress. The Central Association for Commercial Geography and the Promotion of German Interests Abroad (Centralverein für Handelsgeographie und Förderung Deutscher Interessen im Auslande), the West German Association for Colonization and Export (Westdeutscher Verein für Colonisation und Export), and the DKV also participated.

39. BA, DKG, R8023/253, Bl. 67, "Rede des Freiherrn Hermann von Maltzan auf der constituirenden Generalversammlung des Deutschen Kolonialvereins," Frankfurt/M., 6 December 1882.

40. Marschalck, *Deutsche Überseeauswanderung*, 12, 77, 82.

41. BA, DKG, R8023/17, Bl. 108, "Unsere Kolonien auf der Jahrhundert Ausstellung: Führer durch die Kolonial-Aussstellung," ed. Hubert Winkler (Breslau, 1913).

42. BA, DKG, R8023/509, Bl. 440, "Deutschland halte fest an deinen Kolonien!" [1907].

43. BA, DKG, R8023/509, Bl. 247, W. Erhardt, "Kolonial-National" (Wiesbaden: Moritz und Münzel, 1907).

44. On the history of emigration and colonialism as solutions to the social question, see Christine Hansen, "Die deutsche Auswanderung im 19. Jahrhundert—ein Mittel zur Lösung sozialer und sozialpolitischer Probleme?" in *Deutsche Amerikaauswanderung im 19. Jahrhundert: Sozialgeschichtliche Beiträge*, ed. Günter Moltmann (Stuttgart: J. B. Metzler, 1976); Bade, *Fabri*.

45. Hübbe-Schleiden, *Deutsche Colonisation*, 65, 64. See also Bade, *Fabri*, 99–102; Wehler, *Bismarck*, 121.

46. Quoted in Bade, *Fabri*, 98.

47. Hübbe-Schleiden, *Deutsche Colonisation*, 97.

48. Friedrich Fabri, *Bedarf Deutschland der Colonien? Eine politisch-ökonomische Betrachtung*, 3rd ed. (1884; bilingual ed., trans. E. C. M. Breuning and M. E. Chamberlain under the title *Does Germany Need Colonies?* [Lewiston, N.Y.: Edwin Mellen, 1998]), 107; Bade, *Fabri*, 91–94.

49. BA, DKG, R8023/509, Bl. 440, "Deutschland halte fest an deinen Kolonien!" [1907].

50. *AVZ*, 21 April, 8 May 1903.

51. *LVZ*, 8 October 1906.

52. Eduard Bernstein, "Die Kolonialfrage und der Klassenkampf," *SM* 13 (1907): 996.

53. Wilhelm Liebknecht, Reichstag speech, 4 March 1885. Quoted in Müller, *Deutschland–Zanzibar–Ostafrika*, 42–43.

54. Discussions about East Africa begin at the turn of the century and continued up to the World War. BA, DKG, R8023/108, Bl. 41, Bericht über die Sitzung der DKG, 1 December 1900; Bl. 58–60, Bericht über die Sitzung des Ausschußes, 17 May 1901; R8023/109, Bl. 105–7, Bericht über die Sitzung des Ausschußes, 8 May 1903; R8023/54, Bl. 12a–13, Bericht über die

Sitzung des Ausschußes, 21 October 1904; R8023/108, Bl. 142, Bericht über die Sitzung des Vorstandes, 28–29 November 1904; Bl. 149, Hauptversammlung der DKG, 15–16 June 1905; Bl. 151, Bericht über die Sitzung des Vorstandes, 7 June 1906; R8023/21, Bl. 35, Bericht über die Hauptversammlung der DKG, 9–10 June 1911; Bl. 45–46, Bericht über die Sitzung des Ausschußes, 30 June 1911; R8023/17, Bl. 133, Bericht über die Sitzung des Aussschußes, 18 June 1913. The society formed a German East Africa Settlement Committee in 1905 and continued to fund research on rail transportation, climate, soil, disease, altitude, water, etc.

55. According to Fritz Müller, this was mere subterfuge: "The greatest obstacle to the large-scale settlement of German farmers and artisans was not the tropical climate . . . but rather the land policy of the colonial administration, which in all the colonies gave away immense territorial concessions to the large colonial companies" (*Deutschland–Zanzibar–Ostafrika*, 44–45).

56. Buchner, *Kamerun*, vii.

57. Walther Rathenau, "Report on the State of the South West African Colony" (1908), in *Walther Rathenau, Industrialist, Banker, Intellectual, and Politician: Notes and Diaries, 1907–1922*, ed. Hartmut Pogge von Strandmann (Oxford: Oxford University Press, 1985), 83.

58. Helmut Bley, *South-West Africa under German Rule, 1894–1914*, trans. Hugh Ridley (Evanston, Ill.: Northwestern University Press, 1971), 76. Whites worked in the Otavi copper mines, on the railroad, and as dock workers in Swakopmund.

59. "Die neuen deutschen Kolonien," *ÜLuM* 54, no. 33 (October 1884–85): 731.

60. BA, DKG R8023/253, Bl. 67, "Rede des Freiherrn Hermann von Maltzan."

61. BA, DKG, R8023/261, Bl. 18–19. On the Syndikat, see also Pierard, "German Colonial Society, 1882–1914," 154–57.

62. BA, DKG, R8023/602, Bl. 276, Franz Giesebrecht, "Kolonialspekulation," *Neue Deutsche Rundschau* (November 1895): 1084–1100; Bl. 301–14, "Vorläufige Erwiderungen des Syndikats für südwestafrikanische Siedelung auf die Angriffe des Herrn Giesebrecht in der Neuen Deutschen Rundschau unter dem Titel 'Koloniale Spekulationen' " (Berlin, 1895).

63. See, for example, Rathenau, "Report," 88–89.

64. BA, DKG, R8023/171, Bl. 315, "Der Rheinische Verband und die Frauenfürsorge für Deutsch-Südwest-Afrika," *Africa*, no. 2 (February 1898): 37.

65. Rudolf Wagner, "Die deutsche Frau in den Kolonien," *WIDM* 108 (1910): 211.

66. Adda von Liliencron, "Frauenarbeit in Südwestafrika," ibid., 727.

67. Daniel J. Walther, *Creating Germans Abroad: Cultural Policies and National Identity in Namibia* (Athens: Ohio University Press, 2002), 2.

68. Krista O'Donnell, "Home, Nation, Empire: Domestic Germanness and Colonial Citizenship," in *The Heimat Abroad: The Boundaries of Germanness*, ed. Krista O'Donnell, Renate Bridenthal, and Nancy Reagin (Ann Arbor: University of Michigan Press, 2005), 42.

69. Walther, *Creating Germans Abroad*, 29, 34, 37–39.

70. Theodor Leutwein, *Elf Jahre Gouverneur in Deutsch-Südwestafrika* (Berlin: Ernst Mittler & Sohn, 1906), 408; Walther, *Creating Germans Abroad*, 15.

71. André du Pisani, *SWA/Namibia: The Politics of Continuity and Change* (Johannesburg: Jonathan Ball, 1986), 25–26.

72. Walther, *Creating Germans Abroad*, 16, chap. 2 generally.

73. Ibid., 22.

74. On the web of relations linking race, class, gender, and sexuality in the colonial context, see Ann Laura Stoler, "Carnal Knowledge and Imperial Power: Gender, Race, and Morality in Colonial Asia," in *Gender at the Crossroads of Knowledge: Feminist Anthropology in the Postmodern Era*, ed. Micaela di Leonardo (Berkeley: University of California Press, 1991); eadem, *Race and the Education of Desire: Foucault's* History of Sexuality *and the Colonial Order of Things* (Durham, N.C.: Duke University Press, 1995). For the case of German Southwest Africa, see Wildenthal, "Colonizers and Citizens,"; eadem, *German Women for Empire*, chap. 3; eadem,

" 'She Is the Victor': Bourgeois Women, Nationalist Identities, and the Ideal of the Independent Woman Farmer in German Southwest Africa," *Social Analysis* 33 (1993): 68–88.

75. BA, DKG, R8023/980, Bl. 179, E. A. Fabarius, "Die Deutsche Kolonialschule und ihre Aufgabe," special offprint, *WIDM* (January 1908). Similarly, in a lecture before the ADV Hannover, Colonial School director Fabarius called for colonizers "from the best circles of the people, from the educated middle and higher estates." BA, DKG, R8023/113, Bl. 42, *Der Deutsche Auswanderer*, no. 2 (1902). On schools for educating settlers see Jake W. Spidle, "Colonial Studies in Imperial Germany," *History of Education Quarterly* 13 (Fall 1973): 231–47.

76. Quoted in Walther, *Creating Germans Abroad*, 22.

77. On the women's emigration program, see O'Donnell, "The Colonial Woman Question"; Richard V. Pierard, "The Transportation of White Women to German Southwest Africa, 1898–1914," *Race* 12 (1970–71): 317–22; Wildenthal, "Colonizers and Citizens," 194–99.

78. Wildenthal, "Colonizers and Citizens," 182–83.

79. BA, DKG, R8023/606, unnumbered, "Eine Lehrfarm in Deutsch-Südwest," *Deutsche Zeitung*, 22 March 1909.

80. BA, DKG, R8023/22, Bl. 1, Bericht über die Sitzung des Vorstandes der DKG, 4 June 1912.

81. Quoted in O'Donnell, "Colonial Woman Question," 47. See also Walther, *Creating Germans Abroad*, 49.

82. Wagner, "Die deutsche Frau," 202.

83. On the class position of women sent to Southwest Africa, see Chickering, " 'Casting Their Gaze,' " 178; O'Donnell, "Colonial Woman Question," 81–92; Pierard, "Transportation of White Women," 319.

84. Lucie Böttcher to DKG, BA, DKG, R8023/171, Bl. 51–52, 18 January 1898.

85. Hedwig Standte to DKG, BA, DKG, R8023/171, Bl. 11, 11 January 1898.

86. Ida Hofter to Colonial Department, Foreign Office, BA, DKG, R8023/171, Bl. 204, 7 May 1898.

87. This was hardly the "army" of white-collar employees, technicians, small businessmen, and shopkeepers who, according to Fritz Müller, formed a "mass basis" for a colonial "Volksbewegung" in the 1870s and 1880s. Müller, *Deutschland–Zanzibar–Ostafrika*, 48–49.

88. Wildenthal, *German Women for Empire*, 146; Pierard, "German Colonial Society," 287–88.

89. Renamed *Die deutschen Kolonien* by at least 1905.

90. SAN, C7/V, 3513, Vereinspolizeiakten, Verein Deutscher Kolonisten (1904).

91. BHStA, MInn 74204, Auswanderung nach Afrika (1838–1908).

92. On veterans' associations in imperial Germany, see Hansjoachim Henning, "Kriegervereine in den preußischen Westprovinzen: Ein Beitrag zur preußischen Innenpolitik zwischen 1860 und 1914," *Rheinische Vierteljahrsblätter* 32 (1968): 430–75; Thomas Rohkrämer, *Der Militarismus der "kleinen Leute": Die Kriegervereine im Deutschen Kaiserreich, 1871–1914* (Munich: Oldenbourg, 1990); Klaus Saul, "Der 'Deutsche Kriegerbund': Zur innenpolitischen Funktion eines 'nationalen' Verbandes im kaiserlichen Deutschland," *Militärgeschichtliche Mitteilungen* 2 (1969): 95–159. None of these deals with the colonial veterans' associations in particular.

93. Rohkrämer, *Militarismus*, 34–35.

94. Ibid., 35. There were some exceptions, for example in the Rhineland and Westphalia, where the core membership consisted of middle and small property owners, master artisans, non–academically trained bureaucrats: middle- to lower middle-class men mindful of distinctions separating them from workers. See Henning, "Kriegervereine in den preußischen Westprovinzen," 470.

95. Henning, "Kriegervereine in den preußischen Westprovinzen," 464, 470; Rohkrämer, *Militarismus*, 36–37.

96. BHStA MInn 65944, Veteranen- und Kriegervereine, 1906–8, Bericht über das 24. Verwaltungsjahr (1907), Bayerischer Veteranen-Verein/Feldzugs-Soldaten der kgl. Haupt- und Residenzstadt München.

97. SAN, C7/V 1300, Vereinspolizeiakten, DKG Abteilung Nürnberg-Fürth, 1888–1928, Mitglieder-Verzeichnis der Abteilung Nürnberg-Fürth der DKG (Nuremberg 1913).

98. Wildenthal, "Colonizers and Citizens," 186 n. 19. The modest dues were just three marks in 1907, raised to four in 1908.

99. Wildenthal, *German Women for Empire*, 150.

100. SAN, E6 292, Vereinsarchive, Veteranen-Vereinigung der Ostasiatischen Expedition 1900/1901 Nürnberg und Umgebung, Statuten (1913).

101. Ibid., "Verzeichnis derjenigen Mitglieder" (1 October 1908); Jahresbericht, 1 October 1907–1 October 1908.

102. Ibid., Statuten (1907, 1913); Jahresbericht, 1 October 1907–1 October 1908.

103. SAB, C2 VI 686/10, Vereinigung ehemaliger Angehöriger des ostasiatischen Expeditions-Corps Bamberg u. Umgebung (1904–19). In March 1907, it renamed itself the Vereinigung ehemaliger Angehöriger des ostasiatischen Expeditionskorps und der kaiserlichen Schutztruppen Bamberg und Umgebung.

104. Rohkrämer, *Militarismus*, 55.

105. SAN, E6 292, Vereinsarchive, Veteranen-Vereinigung der Ostasiatischen Expedition 1900/1901 Nürnberg und Umgebung, Statuten (1913). The Deutscher Kolonialkriegerbund and the Kolonialkriegerdank founded the monthly *Kolonialpost* in Berlin in 1907. See Adolf Dresler, *Die deutschen Kolonien und die Presse* (Würzburg: Konrad Triltsch, 1942), 14.

106. Francke, *Festschrift zum 25-jährigen Bestehen der Abteilung München*, 46.

107. SAB, C2 VI 686/10, Vereinigung ehemaliger Angehöriger des ostasiatischen Expeditions-Corps Bamberg u. Umgebung (1904–19), Vereinigung to Stadtmagistrat Bamberg, 18 June 1909.

108. "Eine Marine- und Kolonial-Ausstellung," *DKZ*, 3 July 1909.

109. "Ein Kolonialkriegerdenkmal in München," *MAAZ*, 7 October 1912.

110. "Die Deutsch-Südwester in Leipzig," *DKZ*, 25 October 1913; SAL, Kap. 26A/104, Das Kolonialkrieger-Denkmal; Kap. 35/1083, Kgl. Sächs. Militärverein ehemaliger kaiserl. Schutztruppen für Leipzig und Umgebung (1913); Kap. 35/1095, Sächsischer Militärverein "China- und Afrika-Krieger" (1914).

111. Arendt, *Origins of Totalitarianism*, 150–55.

112. George W. F. Hallgarten, *Imperialismus vor 1914: Die soziologischen Grundlagen der Außenpolitik europäischer Großmächte vor dem Ersten Weltkrieg*, 2 vols. (Munich: C. H. Beck, 1963), 360.

113. Müller, *Deutschland–Zanzibar–Ostafrika*, 46–49. The theme of a manipulated, decaying *Mittelstand*—if not the contemptuous language—survives in the much more balanced, nuanced work of Wehler and also Woodruff Smith. Wehler discusses "the Kleinbürgertum of craftsmen and small tradesmen, parts of the industrial working class, the rural *Mittelstand*" affected by crisis and afraid of the future. See Wehler, *Bismarck*, 473, 480–81. Woodruff Smith describes the appeal of settlement colonialism to "the self-consciously anti-industrial segment of the middle class." Smith, *The German Colonial Empire*, 144–45.

4. Carnival Knowledge

1. Penny, *Objects of Culture*, esp. 102–6; Zimmerman, *Anthropology and Antihumanism*.

2. On the rise of mass culture in the Kaiserreich, see Lynn Abrams, "From Control to Commercialization: The Triumph of Mass Entertainment in Germany, 1900–25?" *German History*

8 (1990): 278–93; idem, *Workers' Culture in Imperial Germany: Leisure and Recreation in the Rhineland and Westphalia* (London: Routledge, 1992); Peter U. Hohendahl, ed., *Mass Culture in Imperial Germany, 1871–1918*, special issue of *New German Critique* 29 (1984); Lisa Kosok and Mathilde Jamin, eds., *Viel Vergnügen: Öffentliche Lustbarkeiten im Ruhrgebiet der Jahrhundertwende* (Essen: Ruhrlandmuseum and Verlag Peter Pomp, 1992).

3. Ciarlo, *Advertising Empire*.

4. By the end of the nineteenth century, some 90 percent of Germans could read. See Rudolf Schenda, *Volk ohne Buch: Studien zur Sozialgeschichte der populären Lesestoffe, 1770–1910* (Frankfurt/M.: Klostermann, 1970), 444.

5. On colonial themes in mass-consumption colportage literature, see below, chap. 5, and my article "Everyman's Colonial Library: Imperialism and Working-Class Readers in Leipzig, 1890–1914," *German History* 21 (2003): 445–75.

6. *AAZ*, 6 July 1911. The paper ran both an article and an advertisement that day. There is no trace of the exhibition in the local SPD paper, the *Schwäbische Volkszeitung* (until April 1905 the *Augsburger Volkszeitung*).

7. SAA, 10/132, 1, Kapitän Köster to Stadtmagistrat Augsburg, 24 May 1911.

8. *ANN*, 4 July 1911.

9. On both moral and police surveillance and censorship of popular and mass culture in imperial Germany, see Georg Jäger, "Der Kampf gegen Schmutz und Schund: Die Reaktion der Gebildeten auf die Unterhaltungsindustrie," *Archiv für Geschichte des Buchwesens* 31 (1988): 163–91; Peter Jelavich, *Munich and Theatrical Modernism: Politics, Playwriting, and Performance, 1890–1914* (Cambridge, Mass.: Harvard University Press, 1985); Robin Lenman, "Art, Society, and the Law in Wilhelmine Germany: The Lex Heinze," *Oxford German Studies* 8 (1973): 86–113; idem, "Mass Culture and the State in Germany, 1900–26," in *Ideas into Politics: Aspects of European History, 1880–1950*, ed. R. J. Bullen, H. Pogge von Strandmann, and A. B. Polansky (London: Croom Helm, 1984); Kaspar Maase, "Die soziale Konstruktion der Massenkünste: Der Kampf gegen Schmutz und Schund 1907–1918," in *Kunst und Sozialgeschichte*, ed. Martin Papenbrock, Gisela Schirmer, Anette Sohn, and Rosemarie Sprute (Pfaffenweiler: Centaurus, 1995); Elaine Glovka Spencer, "Policing Popular Amusements in German Cities: The Case of Prussia's Rhine Province, 1815–1914," *Journal of Urban History* 16 (1990): 366–85; Gary D. Stark, "Cinema, Society, and the State: Policing the Film Industry in Imperial Germany," in *Essays on Culture and Society in Modern Germany*, ed. Gary D. Stark and Bede Karl Lackner (College Station: Texas A&M University Press, 1982).

10. BA, DKG, R8023/17, Bl. 263.

11. *MNN*, 27 November, 2 December 1886. In Hamburg, a "traveler through Africa who probably never saw Africa" was sentenced to a year in jail for selling counterfeit travelogues. He had "fabricated accounts of Africa from his imagination and assorted papers and sold them to the newspapers with the assurance that the descriptions were of his own experiences."

12. SAA, 10/132, 1, Kapitän Köster to Stadtmagistrat Augsburg, 24 May 1911.

13. SAA, 10/132, 7, Staatssekretär des Reichsmarineamts to Stadtmagistrat Augsburg.

14. BA, DKG, R8023/17, Bl. 336, Kapitän Köster to DKG, 2 December 1910; R8023/1089, Bl. 58, Sitzung der Werbekommission, 16 February 1911.

15. BA, DKG, R8023/17, Bl. 263, "Marine- u. Kolonial-Ausstellung," Kapitän Köster to DKG, 9 December 1911.

16. SAA, 10/132, "Bescheid . . . in der Sache Marine- und Kolonial-Ausstellung," Kammer des Innern, 22 December 1911.

17. *AAZ*, 8 July 1911.

18. *ANN*, 9 July 1911.

19. SAA, 10/132, "Bescheid . . . in der Sache Marine- und Kolonial-Ausstellung."

20. SAA, 10/132, "Führer durch Kapitän Kösters Marine- und Kolonial-Ausstellung."

21. *AAZ*, 16 June 1911.

22. Ibid. Its supporters included the Imperial Naval Office, the Imperial Shipyards, Krupp, the Germania Shipyards in Kiel, the Vulkan Shipyards in Stettin, and "a series of other large shipbuilding and shipping companies."

23. SAA, 10/132, 7, Staatssekretär des Reichs-Marine-Amts to Stadtmagistrat Augsburg.

24. *ANN*, 9 July 1911.

25. BA, DKG, R8023/17, Bl. 265, "Zeugnissabdrücke über Käpitan Kösters Marine- und Kolonial-Ausstellung."

26. BA, DKG, R8023/17, Bl. 335, "Führer durch Kapitän Kösters völkerkundliche und entomologische Ausstellung."

27. Among works on the *Völkerschauen*, see Eric Ames, *Carl Hagenbeck's Empire of Entertainments* (Seattle: University of Washington Press, 2008); Sierra Ann Bruckner, "The Tingle-Tangle of Modernity: Popular Anthropology and the Cultural Politics of Identity in Imperial Germany" (Ph.D. diss., University of Iowa, 1999); Lisa M. Gates, "Images of Africa in Late Nineteenth- and Twentieth-Century German Literature and Culture" (Ph.D. diss., Harvard University, 1996); Stefan Goldmann, "Wilde in Europa: Aspekte und Orte ihrer Zurschaustellung," in *Wir und die Wilden: Einblicke in eine kannibalische Beziehung*, ed. Thomas Theye (Reinbek bei Hamburg: Rowohlt, 1984); idem, "Zwischen Panoptikum und Zoo: Exoten in Völkerschauen um 1900," in *Menschenfresser-Negerküsse: Das Bild vom Fremden im deutschen Alltag*, ed. Marie Lorbeer and Beate Wild (Berlin: Elefanten Press, 1991); Ulrich van der Heyden, "Südafrikanische 'Berliner': Die Kolonial- und Transvaal-Ausstellung in Berlin und die Haltung der deutschen Missionsgesellschaften zur Präsentation fremder Menschen und Kulturen," in *Fremde Erfahrungen: Asiaten und Afrikaner in Deutschland, Österreich und in der Schweiz bis 1945*, ed. Gerhard Höpp (Berlin: Verlag Das Arabische Buch, 1996); Hilke Thode-Arora, *Für fünfzig Pfennig um die Welt: Die Hagenbeckschen Völkerschauen* (Frankfurt/M.: Campus, 1989); Zimmerman, *Anthropology and Antihumanism*, chap. 1.

28. Ames, *Carl Hagenbeck*.

29. Bruckner, "Tingle-Tangle," 253. In his study of colonialism in French mass culture, William Schneider likewise acknowledges the extreme difficulty of reconstructing spectators' responses to ethnographic shows. See *An Empire for the Masses: The French Popular Image of Africa, 1870–1900* (Westport, Conn.: Greenwood, 1982), 146.

30. See, for example, on distraction, fantasy, and illusion in the theatrical spectacles of exotic lands and peoples at Sarrasani's famous Dresden *Welttheater*, Marline Otte, "Sarrasani's Theater of the World: Monumental Circus Entertainment in Dresden, from Kaiserreich to Third Reich," *German History* 17 (1999): 527–42.

31. SAA, 5/630, flyer for "Die Togotruppe."

32. *AAZ*, 14 September 1898.

33. Thode-Arora, *Für fünfzig Pfennig*, 170–74. According to Bruckner, of the at least one hundred shows in Germany between 1884 and 1914, only about a quarter featured performers from the German colonies. "Tingle-Tangle," 252.

34. *AAZ*, 14 September 1898, advertisement.

35. *ANN*, 17 September 1898; *AAZ*, 16 September 1898.

36. *AAZ*, 16 September 1898.

37. "40 Jahre wissenschaftlicher Tätigkeit der Münchener Anthropologischen Gesellschaft, 1870–1910," *Beiträge zur Anthropologie und Urgeschichte Bayerns* 18 (1911): xv.

38. *AAZ*, 9 August 1898. Franz Suppé (1819–95) was a Viennese composer of operetta who had conducted his last work, *Die Afrikareise*, with great success in Germany in 1883.

39. Ibid., 4 December 1898.

40. International imperialist rivalries may have added to the show's appeal: Tripoli had been much in the press the year before, during the Tripolitan War, Italy's bid for colonial conquest in Ottoman North Africa.

41. *AAZ*, 3 August, 18 September 1912.

42. Ames, *Carl Hagenbeck*, 70.

43. In 1904, for example, a "white negress" was displayed along with the wax "abnormalities" and other "curiosities" of a major Berlin wax museum. See "Die weiße Negerin im Berliner Passage-Panoptikum," *LIZ*, 20 October 1904.

44. Ernst Bloch, *Heritage of Our Times*, trans. Neville and Stephen Plaice (Berkeley: University of California Press, 1991), 159.

45. "Die Somali-Neger im Zoologischen Garten zu Berlin," *LIZ*, 2 August 1885.

46. SAA, 5/630, Magistrat der Stadt Augsburg. Schaustellg. v. Riesen, Riesenfrauen, Zwergen, Albinos, Azteken, u. sonst merkw. Pers. (1848–1898). (The name of the file itself suggests a context for interpreting the reception of the ethnographic shows.) The *Menschfisch* had been "captured in 1888, during a violent hurricane, by natives with harpoons and chains off the eastern coast of Zanzibar"—just when German East Africa and Zanzibar were much in the press due to German suppression of the so-called "Arab revolt" along the coast. On the relationship of ethnographic shows and freak shows, see also Bruckner, "Tingle-Tangle," 254–60.

47. Bruckner, "Tingle-Tangle," 381–86; Zimmerman, *Anthropology and Antihumanism*, 20–30.

48. Ames, *Carl Hagenbeck*, 43, 51.

49. Sierra Ann Bruckner, "Spectacles of (Human) Nature: Commercial Ethnography between Leisure, Learning, and *Schaulust*," in *Worldly Provincialism: German Anthropology in the Age of Empire*, ed. H. Glenn Penny and Matti Bunzl (Ann Arbor: University of Michigan Press, 2003).

50. Ibid., 70–71.

51. Bruckner, "Tingle-Tangle;" Zimmerman, *Anthropology and Antihumanism*, chap. 1; Penny, *Objects of Culture*, 103–4; Ames, *Carl Hagenbeck*, 64, 68.

52. Bruckner, "Spectacles of (Human) Nature," 137–39.

53. BHStA, MK 40497, Deutsche Anthropologische Gesellschaft in München (1874–1948), "Das 25-jährige Jubiläum der Münchener Gesellschaft für Anthropologie, Ethnologie und Urgeschichte" (1895), 37–38.

54. On the relationship between German science, entertainment, and freaks more generally, see Nigel Rothfels, "Aztecs, Aborigines, and Ape-People: Science and Freaks in Germany, 1850–1900," in *Freakery: Cultural Spectacles of the Extraordinary Body*, ed. Rosemarie Garland Thomson (New York: New York University Press, 1996); Zimmerman, *Anthropology and Antihumanism*, 73–85. Zimmerman, focusing on the development of anthropology as a discipline, insists on a "contradiction in German anthropology between the role of freaks and the role of ethnographic performers," a contradiction that likely lost its significance among impresarios and the public (85).

55. See Bruckner, "Tingle-Tangle," 282–92; Zimmerman, *Anthropology and Antihumanism*, 18–19.

56. "40 Jahre wissenschaftlicher Tätigkeit," xv–xviii.

57. Ames, *Carl Hagenbeck*, 68.

58. On popular science in Germany, see Andreas W. Daum, *Wissenschaftspopularisierung im 19. Jahrhundert: Bürgerliche Kultur, naturwissenschaftliche Bildung und die deutsche Öffentlichkeit, 1848–1914* (Munich: Oldenbourg, 1998); Alfred Kelly, *The Descent of Darwin: The Popularization of Darwinism in Germany, 1860–1914* (Chapel Hill: University of North Carolina Press, 1981).

59. Glenn Penny makes clear that German anthropology was in no way simply reducible to German colonialism, which it long predated. See Penny, *Objects of Culture*, 3, 11–12.

60. Ibid., 131–32, 144–51, 160–61.

61. Indeed, most were actually travelogues, rather than anthropological studies.

62. Advertisement, *AVZ*, 9 November 1903.

63. Rothfels, "Aztecs, Aborigines, and Ape-People"; Short, "Everyman's Colonial Library;" Zimmerman, *Anthropology and Antihumanism*, 74–75. Zimmerman makes clear that, the popular Darwinism of impresarios and audiences notwithstanding, German anthropologists wholly rejected interpretations of freaks as atavistic "missing links" (chap. 3).

64. SAA, 5/Nr. 627, Magistrat der Stadt Augsburg. Panorama, Wachsfiguren, anatomische u. Naturalien-Kabinetts-Schaukästen (1889–1898), "Kullmann's Museum für Kunst und Wissenschaft." Among the "automatons and plastic art works" were "historical groups" and fairy-tale figures.

65. On both Castan's Panoptikum and the Passage-Panoptikum in Berlin, see Peter Letkemann, "Das Berliner Panoptikum: Namen, Häuser und Schicksale," *Mitteilungen des Vereins für die Geschichte Berlins* 69 (1973): 319–26; Stephan Oettermann, "Alles-Schau: Wachsfigurenkabinette und Panoptiken," in Kosok and Jamin, *Viel Vergnügen*. On the relationship of Castan's *Panoptikum* to contemporary anthropology in particular, see Bruckner, "Tingle-Tangle," 250–51; Goldmann, "Wilde in Europa," 259–61; Zimmerman, *Anthropology and Antihumanism*, 16–20.

66. SAA, 5/Nr. 627, Magistrat der Stadt Augsburg. Panorama, Wachsfiguren, anatomische u. naturalien Kabinetts Schaukästen (1889–1898), "Katalog zu dem Panoptikum à la Castan."

67. Bruckner, "Spectacles of (Human) Nature"; Ames, *Carl Hagenbeck*, 79, 88, 94–102.

68. The most stimulating work on colonial exhibitions is Timothy Mitchell, "The World as Exhibition," *Comparative Studies in Society and History* 31 (1989): 217–36. See also Yaël Simpson Fletcher, "'Capital of the Colonies': Real and Imagined Boundaries between Metropole and Empire in 1920s Marseilles," in *Imperial Cities: Landscape, Display and Identity*, ed. Felix Driver and David Gilbert (Manchester: Manchester University Press, 1999).

69. On the 1896 Colonial Exhibition, see Stefan Arnold, "Propaganda mit Menschen aus Übersee: Kolonialausstellungen in Deutschland, 1896 bis 1940," in *Kolonialausstellungen—Begegnungen mit Afrika?* ed. Robert Debusmann and János Riesz (Frankfurt/M.: IKO, 1995); Bruckner, "Tingle-Tangle," chap. 4; Roland Richter, "Die erste deutsche Kolonial-Ausstellung 1896: Der 'amtliche Bericht' in historischer Perspektive," in Debusmann and Riesz, *Kolonialausstellungen*.

70. SAA, Hassler-Archiv 19/DKG, Jahresbericht der Deutschen Kolonialgesellschaft (1895), 34–35.

71. Simmel, "Berliner Gewerbe-Ausstellung," 59.

72. Lindenberg, *Pracht-Album*, 54.

73. Arbeitsausschuß der Deutschen Kolonial-Ausstellung, *Deutschland und seine Kolonien im Jahre 1896: Amtlicher Bericht über die erste deutsche Kolonial-Ausstellung* (Berlin: Dietrich Reimer, 1897), 15.

74. Pierard, "German Colonial Society, 1882–1914," 207.

75. In 1893, for example, Franz Stuhlmann displayed two Aka Pygmy women to raise funds for the DKG. See Wildenthal, *German Women for Empire*, 50.

76. Arbeitsausschuß der Deutschen Kolonial-Ausstellung, *Deutschland und seine Kolonien*, 7.

77. Ibid., 35.

78. Ibid., 37.

79. *DKZ*, 2 May 1896.

80. Lindenberg, *Pracht-Album*, 180–82.

81. Kühnemann et al., *Berlin und seine Arbeit*, 181.

82. *DKZ*, 24 October 1896.

83. Kühnemann et al. *Berlin und seine Arbeit*, 181.

84. Ames, *Carl Hagenbeck*, 98.

85. Ibid., 98–100; Bruckner, "Spectacles of (Human) Nature," 129, 140–44, 148–55.

86. BA, DKG, R8023/644, Bl. 97, clipping, "Der Schluß der Kolonial-Ausstellung," *DKZ*, 24 October 1896.

87. Prager, *Deutsche Kolonialgesellschaft*, 120.

88. "Das Kolonial-Museum in Berlin," *DKZ*, 19 October 1899; "Entstehung und Zweck der ständigen Berliner Kolonial-Ausstellung," ibid., 30 November 1899; Pierard, "German Colonial Society, 1882–1914," 206–7.

89. Penny, *Objects of Culture*, 42–43.

90. "Deutsches Kolonial-Museum, Berlin," *DKZ*, 15 July 1911. The total of 481,259 paying visitors supposedly excluded thousands of schoolchildren and poorer association members who received free admission.

91. BA, DKG, R8023/646, Bl. 276–77. Promotional material highlighted the testimonials of teachers who had visited the museum (presumably with their pupils).

92. BA, DKG, R8023/646, 915, Bl. 166, Bericht über die Sitzung des Ausschußes, 20 March 1903.

93. *DKZ*, 7 April 1904.

94. "Deutsches Kolonialmuseum," ibid., 10 July 1909.

95. It was fitting that the former panorama had depicted a North German Lloyd steamship entering New York harbor, the destination of the many hundreds of thousands of German emigrants so often lamented by settlement colonialists. Oettermann, *The Panorama*, 270–74. For further discussion of panoramas, see below.

96. BA, DKG, R8023/644, Bl.160, "Zeichnungs-Einladung zur Bildung der Actien-Gesellschaft 'Deutsches Kolonial-Museum' zu Berlin."

97. Oettermann, *The Panorama*, 244. Hellgrewe had worked on the earlier Marine-Panorama.

98. BA, DKG, R8023/645, Bl. 9, clipping, *Berliner Neueste Nachrichten* (n.d.). The central rotunda had originally held a panoramic painting 48 feet high and 350 feet long. See Oettermann, *The Panorama*, 270–71.

99. BA, DKG, R8023/645, Bl. 14–15, clipping, *DKZ*, 1897, no. 8.

100. BA, DKG, R8023/645, Bl. 26–29, "Zeichnungs-Einladung zu der Actien-Gesellschaft Deutsches Kolonialmuseum."

101. Oettermann, *The Panorama*, 49.

102. BA, DKG, R8023/645, Bl. 9, clipping, *Berliner Neueste Nachrichten* (n.d.).

103. The device was not original. The rooms of the old Marine-Panorama had been furnished as an ocean steamer, with cabins, portholes, railings, and gangways, from which the viewer emerged, as if onto a ship's deck, to view the breathtaking panorama of New York harbor. See Oettermann, *The Panorama*, 271–72.

104. BA, DKG, R8023/645, Bl. 28, "Zeichnungs-Einladung zu der Actien-Gesellschaft Deutsches Kolonialmuseum."

105. BA, DKG, R8023/645, Bl. 28; Bl. 9, clipping, *Berliner Neueste Nachrichten* (n.d.).

106. BA, DKG, R8023/645, 646, Bl. 191–95, "Führer durch das Deutsche Kolonial-Museum in Berlin."

107. BA, RKA, R1001/6361, Bl. 52. See postcards depicting museum displays and dioramas: "Die Felsengrotte," "Der Chinesische Tempel," "Das arabische Haus mit dem Leuchtthurm," "Die Togohütten," and "Ein Winkel im Neu-Guinea-Dorf."

108. BA, DKG, R8023/646, Bl. 195, "Führer durch das Deutsche Kolonial-Museum in Berlin."

109. Bruckner, "Tingle-Tangle," 125; Penny, *Objects of Culture*, 43.

110. Penny, *Objects of Culture*, 193–96, 201.

111. Bernhard Dernburg, *Zielpunkte des Deutschen Kolonialwesens: Zwei Vorträge* (Berlin: Mittler, 1907), 12.

112. *DKZ*, 27 April 1907.

113. From a memorandum to Chancellor von Bülow with detailed proposals for directing the Bülow bloc's campaign, 14 December 1906. Reproduced in Dieter Fricke, "Der deutsche Imperialismus und die Reichstagswahlen von 1907," *Zeitschrift für Geschichtswissenschaft* 9 (1961): 553. Bülow's response in the margin: "Right."

114. A good example is the propaganda leaflet "Das ist Wahrheit!" with color reproductions of paintings by the ubiquitous "Orientmaler" Rudolf Hellgrewe. The dramatic cover shows the nighttime African sky ablaze in lurid red and yellow as Herero "savages," terrifying in their murderous lust, attack a family of German settlers. BA, R8023/509, DKG, Bl. 316–17.

115. *LVZ*, 1 November 1907. Paul Busch, owner of Zirkus Busch, Hamburg, and Albert Schumann, owner of Zirkus Schumann, Berlin.

5. Ethnographic-Fantastic

1. Habermas, *The Structural Transformation of the Public Sphere*, 23, 29.

2. Ibid., 56.

3. Schenda, *Volk ohne Buch*, 444.

4. Ronald A. Fullerton, "Creating A Mass Book Market in Germany: The Story of the 'Colporteur Novel,' 1870–1890," *JSH* 10 (1977): 265–83.

5. Ronald A. Fullerton, "Toward A Commercial Popular Culture in Germany: The Development of Pamphlet Fiction, 1871–1914," *JSH* 12 (1979): 495–500.

6. Karl Heinrici, "Die Verhältnisse im deutschen Colportagebuchhandel," *Schriften des Vereins für Sozialpolitik* 79 (1899): 203. Heinrici points out such peculiarities of the book market in Leipzig.

7. Rudolf Schenda, *Die Lesestoffe der kleinen Leute: Studien zur populären Literatur im 19. und 20. Jahrhundert* (Munich: C. H. Beck, 1976), 97.

8. Ibid., 205, 209–11.

9. Moritz William Theodor Bromme, *Lebensgeschichte eines modernen Fabrikarbeiters*, ed. Paul Göhre (Jena: Eugen Diederichs, 1905), 285–87.

10. Rudolf Schenda, "Tausend deutsche populäre Drucke aus dem 19. Jahrhundert," *Archiv für Geschichte des Buchwesens* 11 (1971): 1466–1651. For a sense of popular themes, see Schenda's list of a thousand titles, which includes religious tracts, colporteur novels, and diverse ephemera of the period. Among colonial titles on Schenda's list are *Anarkalli, die indische Bajadere, oder der Sepoy-Aufstand in Indien* and *Die Gefangenen unter den Wilden der Südsee-Inseln, oder: Schreckliche Schicksale der Mannschaft des Schiffes Mentor.* As was typical of this sort of literature, most have no date of publication.

11. Fullerton, "Popular Culture," 497–99; Hans Friedrich Foltin, "Zur Erforschung der Unterhaltungs- und Trivialliteratur, insbesondere im Bereich des Romans," in *Studien zur Trivialliteratur*, ed. Heinz Otto Burger (Frankfurt/M.: Klostermann, 1968), 254–55.

12. Hans-Josef Steinberg, "Workers' Libraries in Germany Before 1914," *History Workshop* 1 (1976): 166–80; *Bibliothekar* 1 (1909): 28. This example of a periodicals category encompassing ten titles in a public library in Berlin encapsulates the thematic constellation of discourses and disciplines so typical of the period: science, the mass-cultural encounter with overseas worlds, and colonialism.

13. Heinrici, "Colportagebuchhandel," 215, 217.

14. A. H. Th. Pfannkuche, *Was liest der deutsche Arbeiter?* (Tübingen: Mohr, 1900), 42.

15. On colonialism in the *Gartenlaube*, see Kirsten Belgum, *Popularizing the Nation: Audience, Representation, and the Production of Identity in* Die Gartenlaube, *1853–1900* (Lincoln: University of Nebraska Press, 1998), in particular chapter 6, "Colonialism, Myth, and Nostalgia."

16. Emil Sembritzki, ed., *Der Kolonialfreund: Kritischer Führer durch die volkstümliche deutsche Kolonial-Literatur* (Berlin: Kolonie und Heimat, 1912), 5–6, 19–20, 32.

17. Ibid., 5–6, 19–20, 32, 21.

18. On the broad range of works sold by colporteurs see Heinrici, "Colportage," 215.

19. Advertisement in *ÜLuM*, 65, no. 25 (1891), 542; Konrad Haenisch, "Was lesen die Arbeiter?" *Die Neue Zeit* 18, no. 49 (1899–1900): 693.

20. Heinrici, "Colportage," 219–21.

21. Schenda, *Volk ohne Buch*, 318–19; idem, "Tausend populäre Drucke," 1630. See also Sembritzki, *Der Kolonialfreund.*

22. Johannes Olpp, *Erlebnisse im Hinterlande von Angra-Pequena*, Rheinische Missionstraktate (Barmen: Verlag der Rheinischen Missions-Gesellschaft, 1896); H. Riechmann, *Unter den Zwartboois auf Franzfontein: Ein Beitrag zur Missions- und Kolonialgeschichte Südafrikas*, Rheinische Missions-Schriften, no. 83 (Barmen: Verlag des Missions-Hauses, 1899). I am grateful to Wolfram Hartmann for making several of the Rhenish Missionary Society tracts available to me.

23. Tony Kellen, "Der Massenvertrieb der Volksliteratur," *Preußische Jahrbücher* 98 (October–December 1899): 83.

24. Ernst Schultze, *Freie öffentliche Bibliotheken: Volksbibliotheken und Lesehallen* (Stettin: Dannenberg, 1900), 12–13, 16.

25. Walter Hofmann, "Die Organisation des Ausleihdienstes in der modernen Bildungsbibliothek," part 2, "Zur Psychologie des Proletariats," *Volksbildungsarchiv* 1 (1910): 227, 312–44.

26. Among the books listed were Brenner, *Besuch bei den Kannibalen*; Karl Dove, *Südwestafrika: Kriegs- und Friedensbilder aus der ersten deutschen Kolonie* (1896); Kurt von Morgan, *Durch Kamerun von Süd nach Nord: Reisen und Forschungen im Hinterlande, 1889 bis 1891* (1893); Paul Reichard, *Deutsch-Ostafrika: Das Land und Seine Bewohner* (1892); Rochus Schmidt, *Deutschlands Kolonien: Ihre Gestaltung, Entwicklung und Hilfsquellen* (1895); Kurd Schwabe, *Mit Schwert und Pflug in Deutsch-Südwestafrika: Vier Kriegs- und Wanderjahre* (1899); Franz Stuhlmann, *Mit Emin Pascha ins Herz von Afrika: Ein Reisebericht* (1894); Hermann von Wissmann, *Unter deutscher Flagge quer durch Afrika von West nach Ost, von 1880 bis 1883* (1888). Three other workers—a coppersmith, age twenty-nine, a mill worker, twenty-one, and a machinist, nineteen—had similar profiles. Ibid., 313.

27. Ibid., 261.

28. Alberto Martino, *Die deutsche Leihbibliothek: Geschichte einer literarischen Institution, 1756–1914* (Wiesbaden: Otto Harrassowitz, 1990), 376.

29. StAL, AH 2737, Bücher-Verzeichnis der Öffentlichen Bibliothek des Vereins "Volkswohl" in Gautsch, ca. 1905.

30. *Blätter für Volksbibliotheken und Lesehallen* 3 (1902): 84. On Wissmann's popularity, see Cornelia Essner, *Deutsche Afrikareisende im neunzehnten Jahrhundert: Zur Sozialgeschichte des Reisens* (Stuttgart: Steiner, 1985), 116.

31. On the popularity of Gerstäcker in workers' libraries, see Steinberg, "Workers' Libraries."

32. Hofmann, "Psychologie," 261, 270, 291.

33. Dieter Langewiesche and Klaus Schönhoven, "Arbeiterbibliotheken und Arbeiterlektüre im Wilhelminischen Deutschland," *Archiv für Sozialgeschichte* 16 (1976): 151.

34. Martino, *Die deutsche Leihbibliothek*, 306.

35. Rolf Engelsing, *Analphabetentum und Lektüre: Zur Sozialgeschichte des Lesens in Deutschland zwischen feudaler und industrieller Gesellschaft* (Stuttgart: Metzler, 1973), 124–25.

36. SAL, PB 1906, 25–25b.

37. Gustav Hennig, "Proletarisches und bürgerliches Bibliothekwesen in Leipzig im Jahre 1912," *Der Bibliothekar* 5 (1913): 671.

38. Wilhelm Liebknecht, "Wissen ist Macht — Macht ist Wissen," in *Kleine Politische Schriften*, ed. Wolfgang Schröder (Leipzig: Reclam, 1976), 149.

39. *Der Bibliothekar* 3 (1911): 279.

40. Gustav Hennig, *Zehn Jahre Bibliothekarbeit: Geschichte einer Arbeiterbibliothek* (Leipzig: Leipziger Buchdruckerei, 1908), 25.

41. E. Graf, "Die Bildung Berliner Arbeiter," *Zentralblatt für Volksbildungswesen* 9 (1909): 22.

42. Wilhelm Nitschke, "Wie und nach welcher Richtung entwickelt sich das Lesebedürfnis der Arbeiterschaft?" *SM* 19 (January–May 1913): 366.

43. Gottfried Mergner, "Solidarität mit den 'Wilden'? Das Verhältnis der deutschen Sozialdemokratie zu den afrikanischen Widerstandskämpfen in den ehemaligen deutschen Kolonien um die Jahrhundertwende," in *Internationalism in the Labour Movement, 1830–1940*, ed. Frits van Holthoon and Marcel van der Linden (Leiden: E. J. Brill, 1988), 83.

44. *Der Bibliothekar* 5 (1913): 655; 1 (1909): 61–62. The list includes the following (in some cases, dates of publication are not available — also in subsequent notes): Franz von Bülow, *Im Felde gegen die Hereros: Erlebnisse eines Mitkämpfers* (1905); Dove, *Südwestafrika*; Helene von Falkenhausen, *Ansiedlerschicksale: Elf Jahre in Deutsch-Südwestafrika, 1893–1904*; Curt von François, *Deutsch-Südwest-Afrika: Geschichte der Kolonisation bis zum Ausbruch des Krieges mit Witbooi, April 1893* (1899); Graf Gustav von Götzen, *Durch Afrika von Ost nach West: Resultate und Begebenheiten einer Reise von der Deutsch-Ostafrikanischen Küste bis zur Kongomündung in den Jahren 1893/94* (1895); Wilhelm Junker, *Dr. Wilhelm Junkers Reisen in Afrika 1875 bis 1886* (1889–91); David Livingstone, *Entdeckungsreisen in Afrika*; Gustav Nachtigal, *Sahara und Sudan: Ergebnisse sechsjähriger Reisen in Afrika*; Carl Peters, *Im Goldland des Altertums: Forschungen zwischen Zambesi und Sabi* (1902); Magdalene von Prince, *Eine deutsche Frau im Innern Deutsch-Ostafrikas: Elf Jahre nach Tagebuchblättern erzählt* (1903); Gerhard Rohlfs, *Quer durch Afrika: Die Erstdurchquerung der Sahara vom Mittelmeer zum Golf von Guinea, 1865–1867* (1874); Schwabe, *Mit Schwert und Pflug in Deutsch-Südwestafrika*; H. M. Stanley, *Im dunkelsten Afrika*; Hermann von Wissmann, *Im Innern Afrikas: Die Erforschung des Kassai während der Jahre 1883, 1884 und 1885* (1888); idem, *In den Wildnissen Afrikas und Asiens: Jagderlebnisse*; idem, *Meine zweite Durchquerung Äquatorial-Afrikas vom Kongo zum Zambesi während der Jahre 1886 und 1887*; idem, *Unter deutscher Flagge*.

45. Hennig, *Zehn Jahre Bibliothekarbeit*, 10–11. Among most-read titles in the "Reisebeschreibungen und Naturwissenschaften" section: R. Bock, *Unter den Kannibalen Borneos*; G. A. Farini, *Durch die Kalahari-Wüste*; Karl Lumholtz, *Unter Menschenfressern: Eine vierjährige Reise in Australien* (1892); Richard Oberländer, ed. *Westafrika vom Senegal bis Benguela: Reisen und Schilderungen aus Senegambien, Ober- und Niederguinea* (1878); Stanley, *Im dunkelsten Afrika*; Herbert Ward, *Fünf Jahre unter den Stämmen des Kongostaates* (1891); Wissmann, *Unter deutscher Flagge*. Among most-read authors in the youth section were Defoe, *Robinson Crusoe*, and Kipling (three volumes borrowed 129 times). On the peculiar position of Zola's novels, which fit into neither basic category of "entertaining" or "educational" literature, see Langewiesche and Schönhoven, "Arbeiterbibliotheken," 194–95.

46. Pfannkuche, *Was liest*, 21–23.

47. "Bibliotheken für Arbeiter," *Die Gartenlaube*, no. 41 (1889): 707.

48. Eugen Wolf, *Wissmann: Deutschlands Grösster Afrikaner* (Leipzig: Friedrich Wilhelm Grunow, n.d. [1905?]), 2. Joseph Conrad — a more famous example — recalls how, as a young boy in Poland, an arctic exploration account first stirred his geographical imagination. He describes how the book "sent me off on the romantic explorations of my inner self; to the

discovery of the taste of poring over maps; and revealed to me the existence of a latent devotion to geography." His later travels in the Congo began, in a sense, in his boyhood when, as he recalls it, "putting my finger on a spot in the very middle of the then white heart of Africa, I declared that someday I would go there." Joseph Conrad, "Geography and Some Explorers," *Last Essays* (Garden City, N.Y.: Doubleday, 1926), 12, 16–17.

49. Wildenthal, *German Women for Empire*, 29.

50. Fabri, *Bedarf Deutschland der Colonien?* 57, 59.

51. Among works dealing with the themes and ideological subtexts of colonial literature, see Sibylle Benninghoff-Lühl, *Deutsche Kolonialromane 1884–1914 in ihrem Entstehungs- und Wirkungszusammenhang* (Bremen: Übersee-Museum, 1983); Amadou Booker Sadji, *Das Bild des Negro-Afrikaners in der Deutschen Kolonialliteratur, 1884–1945: Ein Beitrag zur literarischen Imagologie Schwarzafrikas* (Berlin: Dietrich Reimer, 1985); Joachim Warmbold, *Germania in Africa: Germany's Colonial Literature* (New York: Peter Lang, 1989).

52. Felix Hänsch, "Weltpolitik, Kolonialpolitik und Schule," *Zeitschrift für Kolonialpolitik, Kolonialrecht und Kolonialwirtschaft* 9, no. 10 (October 1907): 774.

53. Zacher, "Ein Aktionsprogramm für koloniale Volksaufklärung," *Kölnische Zeitung*, 17 February 1908.

54. Hofmann, "Psychologie," 312–44. The book was Adolf Heilborn, *Die deutschen Kolonien* [1905?].

55. Sembritzki, *Kolonialfreund*, 111, 103. Gustav Frenssen, *Peter Moors Fahrt nach Südwest: Ein Feldzugbericht* (Berlin, 1906).

56. SAN C7/V 1300, Vereinspolizeiakten (Acten des Statdmagistrats Nürnberg), Deutsche Kolonialgesellschaft, Abteilung Nürnberg-Fürth, 1888–1928, "Katalog der Bibliothek der Abteilung Nürnberg der Deutschen Kolonialgesellschaft"; "Aus den Abteilungen," *DKZ* 18 (1901); "Deutsche Kolonialgesellschaft," *AAZ*, 9 July 1912.

57. *MNN*, 2 March 1886.

58. BA, R8023/108, Bl. 127. "Bericht über die Sitzung des Vorstandes der Deutschen Kolonialgesellschaft," 28 November 1905.

59. *AAZ*, 2 April 1911.

60. *ANN*, 8 July 1911.

61. See, for example, Karl Dove, *Die deutschen Kolonien*, vol. 1: *Togo und Kamerun*, vol. 2: *Das Südseegebiet und Kiautschou* (Leipzig: Göschen, 1909, 1911).

62. On the origins and development of popular science, see Andreas W. Daum, *Wissenschaftspopularisierung im 19. Jahrhundert: Bürgerliche Kultur, naturwissenschaftliche Bildung und die deutsche Öffentlichkeit, 1848–1914* (Munich: Oldenbourg, 1998); Kelly, *Descent of Darwin*, 10–18.

63. On the contradictions between ideological-pedagogical goals and realist practice in workers' libraries, see Dieter Langewiesche and Klaus Schönhoven, "Arbeiterbibliotheken"; and Steinberg, "Workers' Libraries."

64. *SVZ*, 27 December 1906.

65. *Bibliothekar* 1 (1909): 62; 5 (1913): 571–72. The book was *Vom Kongo zum Niger und Nil: Berichte der deutschen Zentralafrika-Expedition 1910–11*, 2 vols. (Leipzig: Brockhaus, 1912). The duke served as the last German governor of Togo (1912–14).

66. Hans Meyer, *Das Deutsche Kolonialreich: Eine Länderkunde der deutschen Schutzgebiete*, vol. 1 (Leipzig: Verlag des Bibliographischen Instituts, 1909), 7.

67. Kelly, *Descent of Darwin*, chap. 7, "Darwin, Marx, and the German Workers," traces this development among workers; Steinberg, "Workers' Libraries."

68. Manfred Häckel, "Arbeiterbewegung und Literatur," in *100 Jahre Reclams Universal-Bibliothek, 1867–1967*, edited by Hans Marquardt (Leipzig: Reclam, 1967), 398–99.

69. Kelly, *Descent of Darwin*, 134, 132.

70. *Bibliothekar* 4 (1912): 390–91; Pfannkuche, *Was liest*, 22. For further examples of workers reading Darwin, see *Bibliothekar* 1 (1909); 3 (1911): 261–62, 284; J. S. and E. F., "Was lesen die organisirten Arbeiter in Deutschland?" *Die Neue Zeit* 13, no. 5 (1894–95): 154–55; Advocatus [pseud.], "Ein weiterer Beitrag zur Frage: 'Was liest der deutsche Arbeiter?'" ibid., 14, no. 20 (1895–96): 633; Steinberg, "Workers' Libraries." On Stanley, see examples cited above and *Bibliothekar* 4 (1912): 512. See also Daum, *Wissenschaftspopularisierung*, 241, 300–308.

71. Henry Morton Stanley, *In Darkest Africa, or the Quest, Rescue and Retreat of Emin Pasha, Governor of Equatoria*, vol. 1 (London: Sampson Low, 1890), 363, 352.

72. Ernst Haeckel, *The History of Creation: Or the Development of the Earth and Its Inhabitants by the Action of Natural Causes*, vol. 2, trans. E. Ray Lankester (New York: Appleton, 1876), 307, 310–14, 324. Translation of *Die Natürliche Schöpfungsgeschichte* (1868). Cited in Kelly, *Descent of Darwin*, 117.

73. Kelly, *Descent of Darwin*, 108–9, 117, 122.

74. Ludwig Büchner, *Man in the Past, Present and Future: A Popular Account of the Results of Recent Scientific Research*, trans. W. S. Dallas (London: Asher & Co., 1872), 315, 324, 137–38. Translation of *Der Mensch und seine Stellung in der Natur in Vergangenheit, Gegenwart und Zukunft* (1872). Cited in Kelly, *Descent of Darwin*, 117.

75. On the German debate about Stanley, see Essner, *Deutsche Afrikareisende*, 114. On the mixing of science and travel narrative, see ibid., 117–19 and Daum, *Wissenschaftspopularisierung*, 329–30.

76. Essner, *Deutsche Afrikareisende*, 114.

77. Karl Dove, *Südwestafrika: Kriegs- und Friedensbilder aus der ersten deutschen Kolonie* (Berlin: Allgemeiner Verein für Deutsche Literatur, 1896), vii.

78. Conrad, "Geography," 247.

79. Advocatus [pseud.], "Was liest der deutsche Arbeiter?" *Die Neue Zeit* 13, no. 2 (1894–95): 817. As was typical, the "Länder- und Völkerkunde (Reisebeschreibungen)" category was second in popularity to "Romane und Novellen," which included a lot of Zola and "a few *Hintertreppenromane*" of the pop-orientalist subgenre, among them *Der Türkenkaiser und seine Feinde* and *Die Geheimnisse des Hofes von Konstantinopel* (815).

80. Langewiesche and Schönhoven, "Arbeiterbibliotheken," 184–88, 194.

81. Essner, *Deutsche Afrikareisende*, 83.

82. Hermann Wissmann, *Unter deutscher Flagge quer durch Afrika von West nach Ost, von 1880 bis 1883*, 7th ed. (Berlin: Walther & Apolant, 1890); Herbert Ward, *Five Years with the Congo Cannibals* (London: Chatto & Windus, 1891; reprint, New York: Negro Universities Press, 1969), translated as *Fünf Jahre unter den Stämmen des Kongostaates* (Leipzig, 1891); Stanley, *In Darkest Africa*.

83. Hofmann, "Psychologie," 278–79, 284. These were the thirty volumes of Alexander von Humboldt's epic *Travels to the Equinoctial Regions of the New Continent*, first published in French from 1805 to 1834. See Marie Louise Pratt, *Imperial Eyes: Travel Writing and Transculturation* (London: Routledge, 1992), 111–43; Daum, *Wissenschaftspopularisierung*, 269–79.

84. Hofmann's Buchholz, *Reisen in Südwestafrika*, is likely to have been P. Buchholz, *Reisen in Westafrika*; Franz Thonner, *Im afrikanischen Urwald: Meine Reise nach dem Kongo und der Mongalla im Jahre 1896* (1898).

85. Hofmann, "Psychologie," 267, 280.

86. Among the substantial literature on the SPD subculture and its political implications, see Günther Roth, *The Social Democrats in Imperial Germany: A Study in Working-Class Isolation and National Integration* (Totowa, N.J.: Bedminster, 1963). Among criticism of Roth's interpretation, see Richard Evans, "The Sociological Interpretation of German Labour

History," in *The German Working Class 1888–1933: The Politics of Everyday Life*, ed. Richard J. Evans (London: Croom Helm, 1982); and Dick Geary, "Working-Class Culture in Imperial Germany," in *Bernstein to Brandt: A Short History of German Social Democracy*, ed. Roger Fletcher (Baltimore: Edward Arnold, 1987). More recently, Vernon Lidtke has drawn a much sharper distinction between the SPD and other spheres of German culture. See *The Alternative Culture: Socialist Labor in Imperial Germany, 1878–1890* (New York: Oxford University Press, 1985).

87. The philosopher Ernst Bloch speculated on the potentially revolutionary and utopian content of nineteenth-century colportage literature set in faraway places, and particularly in the work of Karl May. See his *Heritage of Our Times*, 154–64.

88. The most influential application of this theory to German history is Wehler, *Bismarck*.

6. The Hottentot Elections

1. Richard J. Evans, *Kneipengespräche im Kaiserreich: Die Stimmungsberichte der Hamburger Politischen Polizei, 1892–1914* (Reinbek bei Hamburg: Rowohlt, 1989), 353–54.

2. John A. Hobson, *Imperialism, A Study* (1902; rev. ed. 1905; reprint, Ann Arbor: University of Michigan Press, 1965), 101.

3. John A. Hobson, *The Psychology of Jingoism* (London: Grant Richards, 1901), 117.

4. *DKZ*, 27 April 1907.

5. V. I. Lenin, *Imperialism, The Highest Stage of Capitalism* (New York: International Publishers, 1939), 109.

6. Hobson, *Imperialism*, 101.

7. Among the considerable literature treating German Social Democracy and imperialism, see Abraham Ascher, "Imperialists within German Social Democracy Prior to 1914," *Journal of Central European Affairs* 20 (1961): 397–422; Roger Fletcher, *Revisionism and Empire: Socialist Imperialism in Germany, 1897–1914* (London: George Allen & Unwin, 1984); Carl E. Schorske, *German Social Democracy, 1905–1917: The Development of the Great Schism* (Cambridge: Harvard University Press, 1955), 59–87; Hans-Christoph Schröder, *Gustav Noske und die Kolonialpolitik des Deutschen Kaiserreichs* (Berlin: J. H. W. Dietz, 1979); idem, *Sozialismus und Imperialismus: Die Auseinandersetzung der deutschen Sozialdemokratie mit dem Imperialismusproblem und der "Weltpolitik" vor 1914* (Hanover: Verlag für Literatur und Zeitgeschehen, 1968); Helmuth Stoecker and Peter Sebald, "Enemies of the Colonial Idea," in Knoll and Gann, *Germans in the Tropics*.

8. For example, Stoecker and Sebald conclude that the "German working class could indeed not be won over to colonial aims," but virtually all their evidence concerns the anticolonialism of SPD leaders, intellectuals, and the press. "Enemies of the Colonial Idea," 66. Conversely, Fletcher's speculation on working-class receptivity to imperialism reflects his interest in SPD revisionism: "Although the workers did not succumb to the populist nationalism of the Navy League and similar non-socialist agitational groups, the aggregate impact of traditional values, uprooting, material and status deprivation, structural change, the work experience, and social controls undoubtedly made many workers more susceptible to the kind of nationalist fare offered by avowedly socialist organs like the *Sozialistische Monatshefte* than historians have hitherto cared to contemplate. This was not a case of workers being betrayed or misled by opportunistic leaders so much as a matter of autonomous working-class radicalism seeking, and to some extent finding, an outlet for its grievances in an avenue that was compatible with social reality as it appeared to the ordinary shop-floor worker." *Revisionism and Empire*, 34.

9. See the police reports on conversations overheard in working-class pubs in Hamburg, transcribed and compiled in Evans, *Kneipengespräche im Kaiserreich*, 341–60; idem, "Proletarian Mentalities: Pub Conversations in Hamburg," in *Proletarians and Politics: Socialism, Protest, and the Working Class in Germany before the First World War* (New York: St. Martin's Press, 1990).

10. On the elections of 1907, see the outstanding recent work by Frank Oliver Sobich, *"Schwarze Bestien, rote Gefahr": Rassismus und Antisozialismus im deutschen Kaiserreich* (Frankfurt/M.: Campus, 2006); Winfried Becker, "Kulturkampf als Vorwand: Die Kolonialwahlen von 1907 und das Problem der Parlamentarisierung des Reiches," *Historisches Jahrbuch* 106 (1986): 59–84; George Dunlap Crothers, *The German Elections of 1907* (New York: Columbia University Press, 1941); Dieter Fricke, "Der deutsche Imperialismus und die Reichstagswahlen von 1907," *Zeitschrift für Geschichtswissenschaft* 9 (1961): 538–76; Wolfgang Reinhard, " 'Sozialimperialismus' oder 'Entkolonisierung der Historie'? Kolonialkrise und 'Hottentottenwahlen' 1904–1907," *Historisches Jahrbuch* 97/98 (1978): 384–417.

11. On the Maji Maji Rebellion, see John Iliffe, "The Effects of the Maji Maji Rebellion of 1905–1906 on German Occupation Policy in East Africa," in *Britain and Germany in Africa: Imperial Rivalry and Colonial Rule*, ed. Prosser Gifford and Wm. Roger Louis (New Haven, Conn.: Yale University Press, 1967); idem, "The Organization of the Maji Maji Rebellion," *Journal of African History* 8 (1967): 495–512; Karl-Martin Seeberg, *Der Maji-Maji-Krieg gegen die deutsche Kolonialherrschaft* (Berlin: Dietrich Reimer, 1989); Marcia Wright, "Maji Maji: Prophecy and Historiography," in *Revealing Prophets: Prophecy in Eastern African History*, ed. David M. Anderson and Douglas H. Johnson (London: James Currey, 1995).

12. On the German-Herero War see Jon M. Bridgman, *The Revolt of the Hereros* (Berkeley: University of California Press, 1981); Horst Drechsler, *"Let Us Die Fighting": The Struggle of the Herero and Nama against German Imperialism, 1884–1915* (London: Zed, 1980); Isabel V. Hull, *Absolute Destruction: Military Culture and the Practices of War in Imperial Germany* (Ithaca: Cornell University Press, 2005); Gesine Krüger, *Kriegsbewältigung und Geschichtsbewußtsein: Realität, Deutung und Verarbeitung des deutschen Kolonialkriegs in Namibia, 1904–1907* (Göttingen: Vandenhoeck und Ruprecht, 1999); Jürgen Zimmerer, *Deutsche Herrschaft über Afrikaner: Staatlicher Machtanspruch und Wirklichkeit im kolonialen Namibia* (Münster: Lit, 2002).

13. Sobich, *"Schwarze Bestien, rote Gefahr."* Among many German Protestants, anti-Catholicism also played an important role in the elections. See Crothers, *German Elections*, 177–78; Jonathan Sperber, *The Kaiser's Voters: Electors and Elections in Imperial Germany* (Cambridge: Cambridge University Press, 1997), 245, 254.

14. Dernburg, *Zielpunkte*, 20.

15. BA, R8023/509, DKG, Bl. 12, President of DKG to local chairmen, 21 December 1906.

16. Soénius, *Koloniale Begeisterung im Rheinland*, 62, 108–9.

17. *DKZ*, 26 January 1907. The DKG distributed some four million pieces of literature altogether. See Richard V. Pierard, "The German Colonial Society," in Knoll and Gann, *Germans in the Tropics*, 31.

18. BA, R8023/509, DKG, Bl. 316–17.

19. Soénius, *Koloniale Begeisterung im Rheinland*, 62.

20. BA, R8023/510, DKG.

21. Carl Severing, *Mein Lebensweg*, vol. 1: *Vom Schlosser zum Minister* (Cologne: Greven, 1950), 155.

22. BA, R8023/510, DKG, Bl. 412–13, "Die Koloniale Lügenfabrik."

23. *FK*, 7 January 1907.

24. Sobich, *"Schwarze Bestien, rote Gefahr,"* 258.

25. Soénius, *Koloniale Begeisterung im Rheinland*, 108–9.

26. Severing, *Mein Lebensweg*, 1:155; Dernburg, *Zielpunkte*, 20; Sobich, "*Schwarze Bestien, rote Gefahr,*" 258, 284–85.

27. Dernburg, *Zielpunkte*, 5.

28. Crothers, *German Elections*, 153, 176–78; Mary Nolan, *Social Democracy and Society: Working-Class Radicalism in Düsseldorf, 1890–1920* (Cambridge: Cambridge University Press, 1981), 177–80.

29. Nolan, *Social Democracy*, 178–79.

30. In his examination of the so-called "Khaki Election" in Britain in 1900, Richard Price emphasizes the election as a chiefly local phenomenon in which there was "very little correlation between imperial appeal and electoral success." Richard Price, *An Imperial War and the British Working Class: Working-Class Attitudes and Reactions to the Boer War, 1899–1902* (London: Routledge & Kegan Paul, 1972), 130.

31. The SPD did not, of course, allow the imperialism debate to obscure longstanding issues like tariffs or social insurance. See, for example, *LVZ*, 15 December 1906.

32. Eduard Bernstein, "Was folgt aus dem Ergebnis der Reichstagswahlen?" *SM* 13 (January–June 1907), 110.

33. StAL, AH Oschatz 17, Reichstagswahl (1907).

34. Sobich, "*Schwarze Bestien, rote Gefahr,*" 300–305.

35. Eduard Bernstein, "The German Elections and the Social Democrats," *Contemporary Review* 91 (April 1907): 489.

36. Fletcher, in his work on imperialism and revisionism in the SPD, observes before 1911 a "general indifference [to imperialism], punctuated by largely formal, hyperbolical and desultory forays against imperialist excesses. . . . Such interest as was expressed in foreign policy problems was usually vague and woolly-minded, reflecting a clear ambivalence in Social Democratic thinking" (*Revisionism*, 34). The idea that the SPD had no consistent response to imperialism and remained indifferent to diplomatic and international matters makes less sense in the *local* context when one considers the SPD press. Beginning in at least 1900, readers of local SPD papers encountered strong, consistent criticism of colonialism over a period of many years. See also Ascher, "Imperialists within German Social Democracy," 402–3; Nolan, *Social Democracy*, 176; Schorske, *German Social Democracy*, 66–68.

37. *LVZ*, 26 June 1900, 8–10 October 1906. The sneering accusation about "Gold für die Tippelskirche und die Wörmänner" refers to a colonial financial scandal in the Tippelskirch firm and to the influential Hamburg shipping and trading firm C. Woermann. See Klaus Epstein, "Erzberger and the German Colonial Scandals, 1905–1910," *English Historical Review* 74 (1959): 644–45.

38. *AVZ*, 12, 16 October 1900.

39. Ibid., 18 October 1904.

40. Ibid., 12 October 1900.

41. *SVZ*, 10 October 1905. The *AVZ* became the *SVZ* on 1 April 1905.

42. Evans, *Kneipengespräche im Kaiserreich*, 357; Bromme, *Lebensgeschichte*, 320.

43. *LVZ*, 14, 15 December 1906. The paper gave a detailed account of the costs of empire, estimating that in 1905 Germany's colonial trade amounted to just 0.5 percent of its entire world trade. Ibid., 15 December 1906.

44. SAL, PB 1907, 113.

45. SAL, PB 1907, 113, 1, 5.

46. *DKZ*, 24 January 1907. The DKG held thirteen meetings altogether in Saxony.

47. SAL, PB 1907, 5.

48. SAL, PB 1907, 101.

49. *LVZ*, 22 January 1907.

50. StAL, AH Oschatz 17, Reichstagswahl 1907.

51. *Bericht über die Tätigkeit des Agitationskomitees der Sozialdemokratischen Partei Leipzigs für das Jahr1906–07* (Leipzig: Agitationskomitee der Sozialdemokratischen Partei Leipzigs, 1907), 5–6, 7.

52. StAL, AH 2675, Öffentliche Versammlungen 1907, Bl. 29–31.

53. Ibid., Bl. 33–35. Trotha had issued the proclamation early in the war, on 2 October 1904.

54. *Bericht*, 6.

55. StAL, AH 2675, Öffentliche Versammlungen 1907, Bl. 167–69; *LVZ*, 24 January 1907.

56. StAL, AH 2675, Öffentliche Versammlungen 1907, Bl. 76–78, 110–11.

57. *Bericht*, 6.

58. *SVZ*, 20 December 1906.

59. Ibid., 21 January 1907.

60. *SVZ*, 27 December 1906.

61. Bernstein, "Was folgt?"; idem, "Die Kolonialfrage und der Klassenkampf," *SM* 13 (July–December 1907): 988–96; Richard Calwer, "Der 25. Januar," ibid. (January–June 1907): 101–7. Of course, it was to the revisionists' advantage to portray colonialism as a decisive issue in the elections.

62. Karl Kautsky, "Der 25. Januar," *Die Neue Zeit* 25, no. 18 (1906–7), 589.

63. Rosa Luxemburg, "Die Lehren der letzten Reichstagswahl," speech delivered 6 March 1907 in Berlin, in Luxemburg, *Gesammelte Werke*, vol. 2 (Berlin [East]: Dietz, 1972), 192, 194.

64. Sperber, *Kaiser's Voters*, 249–51. The SPD lost nearly half of its deputies, falling from 81 to 43 seats. Sobich, "*Schwarze Bestien, rote Gefahr,*" 319–22, 346.

65. Martina Bauernfeind, *Bürgermeister Georg Ritter von Schuh: Stadtentwicklung in Erlangen und Nürnberg im Zeichen der Hochindustrialisierung, 1878–1913* (Nuremberg: Stadtarchiv Nürnberg, 2000), 457.

66. SAL, PB 1907, 3.

67. SAL, PB 1907, 5. Of 42,197 eligible voters in Leipzig-Stadt in 1903, 36,153 (or 86 percent) cast votes.

68. *Bericht*, 6.

69. Ibid., 8.

70. Karsten Rudolph, *Die sächsische Sozialdemokratie vom Kaiserreich zur Republik, 1871–1923* (Weimar: Böhlau, 1995), 66 n. 9.

71. *Bericht*, 9.

72. SAL, PB 1907, 5. Of 96,927 eligible voters in Leipzig-Land in 1903, 79,389 (82 percent) cast votes. PB 1907, 6.

73. *Bericht*, 6.

74. Ibid., 9.

75. Sperber, *Kaiser's Voters*, 249.

76. The SPD won 48 percent of the Saxon vote, down from 58 percent in 1903. Crothers, *German Elections*, 178.

77. SAL, PB 1907, 14, 26–27.

78. Karsten Rudolph, "Das 'rote Königreich': Die sächsische Sozialdemokratie im Wilhelminischen Deutschland," in *Sachsen im Kaiserreich: Politik, Wirtschaft und Gesellschaft im Umbruch*, ed. Simone Lässig and Karl Heinrich Pohl (Weimar: Böhlau, 1997), 77–78.

79. SAL, PB 1911, 33.

80. SAL, PB 1912, 2–3. Nationally, the SPD drew 42 percent of eligible working-class voters in 1912, representing 49 percent of all working-class votes cast. Sperber, *Kaiser's Voters*, 264.

81. SAL, PB 1914, 1.

82. Kautsky, "Der 25. Januar," 589.
83. Sobich, *"Schwarze Bestien, rote Gefahr,"* 13, 346.
84. Ibid., 19–26.
85. Ibid., 26.
86. In, for example, Rudolf Hilferding's 1910 work *Das Finanzkapital: Eine Studie über die jüngste Entwicklung des Kapitalismus.*

Magic Lantern Empire

1. SAA, 5/627, Magistrat der Stadt Augsburg. Panorama, Wachsfiguren, anatomische u. Naturalien-Kabinetts-Schaukästen (1889–1898).
2. A. Woldt, "Deutschlands Interessen im Niger- und Kongogebiet," *WIDM* 58 (April–September 1885), 242, 239.
3. C. Falkenhorst, "Aus dem Reiche Emin Paschas," *Die Gartenlaube,* no. 20 (1888): 636.
4. "Menschenfresser in Ostindien." ibid., no. 18 (1888): 579.
5. *Globus* 48, no. 1 (1885): 14.
6. Ciarlo, *Advertising Empire,* 95–100.
7. Münchener Gesellschaft für Anthropologie, Ethnologie und Urgeschichte, "40 Jahre wissenschaftlicher Tätigkeit der Münchener Anthropologischen Gesellschaft, 1870–1910," *Beiträge zur Anthropologie und Urgeschichte Bayerns* 18 (1911): xi.
8. *DKZ,* 16 May 1914, 338.
9. Zöller, *Als Journalist [sic] und Forscher,* 150.
10. "Die Amazonen von Dahome," *Die Gartenlaube,* no. 13 (1888): 418. See Henrici's book, dedicated to the memory of Gustav Nachtigal, *Das Deutsche Togogebiet und meine Afrikareise 1887* (Leipzig: Carl Reißner, 1888), 57. The *Gartenlaube* text closely paraphrases the book itself, where it does not simply reproduce it.
11. Zöller, *Als Journalist [sic] und Forscher,* 149.
12. Ames, *Carl Hagenbeck,* 15, 106, 125–40; Rothfels, "Aztecs, Aborigines, and Ape-People."
13. Bruckner, "Spectacles of (Human) Nature," 140, 142, 151–55.
14. Penny, *Objects of Culture,* 206–8.
15. *DKZ,* 27 April 1907.
16. Smith, *Ideological Origins of Nazi Imperialism,* 61–62. On scientific colonialism generally, see pp. 144–52. Smith analyzes the fundamental distinction between, on the one hand, an anachronistic settlement colonialism and, on the other, the modernizing economic colonialism of *Weltpolitik,* of which scientific colonialism formed a major strand. See also Spidle, "Colonial Studies in Imperial Germany," 231–47.
17. Zimmerman, *Alabama in Africa,* 190–91.
18. Dernburg, *Zielpunkte,* 5; Zimmerman, *Alabama in Africa,* 192–93.
19. Zimmerman, *Alabama in Africa,* 192–93; Sobich, *"Schwarze Bestien, rote Gefahr,"* 258.
20. Zimmerman, *Alabama in Africa,* 193.
21. Spidle, "Colonial Studies in Imperial Germany," 243.
22. Rudolf Hilferding, *Finance Capital: A Study of the Latest Phase of Capitalist Development,* ed. Tom Bottomore (London: Routledge & Kegan Paul, 1981), 349–50.
23. Lenin, *Imperialism,* 104.
24. For example, Hilferding, *Finance Capital,* 368.

25. Rosa Luxemburg, *The Crisis in German Social Democracy* (New York: Howard Fertig, 1969), 40.

26. Hilferding, *Finance Capital*, 336.

27. On the fund of knowledge and expertise concentrated in the Colonial Council, which bridged state and colonial public sphere, see Hartmut Pogge von Strandmann, *Imperialismus vom Grünen Tisch: Deutsche Kolonialpolitik zwischen wirtschaftlicher Ausbeutung und "zivilisatorischen" Bemühungen* (Berlin: Christoph Links, 2009).

28. Gustav Noske, *Kolonialpolitik und Sozialdemokratie* (Stuttgart: J. H. W. Dietz, 1914), 217.

29. Ascher, "Imperialists within German Social Democracy,", 400.

30. Hilferding, *Finance Capital*, 328, 335.

31. Ibid., 318.

32. Rosa Luxemburg, *The Accumulation of Capital* (London: Routledge, 2003), 426.

33. Ibid., 338–39.

34. Sobich, "*Schwarze Bestien, rote Gefahr,*" 14, 319.

35. Conrad, *Globalization and the Nation*, 79.

36. Zimmerman, *Alabama in Africa*.

37. Ibid., 212, 237.

38. Ibid., 173, 196.

39. Sobich, "*Schwarze Bestien, rote Gefahr,*" 305–6.

40. Geoff Eley argues for the decline of *Honoratiorenpolitik*, and of the National Liberals in particular. See Eley, *Reshaping the German Right*, 10–11.

41. Ibid., 11, 178–79.

42. Conrad, *Globalization and the Nation*, 16, 18.

43. Ciarlo, *Advertising Empire*, 308–9.

44. Sobich, "*Schwarze Bestien, rote Gefahr,*" 247, 260, 273.

45. Ibid., 222, 297, 26.

46. Luxemburg, "Die Lehren der letzten Reichstagswahl," 193; eadem, *The Crisis in German Social Democracy*, 40.

47. Luxemburg, *The Crisis in German Social Democracy*, 40; Sobich, "*Schwarze Bestien, rote Gefahr,*" 316, 346.

48. Eley, *Reshaping the German Right*, 167–68, 176–77, 254–55. Eley observes several contending currents of nationalism, indeed a "wide spectrum of nationalisms."

Bibliography

Archival Sources

Bayerisches Hauptstaatsarchiv

MA 76188, Anpflanzung von Baumwolle in den Kolonien (1904)
MA 76193, Zerstörung der bayerischen Benediktinermission in Ostafrika
MA 76196, Errichtung eines Wissmann-Denkmals (1906)
MA 76202, Das Agitationskomitee für deutsche Kolonialpolitik (1907)
MA 95355, Die Gesellschaft für deutsche Kolonisation (1887–1918)
MA 95356, Unterstützung einer den Entsatz des Afrikaforschers Emin Pascha
    (Dr. Schnitzer) bezweckenden Expedition (1889–1890)
MA 95372, Wolf Eugen, Afrikaschriftsteller (1892–1907)
MInn 65944, Veteranen- und Kriegervereine (1906–1908)
MInn 73496, Die geographische Gesellschaft (1875–1923)
MInn 73515, Deutscher Colonialverein und Colonialgesellschaft (1887–1925)
MInn 73547, Deutsche Flottenvereine (1898–1916)
MInn 73562, Hilfskomitee für die deutsche China-Expedition (1900–1903)
MInn 73567, Die Deutsche Buren-Centrale (Burenvereine) (1902)
MInn 74204, Auswanderung nach Afrika (1838–1908)
MK 40497, Deutsche Anthropologische Gesellschaft in München (1874–1948)
MK 40523, Orientalische Gesellschaft in München (1828–1914)

Bundesarchiv Berlin-Lichterfelde (Abteilung Reich)

Bestand R1001, Reichskolonialamt
Bestand R8023, Deutsche Kolonialgesellschaft
Bestand R8072, Deutsche Landwirtschaftsgesellschaft

Münchner Stadtmuseum

Abteilung Schaustellerei

Sächsisches Staatsarchiv Leipzig

AH Oschatz 17 Reichstagswahl (1907)
AH 2675 Öffentliche Versammlungen (1907)

AH 2737 Volks- und Arbeiterbibliotheken Gautzsch (1905–22)
PP-V 427 Deutsche Kolonialgesellschaft Abteilung Leipzig

Stadtarchiv Augsburg

Archiv der Spinnerei und Weberei Augsburg (SWA-Archiv)
Bestand 5/579, 627, 630 Magistrat der Stadt Augsburg
Bestand 10/132, 1160 Magistrat der Stadt Augsburg
Bestand SAA E IV 3/1492 Deutscher Verein für Krankenpflege in den Kolonien
Theodor von Hassler Papers (Hassler-Archiv)

Stadtarchiv Bamberg

BS 6934/12, Deutsche Kolonialgesellschaft
C2 VI N 675/11, Deutscher Colonialverein Sektion Bamberg 1884–1940
C2 VI N 686/10, Vereinigung ehemaliger China- und Afrikakämpfer 1904–1919

Stadtarchiv Leipzig

GewA 236, Kinematographen, Band I (1913)
Kap. 26A/104, Das Kolonialkrieger-Denkmal (1915)
Kap. 35/182, Südamerikanische Colonisations-Gesellschaft (1887)
Kap. 35/187, Centralverein f. Handelsgeographie (1887)
Kap. 35/275, Evangelischer Arbeiterverein (1891)
Kap. 35/469, Deutsche Kolonialgesellschaft u. Kolonialwirtschaftl. Komitee
Kap. 35/669, Der Deutsche Flottenverein (1902)
Kap. 35/802, Evangelischer Arbeiterverein Leipzig-Gohlis (1906)
Kap. 35/1083, Kgl. Sächs. Militärverein ehemaliger kaiserl. Schutztruppen für
      Leipzig und Umgebung (1913)
Kap. 35/1095, Sächs. Militärverein "China- und Afrika-Krieger" (1914)
Polizeiberichte 1892–1914

Stadtarchiv München

Zeitgeschichtliche Sammlung: Historisches Bildarchiv

Stadtarchiv Nürnberg

C7/I 12690, Kriegsmarine Ausstellung, 1913
C7/V 726, Afrikanische Gesellschaft in Deutschland
C7/V 1300, DKG, Abteilung Nürnberg-Fürth, 1888–1928
C7/V 3513, Verein Deutscher Kolonisten, 1904
C7/V 4355, Zweigverband Nürnberg-Fürth der DKG, 1907–21
C7/V 4840, Gauverband "Bayern-Nord" der DKG, 1912–1920
C7/V 5382, Deutscher Flottenverein, Ortsgruppe Nürnberg-Fürth
E6 292, Veteranen-Vereinigung der Ostasiatischen Expedition 1900/1901

E6 402, Evangelisch-lutherischer Lokal-Missionsverein Nürnberg, 1908–1919
E6 487, Abteilung Nürnberg-Fürth der Deutschen Kolonialgesellschaft
E10/32, Friedrich Stahl Papers

Newspapers and Periodicals

Alldeutsche Blätter
Archiv für Sozialwissenschaft und Sozialpolitik
Augsburger Abendzeitung
Augsburger Neueste Nachrichten
Augsburger Volkszeitung
Beiträge zur Anthropologie und Urgeschichte Bayerns
Beiträge zur Kolonialpolitik und Kolonialwirtschaft
Der Bibliothekar
Blätter für Volksbibliotheken und Lesehallen
Börsenblatt für den deutschen Buchhandel
Deutsche Kolonialzeitung
Fliegende Blätter
Fränkischer Kurier
Die Gartenlaube
Globus
Kölnische Zeitung
Leipziger Illustrierte Zeitung
Leipziger Neueste Nachrichten
Leipziger Tageblatt
Leipziger Volkszeitung
Mitteilungen der Gesellschaft für Erdkunde und Kolonialwesen
Mitteilungen des Vereins für Erdkunde zu Leipzig
München-Augsburger Abendzeitung
Münchner Neueste Nachrichten
Neue Zeit
Schriften des Vereins für Sozialpolitik
Schwäbische Volkszeitung
Sozialistische Monatshefte
Süddeutsche Monatshefte
Über Land und Meer
Volksbildungsarchiv
Vossische Zeitung
Westermanns Illustrierte Deutsche Monatshefte
Zeitschrift für Kolonialpolitik, Kolonialrecht und Kolonialwirtschaft

Published Primary Sources

Achtzehnter Jahresbericht für die Frauen-Hilfsvereine der Evangelisch-lutherischen Mission zu Leipzig. Leipzig: Evangelisch-lutherische Mission, 1913.
Advocatus [pseud.]. "Ein weiterer Beitrag zur Frage: 'Was liest der deutsche Arbeiter?'" *Neue Zeit* 14 (1895–96): 631–35.

———. "Was liest der deutsche Arbeiter?" *Neue Zeit* 13, no. 2 (1894–95): 814–17.

Alldeutscher Verband Leipzig. *Jahresbericht der Ortsgruppe Leipzig des Alldeutschen Verbandes über das Jahr 1900.* Leipzig: Alldeutscher Verband, 1901.

Arbeitsausschuß der Deutschen Kolonial-Ausstellung. *Deutschland und seine Kolonien im Jahre 1896: Amtlicher Bericht über die erste deutsche Kolonial-Ausstellung.* Berlin: Dietrich Reimer, 1897.

Bericht über die Tätigkeit des Agitationskomitees der Sozialdemokratischen Partei Leipzigs für das Jahr 1906–07. Leipzig: Agitationskomitee der Sozialdemokratischen Partei Leipzigs, 1907.

Bericht über die Tätigkeit des Agitationskomitees der Sozialdemokratischen Partei Leipzigs für das Jahr 1907–08. Leipzig: Agitationskomitee der Sozialdemokratischen Partei Leipzigs, 1908.

Bernstein, Eduard. "The German Elections and the Social Democrats," *Contemporary Review* 91 (April 1907): 479–92.

———. "Die Kolonialfrage und der Klassenkampf," *SM* 13 (July–December 1907): 988–96.

———. "Was folgt aus dem Ergebnis der Reichstagswahlen?" *SM* 13 (January–June 1907): 108–14.

Bromme, Moritz William Theodor. *Lebensgeschichte eines modernen Fabrikarbeiters,* edited by Paul Göhre. Jena: Eugen Diederichs, 1905.

Buchner, Max. *Aurora colonialis: Bruchstücke eines Tagebuchs aus dem ersten Beginn unserer Kolonialpolitik 1884–85.* Munich: Piloty & Loehle, 1914.

———. *Kamerun: Skizzen und Betrachtungen.* Leipzig: Duncker & Humblot, 1887.

Calwer, Richard. "Der 25. Januar." *SM* 13 (January–June 1907): 101–7.

Conrad, Joseph. "Geography and Some Explorers." In *Last Essays.* Garden City, N.Y.: Doubleday, 1926.

Coppius, Adolf. *Hamburgs Bedeutung auf dem Gebiete der deutschen Kolonialpolitik.* Berlin: Carl Heymann, 1905.

David, Eduard. *Referenten-Führer: Eine Anleitung zum Erwerb des für die sozialdemokratische Agitationstätigkeit nötigen Wissens und Könnens.* Berlin: Vorwärts, 1908.

Dehn, Richard M. R. *The German Cotton Industry.* Manchester: Sherratt & Hughes, 1913.

Dernburg, Bernhard. *Zielpunkte des Deutschen Kolonialwesens: Zwei Vorträge.* Berlin: Mittler, 1907.

Deutsche Kolonialgesellschaft. *Die Deutsche Kolonialgesellschaft: Zum Handgebrauch für die Vorstandsmitglieder der Abteilungen.* Berlin: Deutsche Kolonialgesellschaft, 1913.

Deutsche Kolonialgesellschaft Abteilung Leipzig. *Verzeichnis der Mitglieder.* Leipzig: Deutsche Kolonialgesellschaft, 1899.

———. *Verzeichnis der Mitglieder.* Leipzig: Deutsche Kolonialgesellschaft, 1910.

Deutsches Kolonial-Handbuch. Berlin: Hermann Paetel, 1909.

Dove, Karl. *Südwestafrika: Kriegs- und Friedensbilder aus der ersten deutschen Kolonie.* Berlin: Allgemeiner Verein für Deutsche Litteratur, 1896.

Fabri, Friedrich. *Bedarf Deutschland der Colonien? Eine politisch-ökonomische Betrachtung.* 3d ed., 1884; bilingual edition, translated by E. C. M. Breuning and M. E. Chamberlain under the title *Does Germany Need Colonies?* Lewiston, N.Y.: Edwin Mellen, 1998.

Francke, Karl. *Festschrift zum 25-jährigen Bestehen der Abteilung München der Deutschen Kolonialgesellschaft, 1887–1912.* Munich: Deutsche Kolonialgesellschaft Abteilung München, 1912.

Graf, E. "Die Bildung Berliner Arbeiter." *Zentralblatt für Volksbildungswesen* 9 (1909): 17–25.

Haeckel, Ernst. *The History of Creation: Or the Development of the Earth and Its Inhabitants by the Action of Natural Causes.* Trans. E. Ray Lankester. 2 vols. New York: Appleton, 1876.

Haenisch, Konrad. "Was lesen die Arbeiter?" *Neue Zeit* 18 (1899–1900): 691–96.

Heinrici, Karl. "Die Verhältnisse im deutschen Kolportagebuchhandel." *Schriften des Vereins für Sozialpolitik* 79 (1899): 183–234.

Helfferich, Karl. *Deutschlands Volkswohlstand, 1888–1913.* Berlin: Georg Stilke, 1913.

Hennig, Gustav. *Zehn Jahre Bibliothekarbeit: Geschichte einer Arbeiterbibliothek.* Leipzig: Leipziger Buchdruckerei, 1908.

Henrici, Ernst. *Das Deutsche Togogebiet und meine Afrikareise 1887.* Leipzig: Carl Reißner, 1888.

Hilferding, Rudolf. *Finance Capital: A Study of the Latest Phase of Capitalist Development*, edited by Tom Bottomore. London: Routledge & Kegan Paul, 1981.

Hofmann, Walter. "Die Organisation des Ausleihdienstes in der modernen Bildungsbibliothek." Part 2, "Zur Psychologie des Proletariats." *Volksbildungsarchiv* 1 (1910): 227–334.

Hübbe-Schleiden, Wilhelm. *Deutsche Colonisation: Eine Replik auf das Referat des Herrn Dr. Friedrich Kapp über Colonisation und Auswanderung.* Hamburg: L. Friedrichsen, 1881.

———. *Überseeische Politik: Eine culturwissenschaftliche Studie.* Hamburg: L. Friedrichsen, 1881.

Juckenburg, Karl. *Das Aufkommen der Großindustrie in Leipzig.* In *Volkswirtschaftliche und wirtschaftsgeschichtliche Abhandlungen*, edited by Wilhelm Stieda. Leipzig: Veit, 1913.

Kautsky, Karl. "Der 25. Januar." *Die Neue Zeit* 25, no. 18 (1906–7), 588–96.

Kellen, Tony. "Der Massenvertrieb der Volksliteratur." *Preußische Jahrbücher* 98 (October–December 1899): 79–103.

Kolonial-Wirtschaftliches Komitee. *Koloniale Produkte: Erläuterungen zu der Schulsammlung.* Berlin: Kolonial-Wirtschaftliches Komitee, 1910.

———. *Unsere Kolonialwirtschaft in ihrer Bedeutung für Industrie, Handel und Landwirtschaft.* Berlin: Kolonial-Wirtschaftliches Komitee, 1910.

Königliche Museen zu Berlin. *Führer durch die Sammlungen des Museums für Völkerkunde.* Berlin: W. Spemann, 1888.

Kühnemann, Fritz, B. Felisch, and L. M. Goldberger, eds. *Berlin und seine Arbeit: Amtlicher Bericht der Berliner Gewerbe-Ausstellung 1896.* Berlin: Dietrich Reimer, 1898.

Leutwein, Theodor. *Elf Jahre Gouverneur in Deutsch-Südwestafrika.* Berlin: Ernst Mittler & Sohn, 1906.

Liebknecht, Wilhelm. "Wissen ist Macht—Macht ist Wissen." In *Kleine Politische Schriften*, edited by Wolfgang Schröder. Leipzig: Reclam, 1976.

Lindenberg, Paul. *Pracht-Album Photographischer Aufnahmen der Berliner Gewerbe-Ausstellung 1896*. Berlin: Werner, 1896.

Luxemburg, Rosa. *The Accumulation of Capital*. London: Routledge, 2003.

——. *The Crisis in German Social Democracy*. New York: Howard Fertig, 1969.

——. "Die Lehren der letzten Reichstagswahl." In *Gesammelte Werke*, vol. 2. Berlin [East]: Dietz, 1972.

Meyer, Hans. *Das Deutsche Kolonialreich: Eine Länderkunde der deutschen Schutzgebiete*. Leipzig: Verlag des Bibliographischen Instituts, 1909.

Michels, Robert. "Die deutsche Sozialdemokratie," part 1, "Parteimitgliedschaft und soziale Zusammensetzung." *Archiv für Sozialwissenschaft und Sozialpolitik* 23 (1906): 471–556.

Nitschke, Wilhelm. "Wie und nach welcher Richtung entwickelt sich das Lesebedürfnis der Arbeiterschaft?" *Sozialistische Monatshefte* 19 (January–May 1913): 364–70.

Noske, Gustav. *Kolonialpolitik und Sozialdemokratie*. Stuttgart: J. H. W. Dietz, 1914.

Oberländer, Richard, ed. *Westafrika vom Senegal bis Benguela: Reisen und Schilderungen aus Senegambien, Ober- und Niederguinea*. Leipzig: Otto Spamer, 1878.

Olpp, Johannes. *Erlebnisse im Hinterlande von Angra-Pequena*. Rheinische Missionstraktate. Barmen: Verlag der Rheinischen Missions-Gesellschaft, 1896.

Peters, Carl. *Gesammelte Schriften*, edited by Walter Frank. 3 vols. Munich: C. H. Beck, 1943.

Pfannkuche, A. H. Th. *Was liest der deutsche Arbeiter?* Tübingen: Mohr, 1900.

Prager, Erich. *Die Deutsche Kolonialgesellschaft, 1882–1907*. Berlin: Dietrich Reimer, 1908.

Riechmann, H. *Unter den Zwartbois auf Franzfontein: Ein Beitrag zur Missions- und Kolonialgeschichte Südafrikas*. Rheinische Missions-Schriften, no. 83. Barmen: Verlag des Missions-Hauses, 1899.

Rönnebeck, R. "Panoramen." In *Berlin und seine Bauten*, edited by Architektenverein zu Berlin and Vereinigung Berliner Architekten. 2 vols. Berlin: Wilhelm Ernst, 1896.

Scheel, Willy. *Deutschlands Kolonien in achtzig farbenphotographischen Abbildungen*. Berlin: Verlagsanstalt für Farbenphotographie Carl Weller, 1914.

Schultze, Ernst. *Freie öffentliche Bibliotheken: Volksbibliotheken und Lesehallen*. Stettin: Dannenberg, 1900.

——. "Schundliteratur und Buchhandel." *Börsenblatt für den deutschen Buchhandel* 76 (April 21, 1909): 4790–94.

Schwabe, Kurd. *Mit Schwert und Pflug in Deutsch-Südwestafrika: Vier Kriegs- und Wanderjahre*. Berlin: Ernst Siegfried Mittler und Sohn, 1899.

Severing, Carl. *Mein Lebensweg*. Vol. 1: *Vom Schlosser zum Minister*. Cologne: Greven, 1950.

Simmel, Georg. "Berliner Gewerbe-Ausstellung." *Die Zeit* (Vienna), 25 July 1896.

Stanley, Henry M. *The Congo and the Founding of Its Free State*. 2 vols. New York: Harper, 1885.

———. *In Darkest Africa, or the Quest, Rescue and Retreat of Emin Pasha, Governor of Equatoria.* London: Sampson Low, 1890.

Stenographischer Bericht über die Verhandlungen der Deutschen Constituierenden Nationalversammlung zu Frankfurt am Main. Edited by Franz Wigard. 9 vols. Leipzig, 1848–49. New edition by Christoph Stoll. 9 vols. Munich: Verlag Moos, 1988.

Ward, Herbert. *Five Years with the Congo Cannibals.* London: Chatto & Windus, 1891; reprint, New York: Negro Universities Press, 1969.

Wolf, Eugen. *Wissmann: Deutschlands Grösster Afrikaner.* Leipzig: Friedrich Wilhelm Grunow, n.d. [1905?].

Winkler, Hubert, ed. *Unsere Kolonien auf der Jahrhundertausstellung: Jahrhundertfeier der Freiheitskriege Breslau 1913.* Breslau: Böhm & Taussig, 1913.

Wissmann, Hermann von. *Unter deutscher Flagge quer durch Afrika von West nach Ost.* Berlin: Globus, 1922.

Wolf, Eugen. *Wissmann: Deutschlands Grösster Afrikaner.* Leipzig: Friedrich Wilhelm Grunow, n.d. [1905?].

Zentralverband christlicher Textilarbeiter Deutschlands. *Geschäftsbericht für die Zeit vom 1. Juli 1912 bis 30. Juni 1914.* Düsseldorf: Zentralverband christlicher Textilarbeiter Deutschlands, 1914.

Zöller, Hugo. *Als Jurnalist [sic] und Forscher in Deutschlands großer Kolonialzeit.* Leipzig: Koehler & Amelang, 1930.

———. *Die deutschen Besitzungen an der westafrikanischen Küste.* Berlin: W. Spemann, 1885.

Statistical, Bibliographical, and Reference Works

Die Deutsche Koloniallitteratur von 1884–1895, compiled by Maximilian Brose. Berlin: Deutsche Kolonialgesellschaft, 1897.

Deutsches Kolonial-Lexikon, edited by Heinrich Schnee. 3 vols. 1920; reprint, Wiesbaden: W. W. A. Bernd Suppes, 1996.

Fage, J. D., and Roland Oliver, eds. *The Cambridge History of Africa.* 8 vols. Cambridge: Cambridge University Press, 1982–84.

Fricke, Dieter, ed. *Lexikon zur Parteiengeschichte: Die bürgerlichen und kleinbürgerlichen Parteien und Verbände in Deutschland, 1789–1945.* 4 vols. Leipzig: VEB Bibliographisches Institut, 1985.

Junge, Peter. *Bibliographie deutscher Kolonialzeitschriften.* Bremen: Übersee-Museum Bremen, 1985.

Keyser, Erich, and Heinz Stoob, eds. *Bayerisches Städtebuch.* 2 vols. Stuttgart: W. Kohlhammer, 1971.

Sembritzki, Emil, ed. *Der Kolonialfreund: Kritischer Führer durch die volkstümliche deutsche Kolonial-Literatur.* Berlin: Kolonie und Heimat, 1912.

Spindler, Max, ed. *Handbuch der Bayerischen Geschichte.* Vol. 4: *Das Neue Bayern, 1800–1970.* Munich: C. H. Beck, 1975.

Statistisches Jahrbuch der Stadt Leipzig. Vol 1. Leipzig: Duncker & Humblot, 1911.

Statistisches Jahrbuch für das Königreich Bayern. Vol. 12. Munich: Königliches Statistisches Landesamt, 1913.

Secondary Sources

Abrams, Lynn. "From Control to Commercialization: The Triumph of Mass Entertainment in Germany, 1900–25?" *German History* 8 (1990): 278–93.

——. *Workers' Culture in Imperial Germany: Leisure and Recreation in the Rhineland and Westphalia.* London: Routledge, 1992.

Adam, Thomas. *Arbeitermilieu und Arbeiterbewegung in Leipzig, 1871–1933.* Cologne: Böhlau, 1999.

——. "How Proletarian Was Leipzig's Social Democratic Milieu?" In *Saxony in German History: Culture, Society, and Politics, 1830–1933,* edited by James Retallack. Ann Arbor: University of Michigan Press, 2000.

Adas, Michael. *Machines as the Measure of Men: Science, Technology, and Ideologies of Western Dominance.* Ithaca: Cornell University Press, 1989.

Ames, Eric. *Carl Hagenbeck's Empire of Entertainments.* Seattle: University of Washington Press, 2008.

Anderson, Benedict. *Imagined Communities: Reflections on the Origin and Spread of Nationalism.* Rev. ed. London: Verso, 1991.

Arendt, Hannah. *The Origins of Totalitarianism.* New York: Harcourt Brace, 1973.

Arnold, Stefan. "Propaganda mit Menschen aus Übersee: Kolonialausstellungen in Deutschland, 1896 bis 1940." In Debusmann and Riesz, *Kolonialausstellungen—Begegnungen mit Afrika?*

Ascher, Abraham. "Imperialists Within German Social Democracy Prior to 1914." *Journal of Central European Affairs* 20 (1961): 397–422.

——. "Professors as Propagandists: The Politics of the Kathedersozialisten." *Journal of Central European Affairs* 23 (1963): 282–302.

——. "'Radical' Imperialists within German Social Democracy, 1912–1918." *Political Science Quarterly* 76 (1961): 555–75.

August, Thomas G. *The Selling of the Empire: British and French Imperialist Propaganda, 1890–1940.* Westport, Conn.: Greenwood, 1985.

Austen, Ralph A. *Northwest Tanzania under German and British Rule: Colonial Policy and Tribal Politics, 1889–1939.* New Haven, Conn.: Yale University Press, 1968.

Aydelotte, William O. *Bismarck and British Colonial Policy: The Problem of South West Africa, 1883–1885.* Philadelphia: University of Pennsylvania Press, 1937.

Bade, Klaus J. "Antisklavereibewegung in Deutschland und Kolonialkrieg in Deutsch-Ostafrika, 1888–1890: Bismarck und Friedrich Fabri." *Geschichte und Gesellschaft* 3 (1977): 31–58.

——. *Friedrich Fabri und der Imperialismus in der Bismarckzeit: Revolution-Depression-Expansion.* Freiburg: Atlantis, 1975.

——. "German Emigration to the United States and Continental Immigration to Germany in the Late Nineteenth and Early Twentieth Centuries." *Central European History* 13 (1980): 348–77.

——. "Imperial Germany and West Africa: Colonial Movement, Business Interests, and Bismarck's 'Colonial Policies." In *Bismarck, Europe, and Africa: The Berlin Africa Conference 1884–1885 and the Onset of Partition,* edited by Stig Förster, Wolfgang J. Mommsen, and Ronald Robinson. New York: Oxford University Press, 1988.

———. "Das Kaiserreich als Kolonialmacht: Ideologische Projektionen und historische Erfahrungen." In *Die Deutsche Frage im 19. und 20. Jahrhundert*, edited by Josef Becker and Andreas Hillgruber. Munich: Ernst Vögel, 1983.

———. "Massenauswanderung und Arbeitsmarkt im deutschen Nordosten von 1880 bis zum Ersten Weltkrieg: Überseeische Auswanderung, interne Abwanderung und kontinentale Zuwanderung." *Archiv für Sozialgeschichte* 20 (1980): 265–323.

———. "Die 'Zweite Reichsgründung' in Übersee: Imperiale Visionen, Kolonialbewegung und Kolonialpolitik in der Bismarckzeit." In *Die Herausforderung des europäischen Staatensystems: Nationale Ideologie und staatliches Interesse zwischen Restauration und Imperialismus*, edited by Adolf M. Birke and Günther Heydemann. Göttingen: Vandenhoeck & Ruprecht, 1989.

———. ed. *Population, Labour and Migration in Nineteenth- and Twentieth-Century Germany*. Providence, R.I.: Berg, 1987.

Bauernfeind, Martina. *Bürgermeister Georg Ritter von Schuh: Stadtentwicklung in Erlangen und Nürnberg im Zeichen der Hochindustrialisierung,1878–1913*. Nuremberg: Stadtarchiv Nürnberg, 2000.

Baumgart, Winfried. "Bismarcks Kolonialpolitik." In *Bismarck und seine Zeit*, edited by Johannes Kunisch. Berlin: Duncker & Humblot, 1992.

———. *Deutschland im Zeitalter des Imperialismus, 1890–1914*. Frankfurt/M.: Ullstein, 1972.

Becker, Winfried. "Kulturkampf als Vorwand: Die Kolonialwahlen von 1907 und das Problem der Parlamentarisierung des Reiches." *Historisches Jahrbuch* 106 (1986): 59–84.

Belgum, Kirsten. *Popularizing the Nation: Audience, Representation, and the Production of Identity in "Die Gartenlaube," 1853–1900*. Lincoln: University of Nebraska Press, 1998.

Bendikat, Elfi. *Organisierte Kolonialbewegung in der Bismarck-Ära*. Heidelberg: Kivouvou, 1984.

Benjamin, Walter. *The Arcades Project*. Cambridge, Mass.: Harvard University Press, 1999.

———. *Berliner Kindheit um neunzehnhundert*. Frankfurt/M.: Suhrkamp, 2000.

———. *Charles Baudelaire: A Lyric Poet in the Era of High Capitalism*. London: Verso, 1976.

Benninghoff-Lühl, Sibylle. *Deutsche Kolonialromane 1884–1914 in ihrem Entstehungs- und Wirkungszusammenhang*. Bremen: Übersee-Museum, 1983.

———. "Völkerschauen—Attraktion und Gefahr des Exotischen." *Sozialwissenschaftliche Informationen* 15 (1986): 41–48.

Berghahn, Volker R. *Imperial Germany, 1871–1914*. Providence, R.I.: Berghahn Books, 1994.

———. *Der Tirpitz-Plan: Genesis und Verfall einer innenpolitischen Krisenstrategie unter Wilhelm II*. Düsseldorf: Droste, 1971.

———. "Zu den Zielen des deutschen Flottenbaus unter Wilhelm II." *Historische Zeitschrift* 210 (1970): 34–100.

Berman, Russell A. *Enlightenment or Empire: Colonial Discourse in German Culture*. Lincoln: University of Nebraska Press, 1998.

———. "German Primitivism/Primitive Germany: The Case of Emil Nolde." In *Cultural Studies of Modern Germany: History, Representation, and Nationhood.* Madison: University of Wisconsin Press, 1993.

Biskup, Peter. "Dr. Albert Hahl—Sketch of a German Colonial Official." *Australian Journal of Politics and History* 14 (1968): 342–57.

Blackbourn, David. "The Discreet Charm of the Bourgeoisie: Reappraising German History in the Nineteenth Century." In *The Peculiarities of German History: Bourgeois Society and Politics in Nineteenth-Century Germany,* edited by David Blackbourn and Geoff Eley. New York: Oxford University Press, 1984.

The Long Nineteenth Century: A History of Germany, 1780–1918. New York: Oxford University Press, 1998.

———. "The *Mittelstand* in German Society and Politics, 1871–1914." *Social History* 2 (1977): 409–33.

Blessing, Werner K. "The Cult of Monarchy, Political Loyalty and the Workers' Movement in Imperial Germany." *Journal of Contemporary History* 13 (1978): 357–75.

———. "Zur Analyse politischer Mentalität und Ideologie der Unterschichten im 19. Jahrhundert." *Zeitschrift für bayerische Landesgeschichte* 34 (1971): 768–816.

Bley, Helmut. *South-West Africa under German Rule, 1894–1914,* translated by Hugh Ridley. Evanston, Ill.: Northwestern University Press, 1971.

Bloch, Ernst. *Heritage of Our Times.* Berkeley: University of California Press, 1991.

Böhm, Ekkehard. *Überseehandel und Flottenbau: Hanseatische Kaufmannschaft und deutsche Seerüstung, 1879–1902.* Düsseldorf: Bertelsmann Universitätsverlag, 1972.

Böhme, Helmut. "Thesen zur Beurteilung der gesellschaftlichen, wirtschaftlichen und politischen Ursachen des deutschen Imperialismus." In *Der moderne Imperialismus,* edited by Wolfgang Mommsen. Stuttgart: Kohlhammer, 1971.

Bowersox, Jeff. *Raising Germans in the Age of Empire: Youth and Colonial Culture, 1871–1914.* New York: Oxford University Press, 2012.

Bridgman, Jon M. *The Revolt of the Hereros.* Berkeley: University of California Press, 1981.

Bristow, Joseph. *Empire Boys: Adventures in a Man's World.* London: HarperCollins, 1991.

Brod, Max. *Über die Schönheit häßlicher Bilder.* Vienna: Paul Zsolnay, 1967.

Bruckner, Sierra Ann. "Spectacles of (Human) Nature: Commercial Ethnography between Leisure, Learning, and Schaulust." In Penny and Bunzl, *Worldly Provincialism.*

———. "The Tingle-Tangle of Modernity: Popular Anthropology and the Cultural Politics of Identity in Imperial Germany." Ph.D. diss., University of Iowa, 1999.

Brunschwig, Henri. *L'expansion allemande outre-mer du XVe siècle à nos jours.* Paris: Presses Universitaires de France, 1957.

Burchardt, Lothar. "The School of Oriental Languages at the University of Berlin— Forging the Cadres of German Imperialism?" In *Science Across the European Empires, 1800–1950,* edited by Benedikt Stuchtey. London: German Historical Institute, 2005.

Calhoun, Craig, ed. *Habermas and the Public Sphere.* Cambridge, Mass.: MIT Press, 1992.

Chickering, Roger. " 'Casting Their Gaze More Broadly': Women's Patriotic Activism in Imperial Germany." *Past and Present,* no. 118 (1988): 156–85.

———. "Patriotic Societies and German Foreign Policy, 1890–1914." *International History Review* 1 (1979): 470–89.

———. *We Men Who Feel Most German: A Cultural Study of the Pan-German League, 1886–1914.* Boston: George Allen & Unwin, 1984.

Ciarlo, David. *Advertising Empire: Race and Visual Culture in Imperial Germany.* Cambridge, Mass.: Harvard University Press, 2011.

Conrad, Sebastian. *Globalization and the Nation in Imperial Germany.* Cambridge: Cambridge University Press, 2010.

Coombes, Annie E. *Reinventing Africa: Museums, Material Culture, and Popular Imagination in Late Victorian and Edwardian England.* New Haven, Conn.: Yale University Press, 1994.

Cooper, Frederick, and Ann Laura Stoler, eds. *Tensions of Empire: Colonial Cultures in a Bourgeois World.* Berkeley: University of California Press, 1997.

Crothers, George Dunlap. *The German Elections of 1907.* New York: Columbia University Press, 1941.

Dabag, Mihran, Horst Gründer, and Uwe-K. Ketelsen, eds. *Kolonialismus, Kolonialdiskurs und Genozid.* Munich: Wilhelm Fink, 2004.

Daum, Andreas W. *Wissenschaftspopularisierung im 19. Jahrhundert: Bürgerliche Kultur, naturwissenschaftliche Bildung und die deutsche Öffentlichkeit, 1848–1914.* Munich: Oldenbourg, 1998.

Debusmann, Robert, and János Riesz, eds. *Kolonialausstellungen—Begegnungen mit Afrika?* Frankfurt/M.: IKO, 1995.

Dedering, Tilman. " 'A Certain Rigorous Treatment of All Parts of the Nation': The Annihilation of the Herero in German South West Africa, 1904." In *The Massacre in History,* edited by Mark Levene and Penny Roberts. New York: Berghahn, 1999.

Djomo, Esaïe. *"Des Deutschen Feld, es ist die Welt!" Pangermanismus in der Literatur des Kaiserreichs, dargestellt am Beispiel der deutschen Koloniallyrik: Ein Beitrag zur Literatur im historischen Kontext.* St. Ingbert: Werner J. Röhrig, 1992.

Dobson, Sean. "Authority and Revolution in Leipzig, 1910–1920." Ph.D. diss., Columbia University, 1996.

Drechsler, Horst. *"Let Us Die Fighting": The Struggle of the Herero and Nama against German Imperialism, 1884–1915.* London: Zed, 1980.

Dreesbach, Anne, and Helmut Zedelmaier, eds. *"Gleich hinterm Hofbräuhaus waschechte Amazonen": Exotik in München.* Munich: Dölling und Galitz, 2003.

Dresler, Adolf. *Die deutschen Kolonien und die Presse.* Würzburg: Konrad Triltsch, 1942.

Driver, Felix, and David Gilbert, eds. *Imperial Cities: Landscape, Display and Identity.* Manchester: Manchester University Press, 1999.

Düding, Dieter. *Der Nationalsoziale Verein, 1896–1903: Der gescheiterte Versuch einer parteipolitischen Synthese von Nationalismus, Sozialismus und Liberalismus.* Munich: Oldenbourg, 1972.

Eley, Geoff. "Defining Social Imperialism: Use and Abuse of an Idea." *Social History* 1 (1976): 265–90.

————. "Nations, Publics, and Political Cultures: Placing Habermas in the Nineteenth Century." In Calhoun, *Habermas and the Public Sphere*.

————. *Reshaping the German Right: Radical Nationalism and Political Change after Bismarck*. New Haven, Conn.: Yale University Press, 1980. Reprint, Ann Arbor: University of Michigan Press, 1991.

————. "Sammlungspolitik, Social Imperialism and the Navy Law of 1898." *Militärgeschichtliche Mitteilungen* 1 (1974): 29–63.

————. "Social Imperialism in Germany: Reformist Synthesis or Reactionary Sleight of Hand?" In Radkau and Geiss, *Imperialismus im 20. Jahrhundert*.

————. "Some Thoughts on the Nationalist Pressure Groups in Imperial Germany." In *Nationalist and Racialist Movements in Britain and Germany before 1914*, edited by Paul Kennedy and Anthony Nicholls. London: Macmillan, 1981.

Eley, Geoff, and Keith Nield. *The Future of Class in History: What's Left of the Social?* Ann Arbor: University of Michigan Press, 2007.

Engelsing, Rolf. *Analphabetentum und Lektüre: Zur Sozialgeschichte des Lesens in Deutschland zwischen feudaler und industrieller Gesellschaft*. Stuttgart: Metzler, 1973.

Epstein, Klaus. "Erzberger and the German Colonial Scandals, 1905–1910." *English Historical Review* 74 (1959): 637–63.

Essner, Cornelia. "Berlins Völkerkunde-Museum in der Kolonialära: Anmerkungen zum Verhältnis von Ethnologie und Kolonialismus in Deutschland." In *Berlin in Geschichte und Gegenwart: Jahrbuch des Landesarchivs Berlin*, edited by Hans J. Reichhardt. Berlin: Siedler Verlag, 1986.

————. *Deutsche Afrikareisende im neunzehnten Jahrhundert: Zur Sozialgeschichte des Reisens*. Stuttgart: Steiner, 1985.

Evans, Richard J. *Kneipengespräche im Kaiserreich: Die Stimmungsberichte der Hamburger Politischen Polizei, 1892–1914*. Reinbek bei Hamburg: Rowohlt, 1989.

————. "Proletarian Mentalities: Pub Conversations in Hamburg," in *Proletarians and Politics: Socialism, Protest and the Working Class in Germany before the First World War*. New York: St. Martin's Press, 1990.

————. "The Sociological Interpretation of German Labour History." In *The German Working Class 1888–1933: The Politics of Everyday Life*, edited by Richard J. Evans. London: Croom Helm, 1982.

Fenske, Hans. "Die Deutsche Auswanderung in der Mitte des 19. Jahrhunderts: Öffentliche Meinung und Amtliche Politik." *Geschichte in Wissenschaft und Unterricht* 24 (1973): 221–36.

————. "Imperialistische Tendenzen in Deutschland vor 1866: Auswanderung, überseeische Bestrebungen, Weltmachtträume." *Historisches Jahrbuch* 97/98 (1978): 336–83.

————. "Ungeduldige Zuschauer: Die Deutschen und die europäische Expansion 1815–1880." In *Imperialistische Kontinuität und nationale Ungeduld im 19. Jahrhundert*, edited by Wolfgang Reinhard. Frankfurt/M.: Fischer, 1991.

Fesser, Gerd. *Der Traum vom Platz an der Sonne: Deutsche "Weltpolitik" 1897–1914*. Bremen: Donat, 1996.

Fletcher, Roger. *Revisionism and Empire: Socialist Imperialism in Germany 1897–1914*. London: George Allen & Unwin, 1984.

———. "Revisionism and Wilhelmine Imperialism." *Journal of Contemporary History* 23 (1988): 347–66.

Fletcher, Yaël Simpson. "'Capital of the Colonies': Real and Imagined Boundaries between Metropole and Empire in 1920s Marseilles." In Driver and Gilbert, *Imperial Cities*.

Foltin, Hans Friedrich. "Zur Erforschung der Unterhaltungs- und Trivialliteratur, insbesondere im Bereich des Romans." In *Studien zur Trivialliteratur*, edited by Heinz Otto Burger. Frankfurt/M.: Klostermann, 1968.

Fraser, Nancy. "Rethinking the Public Sphere: A Contribution to the Critique of Actually Existing Democracy." In Calhoun, *Habermas and the Public Sphere*.

Fricke, Dieter. "Der deutsche Imperialismus und die Reichstagswahlen von 1907." *Zeitschrift für Geschichtswissenschaft* 9 (1961): 538–76.

———. "Gesamtverband evangelischer Arbeitervereine Deutschlands, 1890–1933." In *Lexikon zur Parteiengeschichte: Die bürgerlichen und kleinbürgerlichen Parteien und Verbände in Deutschland, 1789–1945*, edited by Dieter Fricke. Vol. 3. Leipzig: VEB Bibliographisches Institut, 1985.

Friedrichsmeyer, Sara, Sara Lennox, and Susanne Zantop, eds. *The Imperialist Imagination: German Colonialism and Its Legacy*. Ann Arbor: University of Michigan Press, 1998.

Frisby, David. *Fragments of Modernity: Theories of Modernity in the Work of Simmel, Kracauer, and Benjamin*. Cambridge, Mass.: MIT Press, 1986.

Frölich, Michael. *Imperialismus: Deutsche Kolonial- und Weltpolitik 1880–1914*. Munich: Deutscher Taschenbuch, 1994.

Fullerton, Ronald A. "Creating A Mass Book Market in Germany: The Story of the 'Colporteur Novel' 1870–1890." *Journal of Social History* 10 (1977): 265–83.

———. "Toward a Commercial Popular Culture in Germany: The Development of Pamphlet Fiction, 1871–1914." *Journal of Social History* 12 (1979): 489–511.

Gann, L. H., and Peter Duignan. *The Rulers of German Africa, 1884–1914*. Stanford: Stanford University Press, 1977.

———, eds. *African Proconsuls: European Governors in Africa*. New York: Free Press, 1978.

Gates, Lisa Marie. "Images of Africa in Late Nineteenth- and Twentieth-Century German Literature and Culture." Ph.D. diss., Harvard University, 1996.

Geary, Christraud M. *Images from Bamum: German Colonial Photography at the Court of King Njoya, Cameroon, West Africa, 1902–1915*. Washington, D.C.: Smithsonian Institution Press, 1988.

———. "Impressions of the African Past: Interpreting Ethnographic Photographs from Cameroon." *Visual Anthropology* 3 (1990): 289–315.

Geary, Dick. "Working-Class Culture in Imperial Germany." In *Bernstein to Brandt: A Short History of German Social Democracy*, edited by Roger Fletcher. Baltimore: Edward Arnold, 1987.

Geiss, Imanuel. *German Foreign Policy, 1871–1914*. London: Routledge and Kegan Paul, 1976.

———. "The German Version of Imperialism, 1898–1914: *Weltpolitik*." In *Escape into War? The Foreign Policy of Imperial Germany*, edited by Gregor Schöllgen. Oxford: Berg, 1990.

———. "Sozialstruktur und imperialistische Dispositionen im zweiten deutschen Kaiserreich." In *Liberalismus und imperialistischer Staat: Der Imperialismus als Problem liberaler Parteien in Deutschland, 1890–1914*, edited by Karl Holl and Günther List. Göttingen: Vandenhoeck and Ruprecht, 1975.

Gifford, Prosser, and Wm. Roger Louis, eds. *Britain and Germany in Africa: Imperial Rivalry and Colonial Rule.* New Haven, Conn.: Yale University Press, 1967.

Goldmann, Stefan. "Wilde in Europa: Aspekte und Orte ihrer Zurschaustellung." In *Wir und die Wilden: Einblicke in eine kannibalische Beziehung*, edited by Thomas Theye. Reinbek bei Hamburg: Rowohlt, 1984.

———. "Zwischen Panoptikum und Zoo: Exoten in Völkerschauen um 1900." In *Menschenfresser-Negerküsse: Das Bild vom Fremden im deutschen Alltag*, edited by Marie Lorbeer and Beate Wild. Berlin: Elefanten Press, 1991.

Gollwitzer, Heinz. *Europe in the Age of Imperialism, 1880–1914.* N.p.: Harcourt, Brace & World, 1969.

———. *Geschichte des weltpolitischen Denkens.* 2 vols. Göttingen: Vandenhoeck & Ruprecht, 1972–82.

Greenhalgh, Paul. *Ephemeral Vistas: The Expositions Universelles, Great Exhibitions and World's Fairs, 1851–1939.* Manchester: Manchester University Press, 1988.

Gründer, Horst. *Geschichte der deutschen Kolonien.* 3d ed. Paderborn: Schöningh, 1995.

Habermas, Jürgen. *The Structural Transformation of the Public Sphere: An Inquiry into a Category of Bourgeois Society.* Cambridge, Mass.: MIT Press, 1989.

Häckel, Manfred. "Arbeiterbewegung und Literatur." In *100 Jahre Reclams Universal-Bibliothek, 1867–1967*, edited by Hans Marquardt. Leipzig: Reclam, 1967.

Hall, Alex. *Scandal, Sensation and Social Democracy: The SPD Press and Wilhelmine Germany 1890–1914.* Cambridge: Cambridge University Press, 1977.

Hallgarten, George W. F. *Imperialismus vor 1914: Die soziologischen Grundlagen der Außenpolitik europäischer Großmächte vor dem Ersten Weltkrieg.* 2 vols. Munich: C. H. Beck, 1963.

———. "War Bismarck ein Imperialist? Die Außenpolitik des Reichsgründers im Licht der Gegenwart." *Geschichte in Wissenschaft und Unterricht* 22 (1971): 257–65.

———. "Wehler, der Imperialismus, und ich: Eine geharnischte Antwort." *Geschichte in Wissenschaft und Unterricht* 23 (1972): 296–303.

Hampe, Peter. "Sozioökonomische und psychische Hintergründe der bildungsbürgerlichen Imperialbegeisterung." In *Das wilhelminische Bildungsbürgertum: Zur Sozialgeschichte seiner Ideen*, edited by Klaus Vondung. Göttingen: Vandenhoeck & Ruprecht, 1976.

Hansen, Christine. "Die deutsche Auswanderung im 19. Jahrhundert—ein Mittel zur Lösung sozialer und sozialpolitischer Probleme?" In *Deutsche Amerikaauswanderung im 19. Jahrhundert: Sozialgeschichtliche Beiträge*, edited by Günter Moltmann. Stuttgart: J. B. Metzler, 1976.

Hansen, Marcus L. "German Schemes of Colonization before 1860." *Smith College Studies in History* 9 (1923–24): 5–65.

Harhoff, Dorian. *The Wild South-West: Frontier Myths and Metaphors in Literature Set in Namibia, 1760–1988.* Johannesburg: Witwatersrand University Press, 1991.

Hausen, Karin. *Deutsche Kolonialherrschaft in Afrika: Wirtschaftsinteressen und Kolonialverwaltung in Kamerun vor 1914.* Zurich: Atlantis, 1970.

Heine, Peter, and Ulrich van der Heyden, eds. *Studien zur Geschichte des deutschen Kolonialismus in Afrika.* Pfaffenweiler: Centaurus, 1995.

Henderson, W. O. *The German Colonial Empire, 1884–1914.* London: Frank Cass, 1993.

———. "Germany's Trade with Her Colonies, 1884–1914." *Economic History Review* 9 (1938–39): 1–16.

Henning, Hansjoachim. "Bismarcks Kolonialpolitik—Export einer Krise?" In *Gegenwartsprobleme der Wirtschaft und der Wirtschaftswissenschaft*, edited by Karl Erich Born. Tübingen: J. C. B. Mohr, 1978.

———. "Kriegervereine in den preußischen Westprovinzen: Ein Beitrag zur preußischen Innenpolitik zwischen 1860 und 1914." *Rheinische Vierteljahrsblätter* 32 (1968): 430–75.

Hermand, Jost. "Artificial Atavism: German Expressionism and Blacks." In *Blacks and German Culture*, edited by Reinhold Grimm and Jost Hermand. Madison: University of Wisconsin Press, 1986.

Heyden, Ulrich van der. "Südafrikanische 'Berliner': Die Kolonial- und Transvaal-Ausstellung in Berlin und die Haltung der deutschen Missionsgesellschaften zur Präsentation fremder Menschen und Kulturen." In *Fremde Erfahrungen: Asiaten und Afrikaner in Deutschland, Österreich und in der Schweiz bis 1945*, edited by Gerhard Höpp. Berlin: Verlag Das Arabische Buch, 1996.

Hildebrand, Klaus. *Deutsche Außenpolitik 1871–1918.* Munich: Oldenbourg, 1989.

Hobson, J. A. *Imperialism: A Study.* Rev. ed., 1905; reprint, Ann Arbor: University of Michigan Press, 1965.

———. *The Psychology of Jingoism.* London: Grant Richards, 1901.

Hoffmann, Walther G. *Das Wachstum der deutschen Wirtschaft seit der Mitte des 19. Jahrhunderts.* Berlin: Springer, 1965.

Hohendahl, Peter U., ed. *Mass Culture in Imperial Germany, 1871–1918.* Special issue of *New German Critique* 29 (1984).

Holston, Kenneth. "'A Measure of the Nation': Politics, Colonial Enthusiasm and Education in Germany, 1896–1933." Ph.D. diss., University of Pennsylvania, 1996.

Holthoon, Frits van, and Marcel van der Linden, eds. *Internationalism in the Labour Movement, 1830–1940.* Leiden: E. J. Brill, 1988.

Hull, Isabel V. *Absolute Destruction: Military Culture and the Practices of War in Imperial Germany.* Ithaca: Cornell University Press, 2005.

Iliffe, John. "The Effects of the Maji Maji Rebellion of 1905–1906 on German Occupation Policy in East Africa." In Gifford and Louis, *Britain and Germany in Africa.*

———. "The Organization of the Maji Maji Rebellion." *Journal of African History* 8 (1967): 495–512.

———. *Tanganyika under German Rule, 1905–1912.* Cambridge: Cambridge University Press, 1969.

Jäger, Georg. "Der Kampf gegen Schmutz und Schund: Die Reaktion der Gebilde-
    ten auf die Unterhaltungsindustrie." *Archiv für Geschichte des Buchwesens*
    31 (1988): 163–91.
Jelavich, Peter. *Munich and Theatrical Modernism: Politics, Playwriting, and Per-
    formance, 1890–1914.* Cambridge, Mass.: Harvard University Press, 1985.
Johnson, Christine R. *The German Discovery of the World: Renaissance Encoun-
    ters with the Strange and Marvelous.* Charlottesville: University of Virginia
    Press, 2008.
Kaarsholm, Preben. "The South African War and the Response of the International
    Socialist Community to Imperialism Between 1896 and 1908." In van Holt-
    hoon and van der Linden, *Internationalism in the Labour Movement.*
Kelly, Alfred. *The Descent of Darwin: The Popularization of Darwinism in Ger-
    many, 1860–1914.* Chapel Hill: University of North Carolina Press, 1981.
Kennedy, Paul M. "German Colonial Expansion: Has the 'Manipulated Social Im-
    perialism' been Ante-Dated?" *Past and Present*, no. 54 (1972): 134–41.
———. *The Samoan Tangle: A Study in Anglo-German-American Relations, 1878–
    1900.* New York: Harper & Row, 1974.
Kittel, Andrea. "Erbaulich und ergötzlich: Missionswerbung in der Heimat." In
    Der ferne Nächste: Bilder der Mission — Mission der Bilder, 1860–1920,
    ed. Eberhard Gutekunst and Werner Unseld. Ludwigsburg: Landeskirchliches
    Museum, 1996.
Klotz, Marcia. "White Women and the Dark Continent: Gender and Sexuality in
    German Colonial Discourse from the Sentimental Novel to the Fascist Film."
    Ph.D. diss., Stanford University, 1995.
———, ed. *German Colonialism: Another* Sonderweg? Special issue of *European
    Studies Journal* 16 (1999).
Knoll, Arthur J. *Togo under Imperial Germany, 1884–1914.* Stanford, Calif.: Stan-
    ford University, Hoover Institution Press, 1978.
Knoll, Arthur J., and Lewis H. Gann, eds. *Germans in the Tropics: Essays in Ger-
    man Colonial History.* New York: Greenwood, 1987.
Kocka, Jürgen. "The First World War and the 'Mittelstand': German Artisans and
    White-Collar Workers." *Journal of Contemporary History* 8 (1973): 101–23.
Köllmann, Wolfgang, and Peter Marschalck. "German Emigration to the United
    States." *Perspectives in American History* 7 (1973): 499–554.
Koponen, Juhani. *Development for Exploitation: German Colonial Policies in
    Mainland Tanzania, 1884–1914.* Helsinki: Lit Verlag, 1994.
Kracauer, Siegfried. *The Mass Ornament.* Cambridge, Mass.: Harvard University
    Press, 1995.
Krautwurst, Udo R. "Tales of the 'Land of Stories': Settlers and Anti-Modernity in
    German Colonial Discourses on German South West Africa, 1884–1914."
    Ph.D. diss., University of Connecticut, 1997.
Kröll, Ulrich. *Die internationale Buren-Agitation 1899–1902: Haltung der
    Öffentlichkeit und Agitation zugunsten der Buren in Deutschland, Frank-
    reich und den Niederlanden während des Burenkrieges.* Münster: Regens-
    berg, 1973.
Krüger, Gesine. *Kriegsbewältigung und Geschichtsbewußtsein: Realität, Deutung
    und Verarbeitung des deutschen Kolonialkriegs in Namibia, 1904–1907.*
    Göttingen: Vandenhoeck & Ruprecht, 1999.

Kundrus, Birthe. *Moderne Imperialisten: Das Kaiserreich im Spiegel seiner Kolonien.* Cologne: Böhlau, 2003.

——, ed. *Phantasiereiche: Zur Kulturgeschichte des deutschen Kolonialismus.* Frankfurt/M.: Campus, 2003.

Laffey, John F. "Municipal Imperialism in Nineteenth-Century France." *Historical Reflections* 1 (1974): 81–114.

——. "Roots of French Imperialism in the Nineteenth Century: The Case of Lyon." *French Historical Studies* 6 (1969): 78–92.

Langewiesche, Dieter, and Klaus Schönhoven. "Arbeiterbibliotheken und Arbeiterlektüre im Wilhelminischen Deutschland." *Archiv für Sozialgeschichte* 16 (1976): 135–204.

Lässig, Simone, and Karl Heinrich Pohl, eds. *Sachsen im Kaiserreich: Politik, Wirtschaft und Gesellschaft im Umbruch.* Weimar: Böhlau, 1997.

Le Bon, Gustave. *The Crowd: A Study of the Popular Mind.* New York: Viking, 1960.

Lenin, V. I. *Imperialism, The Highest Stage of Capitalism.* New York: International Publishers, 1939.

Lenman, Robin. "Art, Society, and the Law in Wilhelmine Germany: The Lex Heinze." *Oxford German Studies* 8 (1973): 86–113.

——. "Mass Culture and the State in Germany, 1900–1926." In *Ideas into Politics: Aspects of European History, 1880–1950*, edited by R. J. Bullen, H. Pogge von Strandmann, and A. B. Polonsky. London: Croom Helm, 1984.

Letkemann, Peter. "Das Berliner Panoptikum: Namen, Häuser und Schicksale." *Mitteilungen des Vereins für die Geschichte Berlins* 69 (1973): 319–26.

Lidtke, Vernon. *The Alternative Culture: Socialist Labor in Imperial Germany, 1878–1890.* New York: Oxford University Press, 1985.

Maase, Kaspar. "Die soziale Konstruktion der Massenkünste: Der Kampf gegen Schmutz und Schund 1907–1918." In *Kunst und Sozialgeschichte*, edited by Martin Papenbrock, Gisela Schirmer, Anette Sohn, and Rosemarie Sprute. Pfaffenweiler: Centaurus, 1995.

MacDonald, Robert H. *The Language of Empire: Myths and Metaphors of Popular Imperialism, 1880–1918.* Manchester: Manchester University Press, 1994.

MacKenzie, John M. *Propaganda and Empire: The Manipulation of British Public Opinion, 1880–1960.* Manchester: Manchester University Press, 1984.

——, ed. *Imperialism and Popular Culture.* Manchester: Manchester University Press, 1986.

Mah, Harold. "Phantasies of the Public Sphere: Rethinking the Habermas of Historians." *Journal of Modern History* 72 (March 2000): 153–82.

Maler, Anselm, ed. *Exotische Welt in populären Lektüren.* Tübingen: Niemeyer, 1990.

Marchand, Suzanne. *German Orientalism in the Age of Empire: Religion, Race, and Scholarship.* Cambridge: Cambridge University Press, 2009.

——. "Leo Frobenius and the Revolt against the West." *Journal of Contemporary History* 32 (1997): 153–70.

Marschalck, Peter. *Deutsche Überseewanderung im 19. Jahrhundert.* Stuttgart: Ernst Klett, 1973.

Martino, Alberto. *Die deutsche Leihbibliothek: Geschichte einer literarischen Institution, 1756–1914.* Wiesbaden: Otto Harrassowitz, 1990.

Mattheier, Klaus. *Die Gelben: Nationale Arbeiter zwischen Wirtschaftsfrieden und Streik.* Düsseldorf: Schwann, 1973.

McClintock, Anne. "Soft-Soaping Empire: Commodity Racism and Imperial Advertising." Chap. 5 in *Imperial Leather: Race, Gender, and Sexuality in the Colonial Contest.* New York: Routledge, 1995.

Mergner, Gottfried. "Solidarität mit den 'Wilden'? Das Verhältnis der deutschen Sozialdemokratie zu den afrikanischen Widerstandskämpfen in den ehemaligen deutschen Kolonien um die Jahrhundertwende." In van Holthoon and van der Linden, *Internationalism in the Labour Movement.*

Mitchell, Timothy. "The World as Exhibition." *Comparative Studies in Society and History* 31 (1989): 217–36.

Mommsen, Wolfgang J. "Domestic Factors in German Foreign Policy before 1914." In *Imperial Germany,* edited by James J. Sheehan. New York: New Viewpoints, 1976.

———. *Theories of Imperialism.* Chicago: University of Chicago Press, 1980.

———. "Triebkräfte und Zielsetzungen des deutschen Imperialismus vor 1914." In *Kultur und Gesellschaft in Deutschland von der Reformation bis zur Gegenwart,* edited by Klaus Bohnen, Sven-Aage Jørgensen, and Friedrich Schmöe. Copenhagen: Wilhelm Fink, 1981.

Montrose, Louis. "The Work of Gender in the Discourse of Discovery." *Representations* 33 (1991): 1–41.

Mooser, Josef. "Arbeiter, Bürger und Priester in den konfessionellen Arbeitervereinen im deutschen Kaiserreich, 1880–1914." In *Arbeiter und Bürger im 19. Jahrhundert. Varianten ihres Verhältnisses im europäischen Vergleich,* edited by Jürgen Kocka. Munich: R. Oldenbourg, 1986.

Moses, John A., and Paul M. Kennedy, eds. *Germany in the Pacific and Far East, 1870–1914.* St. Lucia: University of Queensland Press, 1977.

Müller, Frank Lorenz. "Imperialist Ambitions in *Vormärz* and Revolutionary Germany: The Agitation for German Settlement Colonies Overseas, 1840–1849." *German History* 17 (1999): 346–68.

Müller, Fritz Ferdinand. *Deutschland–Zanzibar–Ostafrika: Geschichte einer deutschen Kolonialeroberung, 1884–1890.* Berlin [East]: Rütten & Loenig, 1959.

Naranch, Bradley D. " 'Colonized Body,' 'Oriental Machine': Debating Race, Railroads, and the Politics of Reconstruction in Germany and East Africa, 1906–1910." *Central European History* 33 (2000): 299–338.

———. "Inventing the *Auslandsdeutsche*: Emigration, Colonial Fantasy and German National Identity, 1848–71." In *Germany's Colonial Pasts,* edited by Eric Ames, Marcia Klotz, and Lora Wildenthal. Lincoln: University of Nebraska Press, 2005.

Nestvogel, Renate, and Rainer Tetzlaff, eds. *Afrika und der deutsche Kolonialismus: Zivilisierung zwischen Schnapshandel und Bibelstunde.* Berlin: Dietrich Reimer, 1987.

Neumann, Franz. *Behemoth: The Structure and Practice of National Socialism.* New York: Oxford University Press, 1942.

Nietzsche, Friedrich. *The Birth of Tragedy and the Genealogy of Morals.* Trans. Francis Golffing. New York: Doubleday, 1956.

Nipperdey, Thomas. "Verein als soziale Struktur in Deutschland im späten 18. und frühen 19. Jahrhundert." In *Gesellschaft, Kultur, Theorie.* Göttingen: Vandenhoeck & Ruprecht, 1976.

Nishikawa, Masao. "Zivilisierung der Kolonien oder Kolonisierung durch Zivilisation? Die Sozialisten und die Kolonialfrage im Zeitalter des Imperialismus." In Radkau and Geiss, *Imperialismus im 20. Jahrhundert.*

Nolan, Mary. *Social Democracy and Society: Working-Class Radicalism in Düsseldorf, 1890–1920.* Cambridge: Cambridge University Press, 1981.

O'Donnell, Krista. "The Colonial Woman Question: Gender, National Identity, and Empire in the German Colonial Society Female Emigration Program, 1896–1914." Ph.D. diss., State University of New York at Binghamton, 1996.

———. "Home, Nation, Empire: Domestic Germanness and Colonial Citizenship." *The Heimat Abroad: The Boundaries of Germanness.* edited by Krista O'Donnell, Renate Bridenthal, and Nancy Reagin. Ann Arbor: University of Michigan Press, 2005.

Oettermann, Stephan. "Alles-Schau: Wachsfiguren-kabinette und Panoptiken." In *Viel Vergnügen: Öffentliche Lustbarkeiten im Ruhrgebiet der Jahrhundertwende,* edited by Lisa Kosok and Mathilde Jamin. Essen: Ruhrlandmuseum and Verlag Peter Pomp, 1992.

———. *The Panorama: History of a Mass Medium,* translated by Deborah Lucas Schneider. New York: Zone, 1997.

Oksiloff, Assenka. *Picturing the Primitive: Visual Culture, Ethnography, and Early German Cinema.* New York: Palgrave, 2001.

Otte, Marline. "Sarrasani's Theater of the World: Monumental Circus Entertainment in Dresden, from Kaiserreich to Third Reich." *German History* 17 (1999): 527–42.

Otte, Wulf. *Weiß und Schwarz—Black and White: Photos aus Deutsch-Südwestafrika/from Namibia, 1896–1901.* Wendeburg: Verlag Uwe Krebs, 2007.

Pao, Angela C. *The Orient of the Boulevards: Exoticism, Empire, and Nineteenth-Century French Theater.* Philadelphia: University of Pennsylvania Press, 1989.

Penny, H. Glenn. "Fashioning Local Identities in an Age of Nation-Building: Museums, Cosmopolitan Visions, and Intra-German Competition." *German History* 17 (1999): 489–505.

———. *Objects of Culture: Ethnology and Ethnographic Museums in Imperial Germany.* Chapel Hill: University of North Carolina Press, 2002.

Penny, H. Glenn, and Matti Bunzl, eds. *Worldly Provincialism: German Anthropology in the Age of Empire.* Ann Arbor: University of Michigan Press, 2003.

Peters, Michael. *Der Alldeutsche Verband am Vorabend des Ersten Weltkrieges, 1908–1914: Ein Beitrag zur Geschichte des völkischen Nationalismus im spätwilhelminischen Deutschland.* Frankfurt/M.: Peter Lang, 1992.

Pierard, Richard V. "A Case Study in German Economic Imperialism: The Colonial Economic Committee, 1896–1914." *Scandinavian Economic History Review* 16 (1968): 155–67.

———. "The German Colonial Society, 1882–1914." Ph.D. diss., State University of Iowa, 1964.

———. "The German Colonial Society." In Knoll and Gann, *Germans in the Tropics.*

——. "The Transportation of White Women to German Southwest Africa, 1898–1914." *Race* 12 (1970–71): 317–22.

Pisani, André du. *SWA/Namibia: The Politics of Continuity and Change.* Johannesburg: Jonathan Ball, 1986.

Plagemann, Volker, ed. *Übersee: Seefahrt und Seemacht im deutschen Kaiserreich.* Munich: C. H. Beck, 1988.

Plessen, Marie-Louise von, and Ulrich Giersch, eds. *Sehsucht: Das Panorama als Massenunterhaltung des 19. Jahrhunderts.* Basel: Stroemfeld/Roter Stern, 1993.

Pogge von Strandmann, Hartmut. "Domestic Origins of Germany's Colonial Expansion under Bismarck." *Past and Present,* no. 42 (1969): 140–59.

——. *Imperialismus vom Grünen Tisch: Deutsche Kolonialpolitik zwischen wirtschaftlicher Ausbeutung und "zivilisatorischen" Bemühungen.* Berlin: Christoph Links, 2009.

——, ed. *Walther Rathenau, Industrialist, Banker, Intellectual, and Politician: Notes and Diaries 1907–1922.* Oxford: Oxford University Press, 1985.

Porterfield, Todd. *The Allure of Empire: Art in the Service of French Imperialism, 1798–1836.* Princeton, N.J.: Princeton University Press, 1998.

Pratt, Mary Louise. *Imperial Eyes: Travel Writing and Transculturation.* London: Routledge, 1992.

Preston, Rebecca. " 'The Scenery of the Torrid Zone': Imagined Travels and the Culture of Exotics in Nineteenth-Century British Gardens." In Driver and Gilbert, *Imperial Cities.*

Price, Richard. *An Imperial War and the British Working Class: Working-Class Attitudes and Reactions to the Boer War, 1899–1902.* London: Routledge & Kegan Paul, 1972.

Pugach, Sara. *Africa in Translation: A History of Colonial Linguistics in Germany and Beyond, 1814–1945.* Ann Arbor: University of Michigan Press, 2011.

Radkau, Joachim, and Imanuel Geiss, eds. *Imperialismus im 20. Jahrhundert.* Munich: C. H. Beck, 1976.

Rancière, Jacques. *The Nights of Labor: The Workers' Dream in Nineteenth-Century France.* Philadelphia: Temple University Press, 1989.

Reinhard, Wolfgang. " 'Sozialimperialismus' oder 'Entkolonisierung der Historie'? Kolonialkrise und 'Hottentottenwahlen' 1904–1907." *Historisches Jahrbuch* 97/98 (1978): 384–417.

Retallack, James. "Society and Politics in Saxony in the Nineteenth and Twentieth Centuries: Reflections on Recent Research." *Archiv für Sozialgeschichte* 38 (1998): 396–457.

Reuss, Martin. "The Disgrace and Fall of Carl Peters: Morality, Politics, and *Staatsräson* in the Time of Wilhelm II." *Central European History* 14 (1981): 110–41.

Richards, Thomas. "Selling Darkest Africa." Chap. 3 in *The Commodity Culture of Victorian England: Advertising and Spectacle, 1851–1914.* Stanford, Calif.: Stanford University Press, 1990.

Richter, Roland. "Die erste Deutsche Kolonialausstellung 1896: Der 'Amtliche Bericht' in historischer Perspektive." In Debusmann and Riesz, *Kolonialausstellungen—Begegnungen mit Afrika?*

Ridley, Hugh. *Images of Imperial Rule.* London: Croom Helm, 1983.

Ritter, Gerhard A. "Wahlen und Wahlpolitik im Königreich Sachsen, 1867–1914." In Lässig and Pohl, *Sachsen im Kaiserreich*.

Ritter, Gerhard A., and Klaus Tenfelde. *Arbeiter im Deutschen Kaiserreich, 1871 bis 1914*. Bonn: Dietz, 1992.

Rohkrämer, Thomas. *Der Militarismus der "kleinen Leute": Die Kriegervereine im Deutschen Kaiserreich, 1871–1914*. Munich: Oldenbourg, 1990.

Röhl, J. C. G. "The Disintegration of the *Kartell* and the Politics of Bismarck's Fall from Power, 1887–90." *Historical Journal* 9 (1966): 60–89.

Rosenthal, Hildegard. *Die Auswanderung aus Sachsen im 19. Jahrhundert, 1815–1871*. Tübingen: Eugen Göbel, [1931?].

Rossmeissl, Dieter. *Arbeiterschaft und Sozialdemokratie in Nürnberg 1890–1914*. Nuremberg: Stadtarchiv Nürnberg, 1977.

Roth, Günther. "Die kulturellen Bestrebungen der Sozialdemokratie im kaiserlichen Deutschland." In *Moderne deutsche Sozialgeschichte*, edited by Hans-Ulrich Wehler. Cologne: Kiepenheuer & Witsch, 1966.

——. *The Social Democrats in Imperial Germany: A Study in Working-Class Isolation and National Integration*. Totowa, N.J.: Bedminster, 1963.

Rothfels, Nigel. "Aztecs, Aborigines, and Ape-People: Science and Freaks in Germany, 1850–1900." In *Freakery: Cultural Spectacles of the Extraordinary Body*, edited by Rosemarie Garland Thomson. New York: New York University Press, 1996.

Rudolph, Karsten. "Das 'rote Königreich': Die sächsische Sozialdemokratie im Wilhelminischen Deutschland." In Lässig and Pohl, *Sachsen im Kaiserreich*.

——. *Die sächsische Sozialdemokratie vom Kaiserreich zur Republik, 1871–1923*. Weimar: Böhlau, 1995.

Ruppenthal, Jens. *Kolonialismus als "Wissenschaft und Technik": Das Hamburgische Kolonialinstitut, 1908 bis 1919*. Stuttgart: Franz Steiner, 2007.

Rydell, Robert W. *All the World's a Fair: Visions of Empire at American International Expositions, 1876–1916*. Chicago: University of Chicago Press, 1984.

Sadji, Amadou Booker. *Das Bild des Negro-Afrikaners in der Deutschen Kolonialliteratur, 1884–1945: Ein Beitrag zur literarischen Imagologie Schwarzafrikas*. Berlin: Dietrich Reimer, 1985.

Said, Edward. *Culture and Imperialism*. New York: Knopf, 1993.

——. *Orientalism*. New York: Vintage, 1979.

Saul, Klaus. "Der 'Deutsche Kriegerbund': Zur innenpolitischen Funktion eines 'nationalen' Verbandes im kaiserlichen Deutschland." *Militärgeschichtliche Mitteilungen* 2 (1969): 95–159.

Saur, Liselotte. *Die Stellungnahme der Münchner Presse zur Bismarck'schen Kolonialpolitik*. Würzburg: Konrad Triltsch, 1940.

Schenda, Rudolf. *Die Lesestoffe der kleinen Leute: Studien zur populären Literatur im 19. und 20. Jahrhundert*. Munich: C. H. Beck, 1976.

——. "Tausend deutsche populäre Drucke aus dem 19. Jahrhundert." *Archiv für Geschichte des Buchwesens* 11 (1971): 1466–1651.

——. *Volk ohne Buch: Studien zur Sozialgeschichte der populären Lesestoffe 1770–1910*. Frankfurt/M.: Klostermann, 1970.

Schinzinger, Francesca. *Die Kolonien und das Deutsche Reich: Die wirtschaftliche Bedeutung der deutschen Besitzungen in Übersee*. Stuttgart: Franz Steiner, 1984.

Schmitt-Egner, Peter. *Kolonialismus und Faschismus: Eine Studie zur historischen und begrifflichen Genesis faschistischer Bewußtseinsformen am deutschen Beispiel.* Giessen: Andreas Aschenbach, 1975.

Schneer, Jonathan. *London 1900: The Imperial Metropolis.* New Haven, Conn.: Yale University Press, 1999.

Schneider, William H. *An Empire for the Masses: The French Popular Image of Africa, 1870–1900.* Westport, Conn.: Greenwood, 1982.

Schorske, Carl E. *German Social Democracy, 1905–1917: The Development of the Great Schism.* Cambridge, Mass.: Harvard University Press, 1955.

Schramm, Percy. *Deutschland und Übersee: Der deutsche Handel mit den anderen Kontinenten, insbesondere Afrika, von Karl V. bis zu Bismarck.* Braunschweig: Georg Westermann, 1950.

——. *Hamburg, Deutschland und die Welt: Leistung und Grenzen hanseatischen Bürgertums in der Zeit zwischen Napoleon I. und Bismarck.* Munich: Georg D. W. Callwey, 1943.

Schreuder, D. M. *The Scramble for Southern Africa, 1877–1895: The Politics of Partition Reappraised.* Cambridge: Cambridge University Press, 1980.

Schröder, Hans-Christoph. *Gustav Noske und die Kolonialpolitik des Deutschen Kaiserreichs.* Berlin: J. H. W. Dietz, 1979.

——. *Sozialismus und Imperialismus: Die Auseinandersetzung der deutschen Sozialdemokratie mit dem Imperialismusproblem und der "Weltpolitik" vor 1914.* Hanover: Verlag für Literatur und Zeitgeschehen, 1968.

Schulte-Althoff, Franz-Josef. "Koloniale Krise und Reformprojekte: Zur Diskussion über eine Kurskorrektur in der deutschen Kolonialpolitik nach der Jahrhundertwende." In *Weltpolitik, Europagedanke, Regionalismus,* edited by Heinz Dollinger, Horst Gründer, and Alwin Hanschmidt. Münster: Aschendorff, 1982.

Schumpeter, Joseph A. *Imperialism and Social Classes.* Philadelphia: Orion, 1991.

Seeberg, Karl-Martin. *Der Maji-Maji-Krieg gegen die deutsche Kolonialherrschaft.* Berlin: Dietrich Reimer, 1989.

Senger und Etterlin, Stefan von. *Neu-Deutschland in Nordamerika: Massenauswanderung, nationale Gruppenansiedlungen und liberale Kolonialbewegung, 1815–1860.* Baden-Baden: Nomos Verlagsgesellschaft, 1991.

Short, John Phillip. "Colonialism and Society: Class and Region in the Popularization of Overseas Empire in Germany, 1890–1914." Ph.D. diss., Columbia University, 2004.

——. "Everyman's Colonial Library: Imperialism and Working-Class Readers in Leipzig, 1890–1914." *German History* 21 (2003): 445–75.

——. "Novelty and Repetition: Photographs of South West Africa in German Visual Culture, 1890–1914." In *Hues between Black and White: Historical Photography from Colonial Namibia, 1860s to 1915,* edited by Wolfram Hartmann. Windhoek: Out of Africa, 2004.

Sippel, Harald. "Rassismus, Protektionismus oder Humanität? Die gesetzlichen Verbote der Anwerbung von 'Eingeborenen' zu Schaustellungszwecken in den deutschen Kolonien." In Debusmann and Riesz, *Kolonialausstellungen—Begegnungen mit Afrika?*

Smith, Woodruff D. *The German Colonial Empire.* Chapel Hill: University of North Carolina Press, 1978.

———. *The Ideological Origins of Nazi Imperialism*. New York: Oxford University Press, 1986.

———. "The Ideology of German Colonialism, 1840–1906." *Journal of Modern History* 46 (1974): 641–62.

———. *Politics and the Sciences of Culture in Germany, 1840–1920*. New York: Oxford University Press, 1991.

Sobich, Frank Oliver. "*Schwarze Bestien, rote Gefahr*": *Rassismus und Antisozialismus im deutschen Kaiserreich*. Frankfurt/M.: Campus, 2006.

Soénius, Ulrich S. *Koloniale Begeisterung im Rheinland während des Kaiserreichs*. Cologne: Rheinisch-Westfälisches Wirtschaftsarchiv, 1992.

Spellmeyer, Hans. *Deutsche Kolonialpolitik im Reichstag*. Stuttgart: Kohlhammer, 1931.

Spencer, Elaine Glovka. "Policing Popular Amusements in German Cities: The Case of Prussia's Rhine Province, 1815–1914," *Journal of Urban History* 16 (1990): 366–85.

Sperber, Jonathan. *The Kaiser's Voters: Electors and Elections in Imperial Germany*. Cambridge: Cambridge University Press, 1997.

Spidle, Jake W. "Colonial Studies in Imperial Germany." *History of Education Quarterly* 13 (Fall 1973): 231–47.

Stark, Gary D. "Cinema, Society, and the State: Policing the Film Industry in Imperial Germany." In *Essays on Culture and Society in Modern Germany*, edited by Gary D. Stark and Bede Karl Lackner. College Station: Texas A&M University Press, 1982.

———. *Entrepreneurs of Ideology: Neoconservative Publishers in Germany, 1890–1913*. Chapel Hill: University of North Carolina Press, 1981.

Stegmann, Dirk. *Die Erben Bismarcks: Parteien und Verbände in der Spätphase des Wilhelminischen Deutschlands. Sammlungspolitik 1897–1918*. Cologne: Kiepenheuer & Witsch, 1970.

Steinberg, Hans-Josef. "Workers' Libraries in Germany Before 1914." *History Workshop* 1 (1976): 166–80.

Steinmetz, George. " 'The Devil's Handwriting': Precolonial Discourse, Ethnographic Acuity, and Cross-Identification in German Colonialism." *Comparative Studies in Society and History* 45 (2003): 41–95.

———. *The Devil's Handwriting: Precoloniality and the German Colonial State in Qingdao, Samoa, and Southwest Africa*. Chicago: University of Chicago Press, 2007.

———. "Precoloniality and Colonial Subjectivity: Ethnographic Discourse and Native Policy in German Overseas Imperialism, 1870s–1914." *Political Power and Social Theory* 15 (2002): 135–228.

Stoecker, Helmuth, ed. *German Imperialism in Africa: From the Beginnings until the Second World War*, translated by Bernd Zöllner. London: C. Hurst, 1986.

Stoecker, Helmuth, and Peter Sebald. "Enemies of the Colonial Idea." In Knoll and Gann, *Germans in the Tropics*.

Stoler, Ann Laura. "Carnal Knowledge and Imperial Power: Gender, Race, and Morality in Colonial Asia." In *Gender at the Crossroads of Knowledge: Feminist Anthropology in the Postmodern Era*, edited by Micaela di Leonardo. Berkeley: University of California Press, 1991.

——. *Race and the Education of Desire: Foucault's* History of Sexuality *and the Colonial Order of Things*. Durham, N.C.: Duke University Press, 1995.

Teuteberg, Hans-Jürgen. "Die Nahrung der sozialen Unterschichten im späten 19. Jahrhundert." In *Ernährung und Ernährungslehre im 19. Jahrhundert*, edited by Edith Heischkel-Artelt. Göttingen: Vandenhoeck & Ruprecht, 1976.

——. "Wie ernährten sich Arbeiter im Kaiserreich?" In *Arbeiterexistenz im 19. Jahrhundert: Lebensstandard und Lebensgestaltung deutscher Arbeiter und Handwerker*, edited by Werner Conze and Ulrich Engelhardt. Stuttgart: Klett-Cotta, 1981.

Theiner, Peter. *Sozialer Liberalismus und deutsche Weltpolitik: Friedrich Naumann im Wilhelminischen Deutschland, 1860–1919*. Baden-Baden: Nomos, 1983.

Thode-Arora, Hilke. *Für fünfzig Pfennig um die Welt: Die Hagenbeckschen Völkerschauen*. Frankfurt/M.: Campus, 1989.

Tilley, Helen, with Robert J. Gordon, ed. *Ordering Africa: Anthropology, European Imperialism and the Politics of Knowledge*. Manchester: Manchester University Press, 2007.

Townsend, Mary Evelyn. *Origins of Modern German Colonialism, 1871–1885*. New York: Columbia University, 1921.

——. *The Rise and Fall of Germany's Colonial Empire, 1884–1918*. New York: Howard Fertig, 1966.

Turner, Henry Ashby, Jr. "Bismarck's Imperialist Venture: Anti-British in Origin?" In Gifford and Louis, *Britain and Germany in Africa*.

Volberg, Heinrich. *Deutsche Kolonialbestrebungen in Südamerika nach dem Dreißigjährigen Kriege, insbesondere die Bemühungen von Johann Joachim Becher*. Cologne: Böhlau, 1977.

Walker, Mack. *Germany and the Emigration, 1816–1885*. Cambridge, Mass.: Harvard University Press, 1964.

Walther, Daniel J. *Creating Germans Abroad: Cultural Policies and National Identity in Namibia*. Athens: Ohio University Press, 2002.

——. "Creating Germans Abroad: The Policies of Culture in Southwest Africa, 1894–1939." Ph. D. diss., University of Pennsylvania, 1996.

——. "Creating Germans Abroad: White Education in German Southwest Africa, 1894–1914." *German Studies Review* 24 (2001): 325–51.

Warmbold, Joachim. *Germania in Africa: Germany's Colonial Literature*. New York: Peter Lang, 1989.

Warner, Michael. "The Mass Public and the Mass Subject." In Calhoun, *Habermas and the Public Sphere*.

Washausen, Helmut. *Hamburg und die Kolonialpolitik des Deutschen Reiches, 1880–1890*. Hamburg: Hans Christian, 1968.

Weber, Max. *From Max Weber: Essays in Sociology*, edited by H. H. Gerth and C. Wright Mills. New York: Oxford University Press, 1946.

Wehler, Hans-Ulrich. "Bismarck's Imperialism 1862–1890." *Past and Present*, no. 48 (1970): 119–55.

——. *Bismarck und der Imperialismus*. Cologne: Kiepenheuer & Witsch, 1969; reprint, Frankfurt/M.: Suhrkamp, 1984.

——. *The German Empire, 1871–1918*, translated by Kim Traynor. Providence, R.I.: Berg, 1985.

Welch, David A. "Cinema and Society in Imperial Germany, 1905–1918." *German History* 8 (1990): 28–45.

Wernecke, Klaus. *Der Wille zur Weltgeltung: Außenpolitik und Öffentlichkeit im Kaiserreich am Vorabend des Ersten Weltkrieges.* Düsseldorf: Droste, 1970.

Wildenthal, Lora. "Colonizers and Citizens: Bourgeois Women and the Woman Question in the German Colonial Movement, 1886–1914." Ph.D. diss., University of Michigan, 1994.

——. *German Women for Empire, 1884–1945.* Durham, N.C.: Duke University Press, 2001.

——. " 'She Is the Victor': Bourgeois Women, Nationalist Identities, and the Ideal of the Independent Woman Farmer in German Southwest Africa." *Social Analysis* 33 (1993): 68–88.

Winkler, Heinrich August. *Mittelstand, Demokratie und Nationalsozialismus: Die politische Entwicklung von Handwerk und Kleinhandel in der Weimarer Republik.* Cologne: Kiepenheuer & Witsch, 1972.

——. "Der rückversicherte Mittelstand: Die Interessenverbände von Handwerk und Kleinhandel im deutschen Kaiserreich." In *Zur soziologischen Theorie und Analyse des 19. Jahrhunderts*, edited by Walter Rüegg and Otto Neuloh. Göttingen: Vandenhoeck & Rupprecht, 1971.

Wright, Marcia. "East Africa, 1870–1905." In *The Cambridge History of Africa*, Vol. 6: *From 1870 to 1905*, edited by Roland Oliver and G. N. Sanderson. Cambridge: Cambridge University Press, 1985.

——. *German Missions in Tanganyika 1891–1941: Lutherans and Moravians in the Southern Highlands.* Oxford University Press, 1971.

——. "Maji Maji: Prophecy and Historiography." In *Revealing Prophets: Prophecy in Eastern African History*, edited by David M. Anderson and Douglas H. Johnson. London: James Currey, 1995.

Zantop, Susanne. *Colonial Fantasies: Conquest, Family, and Nation in Precolonial Germany, 1770–1870.* Durham, N.C.: Duke University Press, 1997.

——. "Colonial Legends, Postcolonial Legacies." In *A User's Guide to German Cultural Studies*, edited by Scott Denham, Irene Kacandes, and Jonathan Petropoulos. Ann Arbor: University of Michigan Press, 1997.

Zimmerer, Jürgen. *Deutsche Herrschaft über Afrikaner: Staatlicher Machtanspruch und Wirklichkeit im kolonialen Namibia.* Hamburg: Lit, 2002.

Zimmerman, Andrew. "Adventures in the Skin Trade: German Anthropology and Colonial Corporeality." In Penny and Bunzl, *Worldly Provincialism.*

——. *Alabama in Africa: Booker T. Washington, the German Empire, and the Globalization of the New South.* Princeton, N.J.: Princeton University Press, 2010.

——. *Anthropology and Antihumanism in Imperial Germany.* Chicago: University of Chicago Press, 2001.

——. "Science and *Schaulust* in the Berlin Museum of Ethnology." In *Wissenschaft und Öffentlichkeit in Berlin, 1870–1930*, edited by Constantin Goschler. Stuttgart: Franz Steiner, 2000.

Zwahr, Hartmut. *Zur Konstituierung des Proletariats als Klasse: Strukturuntersuchung über das Leipziger Proletariat während der industriellen Revolution.* Berlin: Akademie-Verlag, 1978.

Index

Page numbers in *italics* indicate illustrations.